Multimodality, Poetry and Poetics

This groundbreaking work takes multimodality studies in a new direction by applying multimodal approaches to the study of poetry and poetics. The book examines poetry's visual and formal dimensions, applying framing theory to such case studies as Aristotle's *Poetics* and Robert Lowell's 'The Heavenly Rain' to demonstrate both the implied, because of the form's unique relationship with structure, imagery and rhythm, and the explicit forms of multimodality at work—an otherwise little-explored research strand of multimodality studies. The volume explores the theoretical implications of a multimodal approach to poetry and poetics to other art forms and fields of study, making this essential reading for students and scholars working at the intersection of language and communication, including multimodality, discourse analysis and interdisciplinary literary studies.

Richard Andrews is Professor in English Education at the University of East Anglia, UK. He is the author of several books for Routledge, including *Re-framing Literacy*, *A Theory of Contemporary Rhetoric* and *A Prosody of Free Verse: Explorations in Rhythm*.

Routledge Research in Language and Communication

The Role of Language in the Climate Change Debate
Edited by Kjersti Fløttum

Multimodality, Poetry and Poetics
Richard Andrews

Multimodality, Poetry and Poetics

Richard Andrews

NEW YORK AND LONDON

First published 2018
by Routledge
711 Third Avenue, New York, NY 10017

and by Routledge
2 Park Square, Milton Park, Abingdon, Oxon OX14 4RN

Routledge is an imprint of the Taylor & Francis Group, an informa business

© 2018 Taylor & Francis

The right of Richard Andrews to be identified as author of this work
has been asserted by him in accordance with sections 77 and 78
of the Copyright, Designs and Patents Act 1988.

All rights reserved. No part of this book may be reprinted or
reproduced or utilised in any form or by any electronic, mechanical,
or other means, now known or hereafter invented, including
photocopying and recording, or in any information storage or
retrieval system, without permission in writing from the publishers.

Trademark notice: Product or corporate names may be trademarks
or registered trademarks, and are used only for identification and
explanation without intent to infringe.

Library of Congress Cataloging-in-Publication Data
A catalog record for this book has been requested

ISBN: 978-1-138-69660-0 (hbk)
ISBN: 978-1-315-52389-7 (ebk)

Typeset in Sabon
by Apex CoVantage, LLC

For Gunther Kress

Contents

	List of Figures	viii
	Acknowledgements	ix
1	Classical Precedents and Contemporary Multimodality	1
2	Poetry in Multimodal Presentations	17
3	The Forms and Functions of Rhythm in Poetry: From Metrical to Free Verse	38
4	Imagery in Poetry: Implicit and Explicit	51
5	The Framing of a Poem	65
6	The Basis of a New Poetics	76
7	Implications for Poetics	93
8	A Further Look at the Imaginative and Fictive	105
9	What Part Do Rhetoric and Politics Play in the Relationship between Multimodality and Poetics?	119
10	A New Approach to Literary Study?	133
11	Poetry, Writing Process and the New Poetics	146
12	Implications for Multimodality and Learning Theory	165
	References and Bibliography	178
	Index	184

Figures

1.1	William Blake, 'London' From *Songs of Innocence and Experience* (1794)	10
2.1	The Opening Bars of Handel's *L'Allegro, Il Penseroso ed Il Moderato*	26
2.2	Ira Lightman, 'Vista'	32
2.3	Verónica Gerber Bicecci and Anna Milsom, 'Inverted (and Translated) Poem (2017) Visual Essay'	34
2.4(i)	Clive Scott, 'Dimanches'	35
2.4(ii)	Clive Scott, 'Au Cabaret-Vert'	36
4.1	Multimodal Poetics	61
6.1	'Build: Aspects of Construction, Catalogue 13', Janette Ray Booksellers	78
6.2	Centre of Ceramic Art Brochure: Cover	79
6.3	Art in York	80
6.4	Sweet Cream of Carrot Soup	82
6.5	Text and Image From 1873 Newspaper	83
6.6	Linda Combi, 'Herb Garden Melody'	84
6.7	Linda Combi, 'Mosque'	85
6.8	Linda Combi, 'Politics and Rhetoric'	86
6.9	Linda Combi, 'Flexible Language'	87
6.10	Linda Combi, 'Shipping Forecast'	88
9.1	John Christie and Gael Turnbull, 'Poem, Print, Note'	123
11.1	Mary Webb, 'Dunwich Study 2, 1977, Charcoal on Paper'	158
11.2	Mary Webb, 'New York 1980, Photograph'	159
11.3	Mary Webb, 'Circle Line Series: The Isle of Manhattan 18, 1984, Collage'	160
11.4	Mary Webb, 'Yellow, Black and White 1976, Oil on Canvas'	161

* Where the figures were originally in colour, these are collected and reproduced in colour at the end of the book.

Acknowledgements

Poetry is neither an elitist nor 'high' art. It is grounded in song, visual presence and rhythm. The resource of words—in whatever language—combined with physical expression in oral form, and with the white page or screen in written form, is a compelling and low-budget mix. Work it in with a cocktail of other modes—dance, movement, gesture, voice, still and moving images—and in a range of media, including film, and the concoction is headier still.

My debt is greatest to Gunther Kress and colleagues at the Centre for Multimodal Research at UCL Institute of Education, London: Carey Jewitt, Jeff Bezemer, Andrew Burn, Anton Franks, Myrrh Domingo and Sara Price. They taught me that multimodality was the norm in the social semiotics of communication and helped to provide a lens through which to re-interpret the world of poetry and literature more generally. In my own offbeat way, I have pursued a more literary, rhetorical path in multimodal studies and found their intellectual companionship and insights to be inspiring. Along the way, I have found that the work of John Berger, who died during the writing of this book, provides an open window to the interfaces of writing (specifically poetry), photography, painting and film. In many ways, he was a precursor of contemporary multimodality. Another great debt is to Anna Milsom at the University of Leicester and Eugenia Loffredo at the University of East Anglia, co-curators (with Manuela Perteghella) of the travelling exhibition *Transartation!* who introduced me to the work of the artists, some of whom are cited in the present book. In particular, I am grateful to Kirsteen Anderson, Calvin Crowe, Verónica Gerber Bicecci, Ira Lightman, Clive Scott, Ricarda Vidal and Maria-Jose Blanco for references to their work. Ira Lightman's work 'Vista' was first commissioned for *One Poem in Search of a Translator: Rewriting Les Fenêtres by Apollinaire* (Peter Lang, 2008). I am also grateful to John Christie for his generosity in permitting me to reproduce pages 144–5 from *Lapwing & Fox* published by Objectif in 2016 (www.objectifpress.co.uk), which are copyright © by John Christie. The text reproduced from page 171 of *Lapwing & Fox* is copyright © by the estate of John Berger; and thanks also to Victoria Fox at Farrar, Straus,

x   *Acknowledgements*

Giroux for permission to reprint Robert Lowell's 'The Heavenly Rain' in its versions from *Notebook* (1970) and *History* (1973).*

I also want to pay tribute to the many students I have worked with on poetry, both at school and university levels; great teachers and poets themselves, Ian Bentley, Terry Locke, Peter Medway and Andrew Stibbs; the Arvon Foundation; New York University and its summer schools, especially Jim Fraser, Myrrh Domingo, Jill Jeffery and Sarah Beck; and the New York City Writing Project through Richard Sterling and Carla Asher. To Jeni Smith at the University of East Anglia and to Simon Wrigley for their continued work in inspiring teachers to write and to see themselves as writers. To Linda and Peter Combi, Nick Allen and Barbara Webb for a weekend touring York Open Studios in the spring of 2016 and especially to Linda for her artwork that is included in Chapter 6.

To Jane Duru at Wardour, Steve Woodward at A New Direction and especially to Selina Nwulu for permission to reprint 'A Strange Kind of Beauty' in its entirety. The poem is by the Young Poet Laureate for London 2015/16, commissioned by A New Direction, London's flagship cultural education agency, as a response to the challenges young Londoners face in engaging and contributing to the creative and cultural life of their city. The Young Poet Laureate for London is managed by Spread the Word, London's Writer Development Agency, as part of the London Laureates programme, with generous support from Foundation for FutureLondon. An animated version of the poem can be viewed at www.anewdirection.org.uk/a-strange-kind-of-beauty.

Thanks must go to Mary Webb, artist, for her exhibitions at the University of East Anglia in 2011 and 2017/18, and for her generosity in supplying images of her work. I am grateful to Janette Ray for permission to reprint the cover of *Build: Aspects of Construction*; to Fiona Green at the Centre for Ceramic Art, York, for permission to reprint the catalogue cover of August 2015–February 2016; to York Galleries Group and the Lotte Inch Gallery for the map of York, 2015. The image from the *New York Daily Graphic* of December 1873, although available freely on the Net, is from a blog by Martin Fox accessed in May 2016. Thank you, too, to Barbara Friedlander and Bob Cato for the recipe and photograph from *Earth Water Fire Air*, a book I have used much, but whom I have been unable to contact.

The section on Robert Lowell as part of Chapter 5 was first presented as a paper at a conference on Multimodality and Learning in 2010, run by the Centre for Multimodal Research at UCL Institute of Education. The poem by Edwin Morgan in Chapter 7 from *Instamatic Poems* is reprinted courtesy of Foichl Miah at Carcanet Press.

I am grateful to Belarus Free Theatre and especially to its director, Vladimir Shcherban, and the actors, Grace Andrews, Oliver Bennett, Emily Houghton, Samantha Pearl and Alex Robertson for the performance of *Tomorrow*

---

*   "The Heavenly Rain" from *Collected Poems* by Robert Lowell. Copyright © 2003 by Harriet Lowell and Sheridan Lowell. Reprinted by permission of Farrar, Straus and Giroux. Versions originally published in *Notebook* 1967–1968 and *History* by Robert Lowell.

Acknowledgements xi

I Was Always a Lion at the Arcola Theatre in London in October 2016. To David Kirkland, through inspiring conversations both in New York at New York University and in London at the Institute of Contemporary Arts.

Unattributed poems and fragments are my own.

This book was composed in Beverley, Yorkshire, and in the Adirondack Mountains of upstate New York in 2016 and 2017. It is a sequel to *A Prosody of Free Verse: Explorations in Rhythm*, published by Routledge in 2016. It is based on supported research undertaken at the University of East Anglia, Norwich, and I am grateful to the staff of the library and to colleagues in the School of Education and Lifelong Learning there for their help and encouragement in giving me time to complete the book. I am particularly grateful to Jacqueline Collier; to Victoria Carrington as director of research; to Dominique Bivar-Segurado, who pointed me in the direction of the 2016 film on John Berger by Cordelia Dvořák; to John Gordon; to Terry Haydn for giving me pockets of time to finish the book; to Calvin Winner, curator at the Sainsbury Centre for Visual Arts; and to Kajsa Berg. I am also grateful to Karen Glass of the Keene Valley Library, New York.

Elysse Preposi and Allie Simmons at Routledge, New York, have been a continued inspiration and support.

1 Classical Precedents and Contemporary Multimodality

Introduction

This chapter draws on Aristotle's *Poetics* as well as other classical sources to explore what they imply about multimodality. It also refers to the *Rhetoric* in order to make the connection between speech, writing and other modes such as gesture, movement and image. Such public communication has an important bearing on the conception of poetics and poetry that runs through the present book: poetry is seen not as a merely private, individual voice, but as an array of public voices whose function is partly to persuade the reader/audience. Despite the fact that Aristotle did not write much about the lyric form, it is discussed here (his focus was on drama, plot, characters). The classical emphasis on beauty—the aesthetic dimension—is explored, as is the emphasis on form and genre. As an example of multimodality in action, two versions of Blake's poem 'London' are discussed. The account of classical poetics and discussion of Blake are followed by a review of studies of existing applications of contemporary multimodality.

Aristotle's *Poetics*

There is a statement close to the start of Aristotle's *On the Art of Poetry*—also known as the *Poetics*, from its Latin title *De Poetica*—that could come, with some adjustment for contemporary vocabulary and the vagaries of translation, from a book on multimodality: the major poetic genres differ not only in form but also "either in using different media for the representation, or in representing different things, or in representing them in entirely different ways" (Aristotle 1965: 31). The first difference could be re-phrased as "using different *modes and* media for the representation".

Behind Aristotle's thinking is a belief in poetry as imitation: the notion that the thing to be represented is outside language, and language operates to express the thing through imitation. There is no conception of the 'verbal construct', let alone a 'multimodal construct'. Nevertheless, the notion that poetry can not only take different forms/genres but also operate in different modes/media is established at the very beginning of the work. Indeed, in the

2 Classical Precedents

first chapter on the media of poetic imitation, it is asserted that "imitation is produced by means of rhythm, language, and music, these being used either separately or in combination" (1965: 32). Aristotle's thinking here is not systematic in its categorization: rhythm is a different category from language or music. Rhythm is the relation of movement to time. Language itself needs to be broken down into spoken or written language. But the characterization of 'imitation' as being represented by a combination of rhythm, language and music suggests, at the very least, multimodal awareness if not a fully fledged conception of multimodality.

In choosing to focus on dramatic and epic poetry in the *Poetics*, Aristotle was concentrating on the emerging major public genres of his time, which had political as well as aesthetic significance, rather like the plays of Shakespeare at the turn of the seventeenth century with their multi-layered, metaphysical and political references. For the moment, let us define exactly how Aristotle has focused on these genres from a poetics point of view. Later, the book will return to the rhetorical and political dimensions. The art of poetry for Aristotle has broad reference. It refers to artistic expression and includes plot and narrative structure. It thus has closer parallels to what could be now termed something more specific within literary stylistics: narratology. At the same time, it takes in the area now considered distinctive features of poetry: metricality, rhythm, the 'music' of language. In addition, it focusses specifically on tragic and epic narrative poetry. This specific focus gives Aristotle his own contemporary context, and although he uses the foundation of his discussion for generalizing principles, the foundation is, in relation to contemporary poetics, narrow.

Within that narrow spectrum—tragedy, comedy, epic—Aristotle identifies six elements of tragedy. Two are modes/media of communication: diction and song. There is another that "involves the manner of presentation" (1965: 39): spectacle. The other three are the 'objects' of representation: thought, plot and character. The first three are modal: they could be identified in current terms as speech/dialogue, song and the visual (including still images; e.g. the theatrical set and moving images, the movement of the actors). In an aesthetic theory that foregrounds imitation, the elements that take precedence are plot, character and thought, and the other modal elements are merely expressive or representational. In a contemporary multimodal aesthetic, there is no 'substance' that is framed within the expressive elements. Rather, the composition of elements within a frame provides a meaning/modal nexus, creating a situation in which the elements of communication are more equal than in Aristotelian theory. What is presented as art is the representation of a possible world. Even with photography, the framing of the image sets it apart from the real world and demands our special attention. But the real world, in its moment-to-moment unfolding, is also a world of possibilities. Within this philosophy of possible worlds, multimodality and rhetoric operate to define meaning. Poetics operates as a subcategory of rhetoric, and poetry is a concrete example of poetics in action.

Classical Precedents 3

To debate which is the better art form—tragedy or epic—would be pointless from a multimodal perspective. Each has its own affordances.

The closest Horace (1965) comes to commentary on the potential multimodality of poetry, or any more explicit statement, is through analogy:

> A poem is like a painting: the closer you stand to this one the more it will impress you, whereas you have to stand a good distance from that one; this one demands a rather dark corner, but that one needs to be seen in full light, and will stand up to the keen-eyed scrutiny of the art critic; this one pleased you only the first time you saw it, but that one will go on giving pleasure however often it is looked at.
>
> (1965: 91–2)

The point here is more about framing and perspective than a comparison or combination of modes. The statement has also been used to illustrate the notion of *ut pictura poesis*, again an analogistic proposition. It says little more than words in a poem invoke the imagination and, conversely, painting may be seen as having the suggestive and interpretive intensity of poetry. See Rensselaer 1967 and further discussion in Chapter 4 of the present book.

Possible World Semantics and Modal Logic

Classical rhetoric and poetics did not have much to say about modes, other than in relation to genres. If 'mode' is taken, in its most basic sense, as a 'way' of doing something, then modes of transport, fashion modes (and its models) and modes of being can all be classed under the term 'mode'. 'Mode', in these senses, means 'type' or 'way' or 'means'. It is essentially dynamic and concerned with actual or potential *movement*, even in its apparently most static senses of 'state' or 'dimension' (as in 'modes of being').

More specifically, in philosophy, a modal is an expression such as 'probably' or 'necessarily' that is used to qualify the truth of a statement. In linguistics, a modal verb is used to indicate likelihood, possibility, provisionality and expressed intention. For example, the verbs 'can/could', 'may/might', 'shall/should' and 'will/would' all come under the category of modal verbs and are always used in conjunction with more active verbs, hence their further definition as modal auxiliary verbs.

The close association between modal logic in philosophy and possible world semantics[1] in the second half of the twentieth century found application in poetics in the work of Eco (1984), Pavel (1986) and Doležel (1998). Eco's notion is that a literary work cannot be seen as representing a single possible world but "as a *machine for producing possible worlds*" [italics in original] (1984: 246). His notion is based on the idea of the literary work as a process tool rather than a framed artistic work. Pavel's contribution was to perceive that a literary text was not dependent on the validity of individual propositions; that literariness, unlike the scientific approach,

4   Classical Precedents

did not eliminate false propositions; and that literature must be examined from three different perspectives: the semantics of salient structures (meaning), the pragmatics of cultural tradition (context) and the stylistics of textual constraint (style). Doležel, through his notion of 'minimal departure', emphasizes the proximity of fictional words to those of the 'real' world and their ontological fullness as objects in the world.

Literary conceptions of possible worlds have exploited the emancipation of possible world semantics from modal logic. Possible worlds have been loosely designated as imagined worlds which have their own—largely narrative—grammars. Little work has been done on drama or poetry.

Most useful for the purposes of exploring the relationship between multimodality and poetics is the difference between the concretist and the abstractionist perspectives on modal discourse. From the concretist perspective, all that exists is the full extent of the real world and its presence in space and/or time. Possible worlds are possible other worlds in time/space dimensions, including the actual. In other words, what is happening here and now in a limited space could have been different and is related to all other nexuses of actuality. The closest analogy in fictional terms is the real-world novel, the kitchen-sink drama and the a-rhythmical, journalistic, descriptive poem. From an abstractionist perspective, on the other hand, what *could* be the case *is* the case. Its focus is on states of affairs with consistency: an example would be a fictional construct with internal consistency. An individual, from an abstractionist point of view, exists in a number of possible worlds, and these actualities are of a different order from those of the concretist.[2]

The best way to see these two perspectives is to conceive of them as the two ends of a spectrum of possibilities. Some worlds are closer and more proximate to the real, tangible, actual, concrete world. Others are further away and have their own internal consistency and logic. All possibilities on this spectrum could be seen in terms of modes of perception and being. Multimodality would thus have to address the concertina-like presence of more than one point on the spectrum being invoked by the fictional work: novel, story, poem or play. Such concertina-like compression and expansion is also akin to the 'layering' effect described and analyzed by Domingo (2011).

Genre

The precepts, suggestions and comments of classical literacy criticism are based on a fascination with the emergence of *genres* within the culture/society of the time: poetry as opposed to everyday language; tragedy and epic as grand, inclusive genres; and comedy as closer to the *quotidian*. What can genre theory, both in its formulations of genre-as-social-action and genre-as-text-type, offer in terms of an exploration of the relationship between multimodality and poetics?

First, and most simply, poetry is an example of a text-type (we will be exploring the parameters of that text-type in the course of this book) and for the most part is distinguishable from prose or 'everyday speech'. In one sense, it is a meta-genre embracing a plethora of genres, such as free verse, metrical verse and blank verse. In a taxonomy of poetic types, the *smorgasbord* is a better metaphor than the hierarchical tree. Individual poems can borrow from a range of types and styles. So, for example, a blank verse sonnet, as in Lowell's *Notebook* (1970) and *History* (1973) or a combination of blank, half-rhymes and full rhymes in Heaney's 'Glanmore sonnets' (in *Field Work* 1979) are variations on the Shakespearian or Petrarchan sonnet. These are all sub-genres of the overarching textual genre 'poetry'.

Second, the picture is more complex if poetry is considered as a genre in social action. From this broader perspective, poems happen in the interaction between the poet, the text and the reader or the listener. Freed from the confines of the written text, poems can be performed orally and read by the author or by others; they can be recorded and listened to via different media; they are tightly framed works that take their place in a multimodal context, whether they are printed on a white page (and surrounded by white space) or they are delivered or performed orally in a pub, at a funeral, in a concert hall or at a book group or literary festival. These wider social framings help to determine the meaning that is generated between rhetor, artwork and audience, and which constitute the more central topic in the present book.

Rhetoric

Aristotle's narrow definition of rhetoric as the 'art of persuasion', as opposed to the present definition of it as 'the arts of discourse', was shared by rhetoricians from Gorgias (c483–375 BC) to the classical periods in Greece and Rome. Although this is not the place for a history or exposition of classical rhetoric, two points must be made: first, oral rhetoric of the classical period manifested itself in oratory which involved more than mere speech. Whether for delivery in the law courts, public gatherings or for 'display', the practical operation of rhetoric must have been accompanied by gesture and movement and informed by audience reaction. That is to say, it was dialogic and multimodal. Second, observations on the use of rhythm in oratory suggested that prose should be rhythmical rather than metrical. This latter distinction, operating at the borders of prose and poetry, and, in parallel, at the borders of rhetoric and poetics, is indicative of a world of communication in which the poetic played a social and political part as well as an aesthetic one.

Other elements of rhetorical theory need not concern us in an exploration of multimodality and poetics, such as the relationship between claim and proof, the three kinds of rhetoric (deliberative, forensic and epideictic), the characteristics of the good orator (wisdom, virtue and goodwill), the play on the emotions and the categorical excesses of textbook rhetoric. Nothing in the present book suggests that reader response, or the primacy of the audience in interpretation, is key to exploring the relationship between multimodality and poetics.

6 Classical Precedents

But other elements, particularly those addressed in Book III of the *Rhetoric*, are crucial because they address the *how* as opposed to the *what*. One of these elements is composition or the art of arrangement; another is the importance of rhythm in composition and a third is narrative. If these three elements alone are considered, it can be seen that one is concerned with the *spatial* arrangement of elements of a composition and that the other two are concerned with the arrangement of words in *time*.

Spatial arrangements of elements are important because meaning is generated more in the relations of the constituent elements in space than from each element itself. An individual element can have multiple meanings; it can be hard to pin down. By locating it alongside other elements, a more precise meaning emerges. If these elements consist not only of words but also of gestures, visual images, sounds and movements, then the meaning that emerges, shaped within the frame that is chosen to separate text from context, becomes clearer. Spatial arrangement is particularly important in poetry—unlike prose—because relative positioning of words is used to generate semantic, musical and choreographic meaning. The emphasis is more on the words themselves as vehicles of meaning than is the case in prose. Both composer and reader are asked to attend more carefully and more intensely to the relationships between the words on the page, or in the air.

Arrangements of words (and of other elements) in time inevitably set up a rhythm, whether in prose or verse. This rhythm works subliminally in the communication in question, affecting emotion and therefore response. The effect is not unlike that of music. Music arranges sounds in time and speaks of the relationship between human perception of time and other less personal models of time, such as metronomic time or 'universal' time. But its arrangement is always deliberate and significant. There are specific examples in Aristotle, the most interesting of which is the *paean*. In its proportionality of three to two, it is related to other metrical rhythms (which have different proportionalities), but "it is the only one of the rhythms mentioned which is not adapted to a metrical system, so that it is most likely to be undetected" (1982: 385). Furthermore,

> At the present day one kind of paean alone is employed, at the beginning as well as at the end; the end, however, ought to be different from the beginning. Now there are two kinds of paeans, opposed to each other. The one is appropriate at the beginning, where in fact it is used. It begins with a long syllable and ends with three short [. . .] the other on the contrary begins with three short syllables and ends with the long one.
>
> (1982: 385)

Narrative to Aristotle (the rhetorician) is the part of the argument that recites 'the facts of the case': a summary of a series of events or incidents that pertain to the overriding argument. To contemporary narratologists and literary theorists, as well as theorists of the folk tale, the sequence of elements in a narrative is more important in not only underpinning universal tropes about human nature and psychology but also speaking in particular ways to circumstance and the logic of *post hoc propter hoc*—'after this, therefore because of this'. It is therefore both associated with arrangement in time and with spatial arrangement. It is of such power within poetics that it deserves separate recognition.

Book III of the *Rhetoric* begins with a consideration of the previously neglected dimension of *delivery*. The neglect was partly the result of an attitude that saw delivery as vulgar and beneath the purview of rhetoric. Aristotle refers to the *Poetics* with regard to the poetic style. Through this reference, he distinguishes rhetorical style as concerned with clarity, perspicuity and persuasion through volume, harmony and rhythm, and the judicious use of metaphor, whether in poetry or prose. The key section, however, and one which pulls together the three elements of spatiality, time and narrative, is on *arrangement*, or *dispositio*. Aristotle makes it clear that although the core of an argument is statement and proof, the actual parts can vary from two to any number. How these parts are arranged is subject to the needs of the oratorical function and of the particular audience. Only the exordium and epilogue as "merely aids to memory" (1982: 427) are peripheral; the rest of the elements can be modulated, arranged and re-arranged according to need and style. In other words, the proscriptions regarding arrangement are flexible; they are not tight sequences to be followed, nor is the *Rhetoric* a textbook.

The exordium, however, is more than an aid to memory:

> The exordium is the beginning of a speech, as the prologue in poetry and the prelude in flute-playing; for all these are beginnings, and as it were a paving the way for what follows.
>
> (1982: 427)

In jazz or free verse, the opening phrases and lines establish a pattern against which the rest of the composition defines itself. Usually, there is a return to this pattern at the end of the composition, whether thematically or more precisely. In some works—notably opera—the exordium takes the form of an overture. The 'aid to memory' tag comes more to the fore in epic poems, where the exordia

> provide a sample of the subject, in order that the hearers may know beforehand what it is about, and that the mind may not be kept in suspense, for that which is undefined leads astray; so then he who puts the beginning, so to say, into the hearer's hand enables him, if he holds fast to it, to follow the story.
>
> (1982: 431)

8   *Classical Precedents*

Thus rhetorical guidance has implications for poetics (the highly conscious arrangement or verbal form) and for multimodality. In the next section, the principle of multimodal arrangement will be discussed.

Multimodal Arrangement

The principal focus of Aristotle's interest, as far as *dispositio* goes, is in the arrangement of parts of an argument. I have explored the range and significance of such arrangements in arguments in Andrews (1995, 2009) and will not pursue that line further here. Rather, the focus of the present section is on multimodal arrangement in poetics and how classical precedents relate to contemporary perspectives.

Whereas the underlying structural paradigm for Aristotle is sequential, and closest to the 'narrative' category noted earlier, in multimodal arrangement, the structural relationship can be both sequential and collage-like. The three-dimensionality for Aristotle would be the argumentative and narrative drive of the orator; the character of the orator in terms of values, integrity and credibility; and the appeals to the hearer. For multimodal composition, the emphasis is on the first of these, plus lateral juxtaposition of modes; rhythm, if the composition contains moving image or sound; and framing.

Arrangement takes place within the frame, which is what makes us, the audience, look at the constituent elements inside the frame. Although 'frames' of experience and perspective are brought to the interpretation of what is inside the frame, the dynamic relationship is not between text and reader, but within the text. Even so, the reader may see one mode as more foregrounded than the other because of his or her predilection and/or training. For example, in an art gallery, the eye of the viewer may be attracted to the caption before he/she looks at the artwork, or vice versa. What follows is a dialogue between the caption and the artwork, each informing the other. This experience can be defined as one of negotiating within the frame formed by the artwork and the caption. Rarely is an artwork seen without a caption, and even more rarely the captions without artworks. It is important, therefore, to give some credence to the 'appeal to the hearer' in thinking about the effect of arrangement in multimodal compositions, because the attention will be drawn in particular directions and to particular modes.

Multimodal arrangement is key to composition. Composition means literally the process of putting texts or elements of texts with one another.

These texts or elements of a text are usually considered as operating within one mode. So, for example, the poet uses a range of linguistic and stylistic literary devices to compose a poem. The mode is written (and/or spoken) language, in any language. There is a wealth of research and resultant literature on poetic composition, just as there is in any mode and its sub-modal genres: architecture, the novel, journalistic writing, etc. These specialist areas have their own *modi operandi*, many of them described in terms derived from linguistic terminology.

When more than one mode is part of the composition, different factors come into play. If one mode is dominant, either through positioning within the frame, or because that mode is the one that the audience *expects* to give primary attention to, then the other mode or modes play a subsidiary role. A clear example is the photograph with a written caption, or the artwork in a gallery with its written plaque.

When there is no dominant mode, but a number of modes in juxtaposition, the audience's focus of attention decides the relationship between primary and secondary focus. The interest in such a situation of a balance between the modes is how the composition takes place and how the designer/composer places the elements in relation to each other. If a state of balance between the modes in a composition can be imagined, what kind of language will be needed to describe and explain it, and what 'rules' of composition will apply?

First, the rhetorical intention of the framed work must be considered; second, the affordances of each mode that is brought inside the frame; third, the other modes that are used; fourth, the interstices of the modes, and the liminal spaces between them; and fifth, the sparks of meaning that are generated by the juxtaposition of a number of modes.

Only when such an exposition and reflection on multimodal composition takes place can it be seen how such an approach can form the basis for a new approach to poetics. In the book, poems will be used to provide examples of how such an approach can work.

An Example: Blake's 'London'

As a preliminary example, here is Blake's 'London' from *Songs of Experience*:

London

> I wander thro' each charter'd street
> Near where the charter'd Thames does flow
> And mark in every face I meet
> Marks of weakness, marks of woe
>
> In every cry of every Man,
> In every Infants cry of fear,
> In every voice, in every ban,
> The mind-forg'd manacles I hear
>
> How the Chimney-sweepers cry
> Every blackning Church appals.
> And the hapless Soldiers sigh
> Runs in blood down Palace walls

10   *Classical Precedents*

   But most thro' midnight streets I hear
   How the youthful Harlots curse
   Blast the new-born Infants tear
   And blights with plagues the Marriage hearse

Simply to array the two versions alongside each other draws attention to the difference between the multimodal version and the ostensibly monomodal version. Although the book will return later to an analysis of the comparison between different versions of the same work, the focus here is on the multimodal version.

Figure 1.1 William Blake, 'London' From *Songs of Innocence and Experience* (1794)

Classical Precedents 11

First, what is the rhetorical intention of the framed work? The illuminated book, *Songs of Experience*, was printed in 1794, with framing of the individual illustrated poems "noticeably more severe" (Blake 1970: xv) than in the earlier *Songs of Innocence* (first published in 1789). The *Songs of Experience* are generally thought to be the result of the experience of London in the wake of the insights and euphoria of *Innocence* and showing, as Blake himself states on the title page of the 1794 edition, "the two Contrary States of the Human Soul". Blake's self-styled 'author and printer' signature on both the 1789 and 1794 books signifies his position as composer/compositor/artist/designer of the poems. He is more than a poet. He is an artist, trained at the Royal Academy, and a craftsman who, through his training in engraving and printing with James Basire, is responsible for both the content and form of his work. The poems themselves are products of an imagination that required expression in the visual as well as verbal mode. Despite historical positioning of Blake as a visionary and an eccentric, his imagination is socially grounded. As a composer, he re-arranged the sequence and categorization of poems in *Innocence* and *Experience*, "transferring a few poems from *Innocence* to *Experience*" (Blake 1970: xv). Furthermore, he "had to live mainly by his work as painter and engraver rather than by his output of poetry" (1970: xvi). The immediate personal context is framed with the social and political context of the time. Most notably, the French Revolution (1789 to 1799) was contemporaneous. In England, reform rather than revolution was the chosen option, although the monarchy came under criticism and protest by the London Corresponding Society and others—so much so that William Pitt the Younger ordered repression of public meetings and arrest of political leaders without trial. Whereas 'égalité' was a founding principle of the French Revolution, a mounting sense of inequality in society was the fuel driving Blake's imagination. Whereas it would be speculative to try to identify the author's intentions, the framework within which Blake was composing was more than one which allowed a mere expression of the human soul; it was driven also by a politically and socially informed sense of injustice, and made possible by Blake's own control over the creation, production and distribution of the work.

Second, within the framed work, there are two primary modes: the still visual imagery, realized through the media of copperplate engraved prints with watercolour decoration and washes, and the handwritten or painted lettering of the words. It is the words that are dominant, taking either central or upper-central position in most of the illustrated poems and less commonly taking the form, as seen earlier, of the image at the top and the words below. Each mode has its own affordances. The poem in the illustrated version is framed not only by the page and the plate but also by the illustration, which wraps itself around the words. The fire which is warming the small figure sends its smoke around the words, perhaps taking the shape of ominous black birds that gather in the top right-hand corner of the poem. The illustration taking up the top third of the page is of an old man with a

12 *Classical Precedents*

crutch—perhaps symbolic of time—being led by a child in a shaft of light through an otherwise dark street. The illustration is not so much a direct depiction of the images in the poem as a complement to them. The images of fire and apparent kindness are shrouded in smoke and darkness, suggestive of the fact that innocence operates within experience as well as being 'contrary' to it (just as, conversely, in 'The Sick Rose', experience, corruption and canker operate within the innocent rose).

The images that are evoked in the illustration are different in nature from those evoked by the words. With the visual image, the starting point of reference for association is provided. Those associations may be verbal, visual, tactile, olfactory or aural. But because their origin is visual, the other senses are invited to come into play to ground the image in the experience of the viewer. With the image that is expressed verbally (e.g. "mind-forged manacles") the reader is asked to bring together more than one idea in a fusion of creative insight. The starting point is more multi-dimensional than with a simple visual image. In the case of this example, it is the mind that is manacled, and yet "mind-forged" (a powerful and prescient image in the period that the Industrial Revolution was fomenting) is the *adjective* used to qualify the manacles. The result is an association that is both visual and abstracted. It describes a state of mind, not a physical phenomenon. Further affordances of the verbal that are often taken for granted are its sentential framing of meaning (despite Blake's lack of punctuation); its arrangement into four statements, themselves frames for rhythmic patterning (reinforced by rhyme) in their tight stanzas; the implication of 'song', as in the title of the book; and the arrangement of abstract ideas enmeshed through the language and the history of the language with actual physical experience. The narrative element is subdued in this poem, given that the poem is set in the present tense, but it is present in the voice and perspective of the narrator who walks through the streets and observes.

Third, what other modes are used or implied by the poem? This is where a spectrum from implied multimodality to explicit multimodality will be useful. It must be acknowledged that there is no such thing as a purely mono-modal work. Even the printed words of a poem have a visual dimension, and it might be interesting to speculate whether the handwritten/painted words in the illustrated version are significantly different from the typeset version. More importantly, the typeset poem is surrounded by white space, as all poems are. This space suggests that in addition to the framing provided by the page itself, the poem consists of words within an invisible frame. There is no need to punctuate this framed work: it is recognized as a poem because the words do not go up to the right-hand edge of the page; they are further framed in stanzas, and the lines are of roughly equal length in iambic tetrameter rhythm. These visual cues reinforce the fact that the reader is not only looking at a poem but also hearing it as a song. In other words, the implicit multimodality of the poem is to include sound—in the head of the reader, or in actual performance as a song.

Classical Precedents 13

What of the interstices of the modes? It has already been noted that the explicitly visual elements of the illustrated poem are wrapped around the poem. They are part of an organic whole, and clearly, such a visual/verbal creation was Blake's intention. He did not publish the poems separately from their illustrations. At the same time, there is a clear line drawn between the illustration at the top of the page and the poem underneath it, as if to suggest that as well as the poem being illustrated, the words of the poem complement and add a different meaning to the illustration. This symbiotic relationship suggests that the visual and verbal elements are not in tension, but complement each other. There is nothing to read into the positioning of the illustration and the poem in this case. In most of the illustrated poems in *Songs of Innocence and Experience*, the illustration decorates the poem by surrounding it.

Fourth, and finally, what are the sparks of meaning that are generated by the juxtaposition of the modes in these illustrated poems? The strong contrast between light and dark in the illustration (with an emphasis on darkness and cold) adds a dimension of the poem and draws our attention to the soot of the child chimney sweepers and "every blackning church". The "Marriage hearse" is also an evocation of blackness, darkness and death in the very heart of joy. But there is no depiction of the chains and "charter'd" nature of the streets that are such powerful images in the poem and none of the fire that is depicted in the illustration, but does not appear in the poem. Each of these powerful images is allowed to speak for itself, thus providing a richer imagery for the illustrated poem than in the seemingly monomodal printed version of the poem.

Modes and Media

Kress and van Leeuwen (2001) and Kress (2010) have discussed the relationship between multimodality and what is often conflated with 'multimedia' approaches. In general terms, modes are "semiotics resources" (2001: 21) which can be combined to suit particular communicative purposes within a specific rhetorical (political and social discourse) context in space and time. Media can be thought of as 'hardware'—"the material resources used in the production of semiotic products and events, including both the tools and materials used" (2001: 22). To put the distinction even more sharply: modes constitute the message and media the vehicle via which that message is delivered. To take the example of the Blake poem discussed earlier, the combination of word and image is multimodal; the mechanism via which the poem is produced and distributed (the copperplate engraved prints and the hand-coloured decoration, the handwritten script, the printing, the distribution in book form) describes the media used. The present book does not use the term 'multimedia' for a number of reasons: first, because of the confusing conflation with 'multimodal'; second, because the affordances of media in the contemporary are a better way of accounting for the power

14 *Classical Precedents*

and ubiquity of a range of media platforms than a simple 'multimedia' label. Kress (2010: 22) sets out clearly the contemporary media landscape, including a characterization that includes the affordances of participation (I would add, marked by spectra of access and use); the global and local reach of media; the possibilities of user-generated content; and the "convergence of *representational, productive and communicational functions* in technologies and devices" (ibid.). Multimodality works very well within this hybrid and fast-changing media landscape, although it was also operational before the advent of the Internet, handheld digital devices, etc.

In terms of poetics, the particular case of film is discussed in Chapter 9 in relation to the work of John Berger.

Contemporary Multimodality and Poetics

What has cognitive poetics to do with multimodality and poetics? Cognitive poetics is a hybrid and "a new science of literature and reading" (Stockwell 2002: 11. See also Stockwell 2007). On the one hand, it draws on the principles of cognitive science, especially the sub-disciplines of cognitive psychology and cognitive linguistics.[3] On the other, it derives from literary stylistics, initially based on poetry, but broadening to include all literary forms (and thus, for example, drawing on narratology). The cognitive element indicates that the field of cognitive poetics is very much concerned with reading and interpretation. Although poetics is generally concerned with both production—the craft of literature—and reception, cognitive poetics emphasizes the reader's perspective and draws on reader response theory. Its associations with rhetoric are tenuous and principally through the effect on an audience. If Aristotle's definition of rhetoric as 'the art of persuasion' is adopted, then the connection is clear: it answers the question, "How do poetry and other literary forms affect the reader?" If, however, a wider and more contemporary definition of rhetoric as 'the arts of discourse' is accepted, then cognitive poetics' emphasis on the reader is less relevant. Cognitive poetics refers to the reader-text relationship, whereas the present study is more concerned with the triad of composer/rhetor, the multimodal work and the audience. My claim in this opening chapter is that a rhetoric/poetics framework for studying artworks through poetics is more inclusive, more integrated and more powerful than the various strands that have combined to form cognitive poetics. Already cognitive poetics is dividing into various additional sub-strands. There are fewer publications in the field than in the 2000s, when the movement was in full flow.

A more promising direction is indicated by the application of cognitive poetics not only to literature but also in "other media such as the visual, haptic, kinetic and acoustic arts".[4] For the purposes of the present book, and more precisely, these can be called the visual, haptic, kinetic and acoustic *modes*. However, the emphasis in published papers in the field is still on cognition, albeit 'embodied cognition'. The approach is more synaesthetic (the effect on the senses) than multimodal (the resources available for making meaning).

Work by Norris and Maier (2014), Shackelford (2014) and Gibbons (2013, 2014) has begun to explore the implications of multimodality for poetics, often with regard to e-literature and e-poetry, and its potential to exploit multimodal software interfaces. Gibbons (2008) claims that the turn of the millennium has seen not only an exploration of multimodality in relation to literature but also "an increase in the inclusion of typography, graphics and illustration in fiction" (2008: 107). As literary analysis is largely receptive, the approach again draws on a cognitive-poetic perspective to make sense of the multimodal properties of the 'imagetext novel', as well as on theories of embodiment. With a focus on poetry, Alghadeer (2014) explores the effect of multimodality and digitization on the reading of poetic forms. Citing Koskimaa (2007), she mentions the "dual challenge" which "involves both acknowledging and maintaining the specificity of the literary discourse and undermining the overall media landscape, including various media forms" (2014: 88). To reframe the challenge, multimodality theory emerged in the 1990s, at the same time as wide access to the Internet, with its multimodal resources to make meaning. This is not to say that multimodality did not exist before the '90s. It simply accelerated and made more available multimodal composition. The challenge for the seemingly monomodal poetic text, then, is a) how to compose and read the traditional poetic text in the light of an awareness of multimodality and b) how to compose and respond to poetic texts that include sound, image, moving image, etc. In the latter category can be included "Twitter and haiku, Instagram and photograph poems, Prezi and virtual poetry, poetry with Movie Maker, poetry blogs, poetry prompts, digital collage poetry, and online poetry posters" (2014: 90).

What is common to the work of Gibbons, Alghadeer, Shackelford and others is a sense that the seemingly static conventional poetic text both embodies and invites *movement*. That movement is made more explicit when other modes are conjoined with print on a page. Such perspectives make us acutely aware that print on a page is part of a dynamic meaning encounter between the reader and the poem. The poem is a vehicle for movement. Hence poetics must embrace the sense of movement. How the dynamic meaning-making of poetry operates within the notion of framing—explored elsewhere in this book—will be a fruitful path to tread.

Notes

1 A very good explication of the relationship between possible worlds and modal logic can be found by Ryan (2013) at www.lhn.uni-hamburg.de/article/possible-worlds, accessed 9 February 2016.
2 There is another perspective that is often cited: that of the combinatorial. It is not of relevance here.

16 *Classical Precedents*

3 It is accepted that cognition is more than the rational operation of the brain or mind, and that in its contemporary sense, it refers to "such processes and phenomena as perception, memory, attention, problem-solving, language, thinking and imagery". See https://www2.bc.edu/~richarad/lcb/fea/tsur/cogpoetics.html, accessed 17 February 2016.

4 See www.semioticon.com/virtuals/poetics/, accessed 17 February 2016.

2 Poetry in Multimodal Presentations

Introduction

Not all poetry confines itself to printed words surrounded by blank white space on a page. In performance, and even in modest readings of poems on the radio or in live performance, there is more than one mode in operation (sounds, speech, movement, gesture, etc.). Furthermore, there is a long tradition of poems being presented alongside illustrations, drawings, paintings, photographs and other highly visual modes of expression. This chapter looks at what kinds of affordances are available when poetry works alongside other modes in a range of different media. Some of the history of the relationship between poems and images will be explored: not only poems alongside illustrations but also the visual dimension of poetry itself. An exemplary account of poems operating in a cross-cultural multimodal format is discussed, and the transformation from written poetic text through libretto, musical composition and dance is traced through works by Milton, Handel and Mark Morris. Contemporary artworks are also used to convey the possibilities of explicit multimodal practice.

The Multimodal Potential of Poetry

Before the exploration of explicit multimodality in poetry, it is necessary to consider the nature of poetry itself and what it *offers* in terms of multimodality. Elsewhere in the book, this has been called *implicit* multimodality, but its implicit nature is a powerful one. It needs to be explored first, as it will suggest why the focus of the book is on multimodality and poetry, and why poetry itself provides a basis for a new poetics.

From the perspective of one social semiotic system with two principal modes—language, as shaped by speech or writing—it could be said that poetry is the closest to a multimodal principle in the making of meaning than any other verbal construct. Poetry, among its many characteristics, arises from intensity. That intensity is not always intensity of feeling; it can also be intensity of looking, of hearing, of sensing some framed experience, of thought, of memory—or a combination of any or all of these. It almost

18 *Poetry in Multimodal Presentations*

always calls on the senses and is sometimes physically driven. Its close association with rhythm is an expression of this intense presence. Most poetry, too, is grounded in the material world. However much it tries to describe the spiritual, it often resorts to physical images or descriptions to convey what it wants to say.

In these senses, it is different from prose. To take the last example, a spiritual text might take poetic form, or it might opt for a less intense exposition in prose. A philosophical text might do the same, largely because it wishes to spell out explicitly logical connections or metaphysical insights.

If the argument is accepted that poetry condenses the complexity of experience by intensifying it (in speech or in writing), what are the tools with which it does so? It uses framing, rhythm, metaphor and a high degree of selection to create the words in the air or on the page/screen. In previous books, I have concentrated on framing and rhythm (Andrews 2011, 2016). Suffice it to say here that the highly framed nature of the poem (a 'boxed' work in which the writing does not go up to the right-hand edge of the page, or the pause before a different style of voice is used to demarcate the oral poem from ordinary everyday speech) is key to its intensity. So is the consciously rhythmic nature of all poetry, whether it is metrical or in freer rhythms inspired by jazz or contemporary choreography. These rhythms, closely allied to the intellectual meanings of the words and providing a rhythmic physicality to the language, shape the experience for the audience/reader.

What of metaphor and selectivity? Metaphor and imagery have long been seen as part of the armoury of poetry. Metaphor provides the multi-levelled exploration of meaning. If framing and rhythm provide the horizontal, lateral movement of the words in time and space, metaphor provides the verticality, thus making the poem a powerful multi-dimensional construct via which to 'say something'. Metaphor is sometimes used to disguise a complex set of meanings, but often is expressed in simple terms. A good example, again, comes from Blake:

> O Rose, thou art sick!
> The invisible worm
> That flies in the night,
> In the howling storm,
>
> Has found out thy bed
> Of crimson joy,
> And his dark secret love
> Does thy life destroy.

(For exegesis of 'The Sick Rose', see, for example, Gardner 1968, 50–1 and 127.) The imagery is simple, but the range of reference wide and profound. The intensity of the poem, partly created by its brevity, draws on the power of the core imagery to the extent that the image becomes a symbol: of a

Poetry in Multimodal Presentations 19

fallen Eden, of beauty and perfection embodied in a closed garden space, of corruption, of blighted love in a pestilent city. There is a similar intensity in 'The Tyger' and other poems from the *Songs of Innocence and Experience*. But it is not just a device used by Blake: poets from different historical periods and different cultures use the metaphorical power of imagery to convey their meanings.

Selectivity manifests in poetry in a number of ways. First, in the very fact that most poems are shorter than most pieces of prose or other literary works, such as plays (longer poems, like epics, draw on prose or storytelling structures such as narrative) means that they are more highly selective. Every word counts in a poem, whereas in prose it is possible to replace one word with an alternative and not notice the difference (because the attention is usually on the meaning, not the language). In poetry, the attention is on the meanings *and the language* at the same time. Second, selectivity sometimes takes the form of a diction, a selection from the language, that operates like a code. Third, the musical and choreographic properties of words are used in poetry, thus linking the abstract 'meaning' of the words to physicality (sound, movement).

If these four elements, framing, rhythm, metaphor and selection, are put together, a distinctive compression of the language is found, which, paradoxically, suggests absence: absence of other words that would help to express the sentiments more explicitly, more abstractly. So what is not said in a poem is as important as what is said. The words of a poem draw in other dimensions of experience, other worlds, other modes. In doing so, they create an explosive, tightly packed entity in which, if the reader is attuned, a crucible is created in which chemical-like reactions may occur. The elements in this crucible are informed by the features described earlier; the reaction is the reader's/listener's, drawing on his/her own experience and previous exposure to poems and other artworks.

In multimodal terms, to say poetry contains other modes *implicitly* is to understate the power of this particular meta-genre. Like its close associate, song, it embodies multimodality, whether orally or in print/on-screen. When it is unpacked, it reveals multi-levelled and multi-dimensional meanings that take semiotic expression in other modes.

Selina Nwulu, 'A Strange Kind of Beauty'

'A Strange Kind of Beauty' (Nwulu 2016) is a poem by Selina Nwulu, Young Poet for London 2015/16. It was commissioned by the cultural education charity *A New Direction* and appeared in *RSA Journal* (the journal of the Royal Society for the encouragement of the Arts, Manufactures and Commerce, London). It's a poem that deserves full reprinting:

Let's play a game.
Let's peel back the skin of this city

20 *Poetry in Multimodal Presentations*

and rearrange its insides till
we have created a strange kind of beauty
we don't recognise. Let's move this city's landmarks
like chess pieces; take the London Eye and
roll it to the edges of the city,
drag the Tate into zone five,
have the Royal Opera House playing
in outskirt basement halls,
grab some chicken and chips via the London Coliseum.

Classrooms becomes their own theatres
so that young people can unfurl their
aches into creative roars. For the shy ones
the pen becomes a microphone
to their power and those words travel further
than the lulls in their stomachs. Instead
those notebook soliloquies become a future
bouquet of verses blossoming into the mouths of thespians.

Art galleries are not echo chambers
of prestige. Instead their doors have become
a fleshy open smile, their tongues speaking in
a language of visual miscellany. Graffiti masterpieces
are hanging with Cézanne and Monet. There are
Dali moustaches on corridors twitching and beckoning
young people to find new works of art to get lost in.
Workshops are being run by Barka,
wide floors and windows for children to paint on.

Young people are composing digital sonatas
in their rooms and we've taken their roofs off.
We've unplugged their headphones so that
those tsks tsks in their ears have now become a siren of noise
the sky has broken into an orchestra of patois symphonies
there's grime-fused electro sprinkled with classical undertones,
rap lyrics chasing bhangra, bouncing off buildings,
the sky a new constellation of sounds
pulsating like shooting stars across this city.

Let's play this game,
Let's play it everywhere.
Till we do not know where the
highs and lows of this city
begin and end,
till the backbone of London is a

helix of hybrid noises, words, neon colours and shapes
for young people to skip and dance across.
So that wherever they go
their footprints will leave traces
of the city they played in.
So that wherever they go
they are left reeking
with this strange kind of beauty

and they will not live less
they will not live less
they will not live less.

There is an animation of the poem at www.anewdirection.org.uk/a-strange-kind-of-beauty which I will come back to. First, though, the poem itself. It already has not only the qualities of potential and implicit multimodality that have been described in this chapter but also direct reference to a multimodal and multimedia world through its synaesthetic sensibility and imagery: "the pen becomes a microphone"; "those notebook soliloquies become a future/bouquet of verses blossoming in the mouths of thespians"; "a/helix of hybrid noises, words, neon colours and shapes/for young people to skip and dance across". There is more, like "rap lyrics chasing bhangra, bouncing off buildings,/the sky a new constellation of sounds/pulsating like shooting stars across this city". The sheer energy of the poem's language, inspired by the city's own multimodal and multimedia environment in which buildings themselves play a part, uses imagery, too, to convey its drive—"like shooting stars".

The animation uses graphics, words, sounds and images alongside the spoken voice of the poem. It's a version of a poem that both spins off the imagination and verve of the words of the original, but which also creates a new genre: the animated poem. Thus it is a separate work in itself, a new creation spawned from an existing one and in response to it. There are different transformations taking place in what has happened to Milton's poems, 'L'Allegro' and 'Il Penseroso', discussed next. Again, these are not tributes or versions, but new works created in different modes and media.

Such transformations and transductions from one mode to another could be grouped as what Selina Nwulu calls "tongues speaking in/a language of visual miscellany", but what this poem also suggests is that the creative impulse can take any modal form and move into any other modes. In the cases described in this chapter, the starting points are printed verbal poems. They could also be works of music or photography or film which can be the starting point for commentary and/or response in other modes—rather like a multi-faceted kaleidoscope of expressive possibility.

'A Strange Kind of Beauty' is a tribute to young people and the creation of youthful energy and imagination. The poetic that is implied is one of

22 *Poetry in Multimodal Presentations*

fast-moving hybridity, interrelated modal energy and conventional poetic (metaphorical) imagination, with the elements of rhythm, framing and selectivity present. Its excited, witty and passionate commitment to the city is infectious; at the same time, it is a fashioned work of art, pushing at the boundaries of expression through sheer drive and zest. It not only suggests, in its juxtaposition of elements of the city, an irreverent spirit but also lays down the ground for poetry that is urban, sensory and invitational. It no longer fits into the category of emotion recollected in tranquility, or the best words in the best order, or notions of the pastoral and/or sublime. This is twenty-first century poetry, and it requires a new poetics.

L'Allegro, Il Penseroso ed Il Moderato

One kind of relation between poetry and the other arts is the successive adaptations of Milton's poems, 'L'Allegro' and 'Il Penseroso'—first, set to music by Handel and second, Handel's version choreographed by Mark Morris as *L'Allegro, Il Penseroso ed Il Moderato*. In each successive adaptation, there is a multimodal layering of one art form upon another.

Milton's poems are dated around 1631 and may have originated from a debate about night and day for an academic audience at Cambridge (Carey 1971: 130). As Carey suggests,

> *L'Allegro* and *Il Penseroso* are metrically almost identical. No precedent has been found in English for such a combination of intricate prelude with couplet continuation. Each poem begins with a prelude of ten lines rhyming *abbacddeec*, with the number of syllables per line, excluding feminine endings, alternately six and ten. This 6/10 pattern of line lengths presumably derives from the seven and eleven syllable lines of the *canzone*, just as the rhyme scheme reflects the Italian sonnet.
>
> (Ibid.)

The intertextual derivation and allusions of the poems—fully discussed by Carey—is not the focus of attention here, except to say that the rich texture of allusion makes each poem more than a lyric representation of states of mind. Rather, the metrical, rhyming and formal features of the poems are the surface indicators of the rhythmic identity and their position as academic descriptions of happiness and melancholy, as in a masque. What is telling as far as the present analysis goes is that the poems can be seen not only as comparisons of day and night, mirth and melancholy but also as a rising sequence of steps in Milton's own development (and more generally) which form an argument as to which sides of one's nature should be suppressed or developed. It is notable, however, that there is no such poem as *Il Moderato* in Milton's canon, which would have been the logical, intellectual (as well as spiritual) conclusion to the trio of poems.

Poetry in Multimodal Presentations   23

L'Allegro opens with the prelude, like an argument, addressed to what it is *not* going to address: "loathed melancholy". It then moves, as if into gear, with the running and rhyming couplets that set the rhythm and tempo of the following 140 or so lines. The poem draws not only on classical and contemporary precedents but also on pastoral tradition. It paints a picture of happiness and jollity, associated with light, simple pleasures and dancing. There is a breathless syntactic drive to the poem (long sentences), for example:

> If the earlier season lead
> To the tanned haycock in the mead,
> Sometimes with secure delight
> The upland hamlets will invite,
> When the merry bells ring round,
> And the jocund rebecks sound
> To many a youth, and many a maid
> Dancing in the chequered shade;
> And young and old come forth to play
> On a sunshine holiday.
>
> (Lines 89–99)

Il Penseroso takes similar form. The diction makes it clear why Milton was revered by Wordsworth and Keats:

> Hide me from day's garish eye,
> While the bee with honied thigh,
> That at her flowery work doth sing,
> And the waters murmuring
> With such consort as they keep,
> Entice the dewy-feathered Sleep;
> And let some strange mysterious dream,
> Wave at his wings in airy stream,
> Of lively portraiture displayed,
> Softly on my eyelids laid.
>
> (Lines 141–50)

This is highly verbal art, drawing on the mellifluousness and sonority of the language. But through its classical allusions, as well as through its depiction of concepts, it paints word pictures too.

The full-text libretto of Handel's *L'Allegro, Il Penseroso ed Il Moderato* (1740) is by Charles Jennens, who added 'Il Moderato' to create a third movement to the pastoral ode. The libretto itself takes selections from Milton's poem and re-works them to accompany, or provide the basis, for Handel's composition. Its re-arrangements (re-compositions) at the verbal

24   *Poetry in Multimodal Presentations*

level are interesting. The libretto opens with the beginnings of each of the Milton poems:

1. Accompagnato

L'Allegro (tenor)
Hence loathed Melancholy
Of Cerberus, and blackest midnight born,
In Stygian cave forlorn
'Mongst horrid shapes, and shrieks, and sights unholy,
Find out some uncouth cell,
Where brooding darkness spreads his jealous wings,
And the night-raven sings;
There under ebon shades, and low-brow'd rocks,
As ragged as thy locks,
In dark Cimmerian desert ever dwell.

2. Accompagnato

Il Penseroso (soprano)
Hence vain deluding joys,
Dwell in some idle brain,
And fancies fond with gaudy shapes possess,
As thick and numberless
As the gay motes that people the sunbeams,
Or likest hovering dreams
The fickle pensioners of Morpheus' train.

Missing from Milton's opening to 'Il Penseroso' are three lines, italicized:

Hence vain deluding Joys,
The brood of Folly without father bred,
How little you bestead,
Or fill the fixed mind with all your toys;
Dwell in some idle brain

And so the first and second movements progress with alternating solos, airs, recitatives and choruses, selecting where thought necessary to suit the music and the voices of the soloists and chorus. The striking addition is the addition of the third movement and of the third element in the title of the libretto: Il Moderato. This movement was added, apparently at Handel's request, to provide a single moral design. Here is a quotation from Jennen's accomplished but sub-Miltonic 'Il Moderato':

Il Moderato (bass)
Come, with native lustre shine,

Moderation, grace divine,
Whom the wise God of nature gave,
Mad mortals from themselves to save.
Keep, as of old, the middle way,
Nor deeply sad, nor idly gay,
But still the same in look and gait,
Easy, cheerful and sedate.

Immediately striking are the shorter sentences, the more English, less Latinate syntax and the reduced allusiveness. The third section is moderate both in subject and style, perhaps fitting to the late Augustan desire for balance and propriety.

The score of Handel's *L'Allegro, Il Penseroso ed Il Moderato* (Figure 2.1) takes traditional form and can be found online (see Handel 1859, for example). The Jennens libretto takes its place along scoring for violoncello, fagotti, bassi and pianoforte. The language of the libretto is both in English and German.

There is no research or evidence on how exactly Handel composed. Either he worked straight from Jennens's libretto to the keyboard and orchestrated the other instruments around that transduction from printed words to musical scoring, or there was an iterative movement between the libretto and actual playing on the keyboard that later developed into the full score or a combination of these compositional practices. Whichever, the transformation is a multimodal one: from words to music, from seemingly two-dimensional words on a printed page to the three-dimensional physical interpretation and creation of musical accompaniment. In turn, if the compositional practice involves physical instrumentation on the keyboard, then the return to the two-dimensional written and then printed score requires further transduction.

Performance of the score requires yet more transduction into a range of interacting modes: the assembling of a baroque orchestra (one is even tempted to think of multimodality in transport logistics terms, with musicians travelling to rehearse and play the piece); the interpretation of the score by the orchestra, whether led by the composer himself or by a member of the orchestra; the production of sound through the various instruments; the exploration of the relationship between the words of the libretto and the music of the score; the integration of the singers; the acoustics of the space in which the rehearsals and performance take place. Although in one sense it may seem banal to catalogue the various elements that make up such a transformation of score to performance, it is important to recognize that a great degree of transduction from mode to mode is taking place, and the combination of modes, from the physical to the verbal to the musical, is rich in significance. The journey from the poetic starting point of Milton's poems to Handel's 'ode' in performance is at once simple and complex, at once an expression of creative energy and brilliance and at the same time a complex combination of different modes of making meaning.

Figure 2.1 The Opening Bars of Handel's *L'Allegro, Il Penseroso ed Il Moderato*

Figure 2.1 (Continued)

Figure 2.1 (Continued)

Figure 2.1 (Continued)

30 *Poetry in Multimodal Presentations*

Versions of Handel's ode can be found on YouTube and in CD format. Listening to it, over 250 years since its composition, via various media (in live performance, in high-quality digital sound on headphones in transit or in a room) re-invents the multi-levelled nature of the work.

Mark Morris, the New York–based chorographer, used Handel's ode to choreograph *L'Allegro, Il Penseroso ed Il Moderato* for his dance company and for the first performance in 1988. Again, this can be accessed via You-Tube or via DVD (Mark Morris Dance Group 2014). The credit list for the production and performance at Teatro Real, Madrid, in addition to 24 dancers, includes, as well as the choreographer himself, a set designer, costume designer and lighting designer; and a conductor of the orchestra and chorus master, with four soloists: two sopranos, a tenor and baritone. The text of the accompanying programme/brochure is presented in English, French and Spanish. The film of the 2014 production has its own credits: director, producer and executive producer, as does the Blu-ray edition on DVD, including authoring, artwork and photos. In short, without even mentioning all the individuals in the teams supporting those principal roles named earlier, hundreds of people are involved in the creation, production and performance of the work, as well as the recording, editing and production (and dissemination) of the DVD.

Such works (this one is seen as Morris's signature work) invite reviews. An example is that by Kisselgoff (1990) in the *New York Times* of 8 October 1990, following a performance at the Brooklyn Academy of Music. Inevitably, in the reflective verbal printed form of dance reviews, the language is impressionistic and abstracted from the work itself, but it still conveys the historical and multimodal layering of the work:

> He choreographs here with a deceptive simplicity, a clarity of pattern in which broad strokes, both in steps and structure, hint at basic emotions and aspirations, not without complexity of feeling.
>
> Visually, 'L'Allegro' has a striking impact, and it is not surprising that the cumulative effect of all its ingredients—the superbly sung passages and overlapping dance sequences, framed by a series of prosceniums on stage—impelled the audience at the end into a roaring standing ovation [. . .]
>
> The brilliance of Morris' approach has been to create a pastoral imagery of his own that harks back to Milton's images without ever literalizing them [. . .]
>
> Morris is less a choreographer of steps than shapes [. . .] Within the American dance tradition, the piece has less to do with the kind of a nonillusionist Neo-Classicism George Balanchine developed in America than the lineage of modern-dance pioneers who saw the circle as a healing and communal round, a symbol of an ideal world.

This review brings us back to words and print, and also to Milton. The perception by the reviewer that the choreographer "creates a pastoral

Poetry in Multimodal Presentations 31

imagery of his own that harks back to Milton's images without ever literalizing them" brings us full circle to the suggestive power of poetry and its multimodal potential—here brilliantly realized by the works of Handel and Morris. To summarize, there is multimodal layering: the imagined intensity of words on a page or in the air in Milton's conception; the paring down of the words, and the addition of a third section in Jennens's libretto; the setting in music, represented by both the score with its own semiotic system and by the music, as performed and heard by Handel; and then the choreographic transformations, harking back to Milton's pastoral imagery but re-imagining it via the lenses of Jennens and Handel and in the media and modes of theatre, artwork, costume design, stage design, lighting design and dance moves. The complexity is not only multimodal and multimedia, with each mode playing its part in an economy of creative production; it is also a series of transformations in time and place.

Transartation!

An exhibition exploring the interface of word, still and moving image and translation (between modes and between languages) took place in 2017 in Dundee, Scotland and Norwich, England. *Transartation!* described itself as "a travelling exhibition of translated 'objects', workshops, artists' talks and site-specific works [. . .] to start an exploration of translation, in the way this reflects how texts and ideas travel and migrate across geographical, cultural and fictional spaces" (*Transartation!* 2017: inside front cover). The principle behind the exhibition is described more fully next:

> Translation is a far-reaching activity, albeit often an invisible one. Translation operates both as a practice and as a metaphor. As a practice, it is the process which allows stories and ideas to travel freely between peoples and cultures. As a metaphor, translation manifests itself as a journey, a moving-across, a transformation, or an interpretive juggling act, often conjured up in discussions that explore nationhood, identity but also creativity. Increasingly, translation is being recognized as a transdisciplinary activity, drawing upon and contributing to a whole range of ideas and practices that include, but can go far beyond, taking a text from one language into another.
>
> (*Transartation!* 2017 catalogue)

Before looking at a few examples of works from this exhibition, it is worth noting the social and political context of the poetic that is behind this exhibition. The formal translational (transductive) moves from word to image, image to word, and the contiguous relationship between the modes is at the core of the multimodal poetic. These are not so much 'stories', although narratives can play a major part in the structuration of words as stories and photos as 'essays'. They are more to do with the modes of communication

32 Poetry in Multimodal Presentations

and their interrelationships. Setting these within a larger frame of the socio-political touches on the wider references to identities, geography, migration and nationhood in a globalized world.

One of the artists, Kirsteen Anderson, describes how her artwork 'Pomegranate Palimpsest' captures

> the way visual and verbal texts "intertranslate" each other: neither has precedence in the creative process—sometimes words came first, sometimes images. The superimposed layers of the palimpsest never entirely blot out those beneath which are positioned so that verbal and visual interpenetrate each other when the palimpsest is viewed from above. In this way the traditional ekphrastic prioritisation of word over image is undermined.
>
> (Ibid.)

Ekphrasis—the verbal description of a work of art or landscape, or the representation of a poem in visual, dramatic form—is close to the project of the present book: to explore the multimodal and translational dimensions of poetry and thus to question the nature of theory about literary production. It is worth noting the artist's sense of the prioritization of the verbal over the visual, despite the different affordances of the two modes; and the way she layers the artwork to undermine the 'traditional' hierarchy. The prioritization of the verbal over the visual seems no longer to be the case.

Ira Lightman's 'Vista' (Figure 2.2) is "a visual translation of Apollinaire's *Les Fenêtres* poem into a digital city map titled *Vista*" (ibid.)

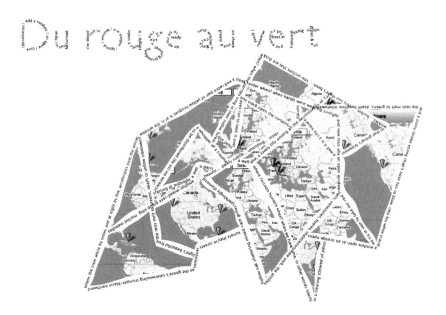

Figure 2.2 Ira Lightman, 'Vista'

Poetry in Multimodal Presentations   33

The catalogue continues:

> The 'pictorial', or better, the 'chromatic' qualities of *Les Fenêtres* are explained by its relationship with Delaunay's series of paintings *Les Fenêtres Simultanées*. In *Vista* the simultaneity of the Apollinaire text and its verbal images and cartography are exemplified into a map. Here the graphic surface of the page yields the multiple square frames, and a fragmented geographical map opens up like cubist windows on the world, onto cities, and possible voyages. The poem-map is exhibited both as a poster and as smaller folded maps which are available to audiences to take home and engage with ideas of poems translated as visual texts.
>
> (Ibid.)

Here there is a Bakhtinian transformation, first from Delaunay (paintings) to Apollinaire (poem) and then from poem in a double translation, from French into English and from poem to poem-map. Furthermore, the poem-map is made available in two media formats: poster and smaller folded map.

Another artist, Verónica Gerber Bicecci, explored the "silences behind a text" (ibid.). Before discussing her work, it is important to acknowledge that silence plays a major and underestimated part in poetic and other literary works, whether in print, on-screen or in performance. To take the silences in free verse, for example: these are key moments in the scoring of a piece of free verse, where rhythm is foregrounded and part of the essence of the work itself. Such jazz-like rhythms cannot be identified, by the composer or the listener/reader, without the time spaces ('rests' in music transcription) between the semiotic elements of the work. Poems, novels, plays, music compositions are inscribed on silence. The silence in poems not only frames the poem (conveyed by the white space around a poem on a printed page) but also enters the poems in the form of line breaks, stanza breaks and verse-paragraph breaks. The duration of these breaks is only indicatively marked in a printed poem: different performances will interpret their duration differently, exactly as in the performance of a piece of music. Such breaks are more a matter of internal rhythmic relativity within the poem than of tempo. Silences can also be critical in plays—and perhaps less so in novels and short stories, where the drive of the narrative is carried in words.

According to the catalogue, the animation

> shows the process in order to exhume the silences of one of the poems in *Four Quartets* by T. S. Eliot. The artist drew straight lines and circles connecting each "comma", "period" and "semicolon", then removed the text. The resulting graphic is a translation gesture to show the invisible machinery behind a text.
>
> (Ibid.)

In the following poem by Bicecci and Anna Milsom, the translation takes on a visual dimension too (Figure 2.3).

34 *Poetry in Multimodal Presentations*

Figure 2.3 Verónica Gerber Bicecci and Anna Milsom, Inverted (and Translated) Poem (2017) Visual Essay

Also displayed at the *Transartation!* traveling exhibition were works by Clive Scott (Figure 2.4). His series from Photography in Translation's Recreation of Reading (2013–16) takes the form of 16 laminated Foamex board panels, each combining paint, photographs and written (verbal) text. Although ostensibly translations from one language to another, these works also explore the multimodality of communication:

> This series of panels asks us what kinds of cross-sensory and associative creativity might be harnessed by literary translation, and asks, too in what ways the exercise of these creative resources allows us to

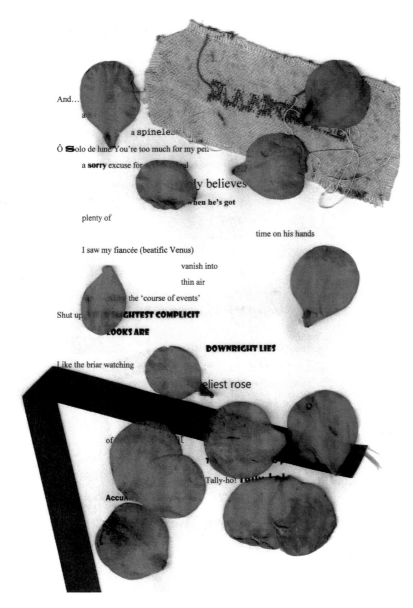

Figure 2.4(i) Clive Scott, 'Dimanches'

re-imagine the ambitions of literary translation. These [. . .] ambitions [. . .] seek to capture the ongoing life of a text in a reading consciousness, permeable to all the solicitations of the hyper-textual, the extra textual and the immediate reading environment.

36 *Poetry in Multimodal Presentations*

Figure 2.4(ii) Clive Scott, 'Au Cabaret-Vert'

What is striking about these works is not only that they are translations from one language to another ('Dimanches' is by Jules Laforgue (1860–87) and 'Au Cabaret-Vert' is by Arthur Rimbaud (1854–91)) but also that the translations are layered. For example, the lines from 'Dimanches' are accompanied by scanned realia: a piece of ribbon, camellia petals and a piece of coarse cloth with the name 'Fidelle' sewn on the reverse.

Finally, another one of the most beautiful of the works on show was an artist book entitled *Translation Games: Still in Translation* (2015) produced by Ricarda Vidal, including work from a number of artists. The conception was to start with an unpublished poem by Denise Riley and give it to an artist (Sam Treadaway) "with the commission to translate the words into imagery". This imagery was not what would be expected from a literary source: not metaphorical read-offs from the printed work on the page, nor a literal depiction of images contained in the writing. Rather, it took the form of similar-sized panels of purely visual response using line, form and colour. Each artist passed on their image to another artist who responded to the image, not the poem. At the end of the visual translation process (word to image, image to image), the final image formed the basis of a competition to retranslate it back into poetry and into three different languages.

3 The Forms and Functions of Rhythm in Poetry
From Metrical to Free Verse

Introduction

Chapter 3 builds on the analysis in Chapter 2 to examine one particular modal aspect of poetry: rhythm. Via a number of examples, the element of rhythm—the arrangement of beats (in their various degrees) in time—is explored. It is argued that rhythmic shape is fundamental to poetry and also plays a part in novels and plays. From simple repetitive rhythms and regular metres at one end of the spectrum to metrical variation, irregular metres and free verse at the other end, rhythmic form is seen as the defining element in poetry and poetics. The function of rhythm is then explored. Thus issues of transduction are raised in moving from a system that is based on beats in time, to a different basis for prosody that tries to capture the relation of time to experience. Examples are provided from translation, in metaphysical poetry and in a poem that is transposed from quatrains to a sonnet and then to prose in order to explore the differences between the various forms.

Rhythm in Translation

In a review by Colin Burrow of Heaney's translation of *Aeneid: Book VI* in *London Reviews of Books* (2016: 13–14), the following passage occurs. It describes in some detail the movements that Heaney has made in the rhythm of the poem as he translates from Latin to English:

> Line lengths vary around the twelve syllable mark, and usually each line contains five main stresses; but every so often Heaney introduces a straight pentameter line. Often these deliberately reverberate with the energy of Milton or of Dryden. So the spirits of the Greeks retreat when they see Aeneas "advance in dazzling armour through the gloom". Generally Heaney reserves regular pentameters to mark heroic violence, as in the description of Salmoneus' punishment for mimicking love—"and blasted Salmoneus headlong down" [. . .] These metrical effects indirectly carry us back to the edgier Virgil of Heaney's earlier writing, in which the *Aeneid* was used both to situate Heaney within the English

The Forms and Functions of Rhythm in Poetry 39

poetic tradition and to push the centre of the tradition in a new direction. This is because very often these "heroic" lines are used to evoke a rugged force which is at odds with the dreamlike marvels of the book as a whole. They seem to embody a very English idiom that does not quite belong within such a sensuous and magical version of the *Aeneid*—one that often seems to have sailed off with Yeats to Byzantium. *A slip in rhythmic gears* can evoke the mismatch between the heavy old world of heroism and the spirits of the underworld. So, when Aeneas tries to embrace Anchises, two pentameter lines are used to describe his corporeal hugging. These are followed by *a sudden rhythmic collapse* as the solid body turns to air:

> Three times he tried to reach arms around that neck.
> Three times the form, reached for in vain, escaped
> *Like a breeze between his hands, a dream on wings.*

The passage is quoted at length, and not just because it is illuminating, incisive critical writing. The italicized phrase reveals the sensitivity to shifts in rhythm and how those shifts are not merely musical but are aligned with—indeed, carry—the sense. The phrases also signify a close association between rhythm (the arrangement of time) and physicality: not only is the content about physicality in the three-line extract but also the ideas are embodied in the rhythm.

Rhythm in Music

The present book is a follow-up to *A Prosody of Free Verse: Explorations in Rhythm* (Andrews 2016), where I attempted to account for the *vers libre* rhythms in late nineteenth and twentieth-century free verse. In that book, I drew on music and contemporary dance to try to forge an appropriate prosody. But rhythm is fundamental to poetry of most kinds and of most periods in history. Conventionally, rhythm is conceived in terms of regularity and beat, with varying lengths of 'feet' in poetry or time signatures in music and varying degrees of beat. The conventional categories of rhythm are isometric and multimetric. In isometric rhythms, time values are multiples or fractions of a beat, and the "measures are equal and are normally accented on the first beat" (Apel 1970: 729)—with that first akin to the pulse that starts the rhythmic line in free verse, or the foot hitting the floor in folk music. These measures are marked by bar lines in Western notation.

It is this tendency to metricality in isometric rhythms that characterizes much of Western music and poetry and

> especially in dance music and in music based on dance rhythms, there is a strong tendency to group the measures in twos and powers of two [. . .] Regularity of phrasing produces a meter on a higher level, so that

40   *The Forms and Functions of Rhythm in Poetry*

isometric groups of measures become units of time, and the space of time measured by these units may in turn become a unit in a yet larger group, and so on.

(Apel 1970: 729)

In other words, dance music and poetry (that follows its patterns in regular metres) have a tendency to build relationships and movements in time in systematic ways, both hierarchically and sequentially.

Multimetric rhythms are less common in poetry, because the multi-layered nature of multimetric rhythm depends on a number of isometric or looser rhythms playing across each other at the same time. Some African and Indian music uses such rhythms, as does Gregorian chant and some of the works of Stravinsky and Bartók. In such music, rhythm is foregrounded: it could be said that the movement of sound in time is foregrounded, rather than providing a foundation for the elaboration of melody, cadence and other features of pitch and harmony.

If an analogy between poetic rhythms and musical rhythms is made, it could be said that poetry follows the range of rhythm in music, but that it does so with different means and in a different mode. First, rhythm is fundamental to poetry as a result of its transformation of the everyday speaking voice into something approaching song. Second, in the written mode, the spatial arrangement of the words on the page in poetry (as opposed to prose) operates like a score in which the visual patterning of lines, stanzas and verse paragraphs suggests a rhythmic dimension. Third, the difference between music and poetry is that poems are composed of words, which have conceptual and abstract content. This is why multimetric rhythm is virtually impossible in poetry: poems in different rhythms could be read at the same time, but the conceptual content would intercut and make comprehension difficult (the device is used occasionally in plays, where characters speak at the same time—but usually for the same duration and to give the impression of cacophony).

It is interesting that modal rhythm in music emerged in the thirteenth century in church music and through close association of music and words in chansons, troubadours' songs and plainsong through uniform note values and the regular variation of long and short values. Music was approximating or moving closer to word patterns, as well as vice versa. The establishment of consistent repetition in simple rhythmic patterns, and the congruence of the metrical foot with the bar in musical notation, helped to shape the metrical categories of trochee, iamb, dactyl, anapaest, spondee, tribrach and other such 'feet' that in turn became the small units of metrical rhythm that have influenced Western poetry. Once modal rhythmic patterns were established, variations such as duple and triple meter or dotted rhythms, triplets and syncopation were introduced to provide entertainment and delight, and to defeat expectation. The development in poetic form could be seen to be

The Forms and Functions of Rhythm in Poetry   41

taking place at the same time as the possible synergies between words and music (and dance) were explored.

This is not the occasion to trace the history of rhythm in poetry from the thirteenth century to the present, but to consider what the implications of the rhythmic connections in music and dance are for poetry and poetics, and how those connections might be illuminated from a multimodal perspective.

Music and Dance

Having proposed that isometric and multimetric rhythms, along with the emergence of modal rhythms, set the template for poetic development from the thirteenth century onwards, what are the distinctive affordances of music and dance that can enrich a new theory of poetics? Apart from the reference to different modes—sound in music and movement in dance—there is a physicality to music and dance that is both implicit and explicit in poetic composition.

A word does not exist in a vacuum, or as a mathematical cipher. It has sonic (phonemic) qualities in speech and graphic, visual qualities in print/on-screen. These qualities are physically rooted in perception and experience and highly subject to context. Although a word is an abstraction from tangible phenomena ('tree' is a conceptual, generic abstraction from any number of actual trees), it has reference to its origins—and the field of etymology traces the origin and evolution of words. As soon as a single word is put alongside another word, the linguistic context begins to pin down the abstraction. Such juxtaposition is or could be purely spatial, but it becomes sequential when syntax is employed to create particular meanings. Sequencing of this kind provides the temporal dimension as well as the spatial. In poetry, as has been suggested earlier, spatial arrangement in significant. It acts as a form of scoring, of determining how the words relate to each other and how they relate, within the framing of the poem, and also with the space beyond the frame.

The musical dimension of poetry inheres in the sound of the words, and different languages carry their own sonorities and dynamics. It is also present in rhythmic patterns and variations, from regular metres through variations on those metres, to free verse, with varying degrees of rhyme (from fully rhymed to half rhymes to blank verse and/or with internal rhyming) whose function is primarily to reinforce the rhythm, as well as provide a soundscape to the poem itself.

The dance dimension is evident in the arrangement of words on a printed/on-screen page. There is pattern, movement and turns from one line-end to the next line. The choreographic nature of poetic composition determines where these articulated moves take place. They are far more prevalent in poetry than in any other form of verbal construct because of the tight

42   *The Forms and Functions of Rhythm in Poetry*

framing of the poem as a work of art. Although turns in large-scale narrative works, such as novels, or even in shorter narrative works such as short stories and prose poems, are significant, they do not operate at word, phrase, line, sentence and stanza/strophe/verse paragraph level in such detailed and in such foregrounded ways.

An Example

The title under which the following poem appears is apt: *Songs and Sonnets* (little songs). John Donne's 1633 collection comes in the wake of English Elizabethan exploration of the sonnet as a form and after a century of close association between music, poetry and dance.

The Good-Morrow

I wonder by my troth, what thou, and I
Did, till we lov'd? were we not wean'd till then?
But suck'd on countrey pleasures, childishly?
Or snorted we in the seaven sleepers den?
T'was so; But this, all pleasures fancies bee.
If ever any beauty I did see,
Which I desir'd, and got, t'was but a dream of thee.

And now good morrow to our waking soules,
Which watch not one another out of feare;
For love, all love of other sights controules,
And makes one little roome, an every where.
Let sea-discoverers to new worlds have gone,
Let Maps to others, worlds on worlds have showne,
Let us possesse one world, each hath one, and is one.

My face is thine eye, thine in mine appeares,
And true plaine hearts doe in the faces rest,
Where can we finde two better hemispheares
Without sharpe North, without declining West?
What ever dies, was not mixt equally;
If our two loves be one, or, thou and I
Love so alike, that none doe slacken, none can die.

A conventional literary reading of the poem would mention its structure (three septets), its rhyme scheme (ABABCCC), its metre, its use of metaphysical imagery and its colloquial voice. These are all embraced within a multimodal interpretation of the poem, but given more focus and significance. Applying the elements of framing, rhythm, intensity/compression and

The Forms and Functions of Rhythm in Poetry   43

reference to other modes, the following can be added. The poem is framed by a social moment as well as a poetic one: a good morning greeting from one lover to another. Formally, it is framed by the use of three two-part septets: seven-line verses with a break between the quatrain and the tercet, not marked by a line break but by a change in rhythm reinforced by a change in rhyme pattern. The three stanzas each contain an argument that work together. Their sequence could be re-arranged without too much dislocation to the meaning or the developing argument. In this sense the poem draws on dance patterning in that each of the stanzas could provide a starting point; each is complete within itself, and as three stanzas, they sit in equal relation to each other. The difference between such spatial patterning and that of the Petrarchan or Elizabethan sonnet is clear, where the internal structure of the sonnet requires or makes possible the development of a single argument.

The metre is basically iambic pentameter. But the rhythmic pattern is varied, giving the impression of a conversational, colloquial voice in action. The first line and a half set the template for such variation: "I wonder by my troth, what thou, and I/Did, till we lov'd?" There is both syntactic variation within the first line, and the emphatic "did" at the beginning of the second sets that line off on a different rhythm, drawing the metrical pattern back to that of a speaking voice. Throughout the poem, there are enjambements to reinforce the prose-like colloquial tone, sometimes punctuated with a comma and sometimes not: "Where can we finde two better hemispheares/ Without sharpe North". And punctuation with question marks, full stops, semicolons and commas, as well as the elisions within and between words ("desir'd", "t'was"), enable the writing to stand in dynamic relation to its musical properties.

Finally, the movement of the language is critical to the sense. In the couplet, "For love, all love of other sights controules,/And makes one little roome, an every where", the very first word is a continuation of the argument via the logical connective 'for'. The metaphysical leap from "one little roome" to "an every where" (the particularization of 'an' makes it all other possible worlds, not just a vague 'everywhere') is managed within one compact line and leads on to further lines about explorers, maps and "worlds on worlds". So syntax, working with metre, indicates moves that are articulated (both in the sense of expressed and joined) within each stanza by musical/dance patterning and within each sentence and line (again working in concert).

Rhythm in Poetry

One could say that poetry is prose with rhythm. But that is not exactly true, as some prose has rhythm. Rather, poetry is language with an ostensibly foregrounded rhythm that is sometimes formalized as metre (including metrical variation). What is the function of rhythm in poetry?

44 *The Forms and Functions of Rhythm in Poetry*

Partly, it is to set the words in time: not so much to situate the poem in a chronological or other time frame, but to arrange the constituent parts of the poem in a time relation to each other. In other words, the rhythmic identity of the poem is internal to the poem. Thus rhythm becomes one of the compositional tools available to the poet. As rhythm is about time relations, the silences of the poem are as key as the words themselves. Such silences are particularly evident when the poem takes the form of free verse and/or when the layout of the poem on the page is indicative of the pauses and silences that take place between the words.

Eliot's *Four Quartets* provides an example of how silences play a part in the overall rhythmic identity/shape of a poem. The opening strophe/verse paragraph of the first part of the poem 'Burnt Norton' establishes a prosaic, free verse form using the thematic keyword 'time' emphatically in the first few lines and then continuing in unrhymed—almost arrhythmic—meditation/reflection/speculation. Then, as the verse paragraph ends in mid-line, there is a pause:

> My words echo
> Thus, in your mind.
> But to what purpose
> Disturbing the dust on a bowl of rose-leaves
> I do not know.
> Other echoes
> Inhabit the garden. Shall we follow?

The caesuras that takes place after "mind" and "know" are further emphasized through the line breaks so that the first verse paragraph (15 lines) and the third (30 lines) are interrupted by the white space on the page that indicates a relatively longer pause before and after the "But to what purpose" sentence. This interruptive sentence is itself disjointed and syncopated: it starts on a half-line and finishes on one. So there is a rhythmic interruption between two long verse paragraphs, itself rich in imagery—"dust on a bowl of rose leaves"—and tentative—"I do not know".

The artist Verónica Gerber Bicecci (2017—see also Chapter 2) has explored *Four Quartets* via the "invisible machinery of silences behind a text" in her animation 'Exhumation'. She drew straight lines and circles connecting each punctuation mark, thus working at the level of sentential punctuation rather than of the larger structural affordances of the poem. But her aim is the same: to see how rhythmic relations at sentence level in the poem could be represented in visual, dynamic format.

The point to be made here is that whereas in the Donne poem the playing with metre and conventional forms give rise to the rhythmic identity of the poem, in Eliot's *Four Quartets*, the rhythmic dynamic is established between words and white space/silences. Whether words are presented in the air, in speech or on paper/screen in 'print', they do not operate in a vacuum.

The Forms and Functions of Rhythm in Poetry   45

Rather, the air is shaped, or the white space is shaped and used to define the rhythmic identity of the artwork—in this case, the poem. Aural or visual silence is used as a positive element in the composition.

Back to the Physical

Eliot's *Four Quartets* is a particularly ethereal work, although its imagery ("dust on a bowl of rose leaves") grounds it lightly in the world. Most poetry is more physically grounded, partly through imagery but also through rhythm. In *A Prosody of Free Verse*, I cited Octavio Paz's 'Recapitulations' in *Alternating Current* (1974, 65–9), especially his opening perception that "rhythm is the original metaphor and encompasses all the others. It says: succession is repetition, time is nontime" (1974: 65). In that book, I was trying to establish rhythm as the key defining element in poetry. But Paz goes further in his argument. He relates the incarnation of the poem (rhythm) to "the reincarnation of the instant":

> The instant dissolves in the succession of other nameless instants. In order to *save it* we must *convert it* into a rhythm.
>
> (1974: 65)

That rhythm is analogous to the incarnation of time in ritual: specifically in rites, 'happenings' that are caught in time and yet which raise experience beyond time so that

> in ordinary discourse one phrase lays the groundwork for the next; it is a chain with a beginning and an end. In a poem the first phrase contains the last one and the last one evokes the first. Poetry is our only recourse against rectilinear time.
>
> (1974: 67)

The chapter in *A Prosody of Free Verse* on embodied cognition could be referred to in order to support the argument that rhythm is not only key to the writing and responding to poetry but also fundamental to a theory of literary stylistics that goes under the name of 'poetics'. At this more general level, artworks are moments (or a series of moments, such as film or animation) in time that lift us outside time, or give us the perspective to see the time relations in a work that enable us to look at everyday experience in a new light. But that insight is ungrounded and ethereal if it is not felt and thus embodied. A poem, because it is compressed and rhythmic, embodies this principle of framing time in order to see, hear and feel time more clearly. Understanding the articulation of time, as in the example from *Four Quartets* discussed earlier, enables us to understand how time is manipulated through rhythm in novels, films, animations, plays, still images (how long does someone look at a painting or photograph and with what degree of attention?) and musical compositions.

46 *The Forms and Functions of Rhythm in Poetry*

From Metrical to Free Verse

What does the move from metrical to free verse signify? Adherence to conventional metrical forms implies that there is safety in using the tried and tested forms, that variation from these forms is interesting and often delightful and that the musicality of these forms, although often forgotten, is an unconscious legacy of poetry's close association with song and music more generally. Experimentation with free verse implies something different: that the 'meaning' of a poem cannot be poured into pre-existing shapes, that different rhythms exist and need to be explored and exploited, that additive rhythm is distinctly different from metrical rhythm and that form and function are inextricably related in poetry and poetics.

Imagine that the period of formal metricality and syllabification (and its variations) lasted from Homer to the twentieth century, and that the resurgent move towards freer forms of poetic expression started in the late nineteenth century and has built up momentum in the twentieth so that in the twenty-first century and beyond it becomes the default, the norm. The significance of such a large-scale move would be multiple.

One consequence would be that the underlying principle of poetic form would be linear, developmental, *additive*. That is to say, poetry could no longer claim to be the art form which lifted us out of the present through repetition; it would take its place alongside other art forms that try to 'say something' in specific modes and media. Additive, emergent rhythm would need to be defined for each poem: there could be no metrical system, no manual, that could guide us as to how to write. What would remain is the clear notion that writing that does not go up to the right-hand edge of the page, or which (in oral delivery) takes a free-form shape in the air, is distinctly different from prose. Such writing might continue to use tone, tempo and other surface features to indicate that this genre is different, distinctive and needs to be listened to/attended to more thoroughly than ordinary discourse. The distinctions from prose would be less clear than between, say, a sonnet and a paragraph of prose in a short story. There would be gradations of form, with the liminal area being between the prose poem and the free verse poem. In rhythmic terms, the poetic side of that dividing line would be marked by rhythmic foregrounding.

Another consequence of the seismic shift to free verse would be a disconnection between poetry and song—at least song that is regularly patterned. Poetry would move closer to jazz rhythms, or the serial rhythms of avant-garde, twentieth-century music.

A third consequence would be the kind of attention that is afforded poetry by the reader/listener. The attention would have to be more intense. It is one thing to listen to the words of the poem knowing that the form is conventional and that certain (rhythmic) expectations will be fulfilled or disappointed for effect. It is another to have to listen or read closely enough

The Forms and Functions of Rhythm in Poetry 47

to pick up the rhythmic shape of a poem, especially, if the shape is restless, fragmented, evolutionary. Poetry would require highly attuned sensitivity to the meaning, sound systems and affordances of words in an arrangement.

Furthermore, in terms of prosody, there is the possibility of a move away from the conventions of 'beat', metrical feet or syllabification as being the defining elements of rhythmic description, to a more expansive, longer unit of rhythm: the line, the verse paragraph, the overall fugue-like work (if the poem is of a longer, multi-sectional type).

Implications for Poetry in the Canon

Chapter 7 explores the implications for poetics, in general, of a multimodal, free verse poetry. Here the focus remains on the implications for poetry itself in relation to other literary art forms and other art forms in general.

Poetry has often been afforded pride of place among the arts for its compression, its multi-levelled significance, its propensity to be able to denote the sublime, its connection to the muses, its other-worldly beauty. Of all the language arts, it is the one that embodies dance, music and imagery. Being one of the language arts, it draws on the cultural, historical and linguistic richness of the languages in which it is couched.

In a new poetic, poetry could have a different place. Alongside the other verbal arts and genres, it could express grounded, experiential and conceptual meaning in time. It would arrange such meaning in compact and compressed ways so that the prism it offers to the reader/listener is less predictable, less distanced from the everyday, but is a lens that offers reconfiguration of the actual. It could play with time in the sense that a novel or a play manipulates time, but it would do so in miniature, and its nuances would have to be attended to closely. It would pick up on the rhythms of everyday existence and combine these in order to show that there was a larger rhythmic set of relationships at play: sometimes harmonic, sometimes fragmented and discordant. Rather than foreground narrative (except in narrative poems), which is the principal tool of the short story, novel and play, it would foreground time relations themselves, multi-levelled significance and compressed summary (either through capturing a single moment and/ or through lyric-like expression or through imagistic, grounded argument).

A Further Example

Earlier in the chapter, a poem by Donne was used to explore the rhythmic relations within the poem within a formal tradition. Here Donne's 'Good Friday, Riding Westward', with its rhyming couplets ("Let mans Soule be a Spheare, and then, in this/The intelligence that moves, devotion is . . .") is taken as an example and answered in twenty-first century terms, both semantically and rhythmically:

48   *The Forms and Functions of Rhythm in Poetry*

Good Friday, Driving Southwards

Against reason or sense we're travelling today
driving south from Yorkshire's wide expanse
to Islington's Upper Street: the Union Chapel.

No sphere or *primum mobile* to impel us
save intelligence of a different sort:
love, familial devotion, a commitment

to eclectic voices of a different sort.
A celebration of youth, the beautiful south
drawing us over the earth's horizon.

Small voices in the universe, a collective spirit
remembering a girl's suicide, drowned migrants,
an aeroplane plunging into the sea.

The strange irony of death-in-life and life-in-death,
our chilled northern spirit in a bright
London morning. On the face of it

a small gesture, evaporating quickly
in southern heat, as if we were obliterated by sunlight
neither here nor there, but somewhere else.

Rhythmically, the rhyming couplets are answered with unrhymed tercets. There is tension between the syntactic structures of the sentences and the formal framing of the poem within tercets. Sometimes the sentences stay within the three-line form; at other times, they transgress it. So there is a de-stabilizing of the form, unlike the regular, argumentational rhythm of Donne's poem. Thus the rhythm reflects the uncertainty, the vacillation, between death and life, between faith and non-faith, between north and south. But there is form: the tercets provide the framework—each verse a vignette either perceptual or abstract. This is not a journey into or affirming faith, but one exploring the uncertainty between opposites.

If the tercets were concertinaed, what would be the effect?

Against reason or sense we're travelling today
driving south from Yorkshire's wide expanse
to Islington's Upper Street: the Union Chapel.
No sphere or *primum mobile* to impel us
save intelligence of a different sort:
love, familial devotion, a commitment
to eclectic voices of a different sort.

The Forms and Functions of Rhythm in Poetry 49

A celebration of youth, the beautiful south
drawing us over the earth's horizon.
Small voices in the universe, a collective spirit
remembering a girl's suicide, drowned migrants,
an aeroplane plunging into the sea.
The strange irony of death-in-life and life-in-death,
our chilled northern spirit in a bright
London morning. On the face of it
a small gesture, evaporating quickly
in southern heat, as if we were obliterated by sunlight
neither here nor there, but somewhere else.

And if further transposed into prose,

> against reason or sense we're travelling today driving south from York-
> shire's wide expanse to Islington's Upper Street: the Union Chapel. No
> sphere or *primum mobile* to impel us save intelligence of a different
> sort: love, familial devotion, a commitment to eclectic voices of a differ-
> ent sort. A celebration of youth, the beautiful south drawing us over the
> earth's horizon. Small voices in the universe, a collective spirit remem-
> bering a girl's suicide, drowned migrants, an aeroplane plunging into
> the sea. The strange irony of death-in-life and life-in-death, our chilled
> northern spirit in a bright London morning. On the face of it a small
> gesture, evaporating quickly in southern heat, as if we were obliterated
> by sunlight neither here nor there, but somewhere else.

The comparison between the three versions—an unrhymed poem in tercets, free verse and prose—brings us closer to the nature and function of
rhythm in poetry. In the first version, the spaces between the tercets provide
more breathing space, more silence, a slower approach and a look back to
the poets who have used this form: Dante, William Carlos Williams and
Heaney. The second version retains the sense of the work being a poem,
with (roughly) the line as the unit of rhythm, the use of enjambement, the
significance of the first and last lines being made clear by the line-endings
and the mirroring of these two lines ("against reason or sense"/"neither
here nor there"). In the last version, such shaping of the underlying feeling,
captured partly in the rhythm, has disappeared and the account (as it now
becomes) is flatter, less sonorous, less consciously multi-levelled and too
compressed for prose, which asks us to read on with narrative insistence.

A Different Poetic

This chapter has explored a different poetic that is manifested principally
through rhythmic shaping by looking briefly at a historical trajectory from
formal, metrical verse to free verse and at a contemporary spectrum from

50   *The Forms and Functions of Rhythm in Poetry*

formal verse at one end to free verse at the other. In doing so, it has suggested that rhythm, whichever way it is shaped, is fundamental to the making and receiving of poetry and that it has been underestimated in the way in which it underpins composition and interpretation. The language that is needed in order to talk about rhythm in poetry is much less a technical language of poetic devices—particularly a prosody based on metricality—and much more a language that can relate notions of time to the actual words on the page or in the air. This is a field that is in its infancy, but which points towards a new poetics that will be explored in Chapters 7 and beyond.

In exploring rhythm, the aim has been to set such a discussion within the broader theme of this book: to investigate the relationship between multimodality, poetry and poetics. Rhythm, whether in poetry, dance or music (and metaphorically in the other modes such as still and moving image, gesture and movement) is a dimension of multimodality that is concerned with relative time relations. It has emerged in the twentieth century from its role in the background of experience and art forms to a position where it is foregrounded as part of the repertoire of expression. In the twenty-first century, it stands beside other forms of expression and meaning-making as not a mode in itself, but as a dimension of modal expression that is different from narrative but equally central to the arts.

4 Imagery in Poetry
Implicit and Explicit

Introduction

Imagery in poetry and poetics is a well-trodden field. This is the level of figurative language—of metaphor, symbol, simile and metonymy—that is, fundamental not only to poetry but also to some kinds of prose and to other kinds of written language. Nevertheless, there is a level of signification in poetry that operates above that of the literal—or alongside it. Poetry seems to use imagery (the default mode is the visual) to evoke imaginative spaces and to add *dimension* to literal description. The chapter draws on existing literature on figurative language, but it also breaks new ground in that it explores how and why images are invoked through the spoken and written word, and how they are deployed by both writer and reader (rhetor and audience) to generate new meaning. In addition, the chapter considers the classical notion of *ut pictura poeisis* and explores the function of imagery in fugue.

Poetic Language

Bruns (1974) explores modern poetry and the idea of language, looking at the keystone role that poetic language has. At the heart of this exploration is the distinction between spoken and written poetic language.

Spoken language is more obviously multimodal: it involves gesture, movement and sound, as well as the physical embodiment of the voice, and is more highly contextualized. There is a more obvious dialogism in spoken communication. Sub-sections of the spoken voice, such as tone and rhythm, are more readily identified, and spoken poetic language is more akin to music and especially song.

But it was "the older grammatical tradition [in Rhetoric, that] took for its object not spoken but written (and most often, literary) language, and as a consequence tended to regard human speech as a wholly spatial and visual affair" (1974: 14). This narrow concentration on printed literary language made for rhetorics and grammars that looked at the way words on the page did all the work of invoking speech and of its attendant modes. Peacham's

52 *Imagery in Poetry*

The Garden of Eloquence (1577, 1977) for example, "a manual devoted to the classification and description of rhetorical figures" (Bruns 1974: 20), suggests that the writer "may set forth any matter with goodly perspecuitie, and paynt out any person, deede or thing, so cunninglye with these coulores [i.e. verbal images, figures] that it shall seem rather a lyvely image paynted" (1557/1977). In other words, a piece of writing could be like a painting, evoking the visual images to excite and define the imagination. This position is close to, and perhaps derives from the notion of *ut pictura poesis*: the power of poetry (and imaginative writing in general) to evoke pictorial scenes and, conversely, the 'poetic' nature of painting.

Shelley, following Coleridge (see later in this chapter), wrote of the language of poetry as "vitally metaphorical, that is, it marks the before unapprehended relations of things and perpetuates their apprehension, until the words which represent them become, through time, signs for portions or classes of thoughts instead of pictures of integral thoughts" (Shelley 1840: 60). Such organic integration of word, image and thought—as, say, in Keats's "sudden a thought came like a full-blown rose in 'The Eve of St. Agnes' where the "sudden" signifies that this is no artificial, but an instantaneous connection, is different from the notion that words evoke pictures and, subsequently, that pictures evoke things, memories, etc. The image is central to the experience, not an illustration of it. Thus literary stylistic usage is no longer seen as intransitive 'deviant utterance', but is at the heart of the poetic process.

The logical conclusion of the integration of word, image and thought/feeling is that words can stand in for experience, rather than depict it. As Bruns puts it,

> The common utterance maintains, if only approximately, an ideal union of word and thing; figurative speech, by contrast, amplifies the distance between word and thing, draining as it does so the mind away [. . .] into a merely verbal universe.
>
> (1974: 72)

Mallarmé is cited as the champion of a universal structure of words that float above everyday life, but which, through the relational structures, symbolize and represent the 'real world' and its own set of complex relations. They do so via the properties of words, again more readily experienced in speech than in writing: sounds, rhythms, tones, associations, nuances of meaning. And yet written language in the form of the printed poem (written poetic language) tries to recreate those structural relations, using all its features such as spacing, capitalization, assonance, alliteration, and scoring as a quasi-musical work. In other words, even with regard to written poetic language, multimodality is at play in the spatial (and thus visual) configuration of the words on the page. The choreography of the printed page *means something*.

Imagery in Poetry 53

Metaphor, Simile, Symbol and Metonymy

Much has been written on poetry's 'dependence' on figurative functions in language, as if the very nature of poetry was the operation of these figurative devices within it. Most simply, metaphor and simile have been the staple of much teaching of poetry, often to the extent of filleting the poem for such devices and then assuming the meaning and nature of the poem has been revealed. Typical of the analysis would be as follows: "Shall I compare thee to a summer's day?/ Thou art more lovely and more temperate./ Rough winds do shake the darling buds of May,/ And summer's lease hath all too short a date" (Sonnet 18) would reveal a comparison between the writer and his lover. The lover is compared to a summer's day and found to be more beautiful: he/she is "more lovely and more temperate" and summer can be fickle, with "rough winds" and with a short 'rental period'. For Shakespeare, this is a witty conceit as well as a tribute, but in (sometimes banal) analysis, the poem is reduced to its metaphorical elements. The same is the case, and perhaps more obviously, with simile, often introduced with 'like' or 'as': "My love is like a red, red rose./That's newly sprung in June:/ My love is like the melody./ That's sweetly played in tune." (Robert Burns). There is no doubt about the direct comparison, but often similes have more limited function and are not developed over a number of lines, as can be the case with metaphor.

With symbol, the metaphor is deeper and the referent often not mentioned. Symbols in an individual's work, or more generally in a culture, accrue deep significance, like a resonant metaphor. Blake's 'The Sick Rose', discussed earlier, is a good example.

O Rose, thou art sick!
The invisible worm
That flies in the night,
In the howling storm,

Has found out thy bed
Of crimson joy,
And his dark secret love
Does thy life destroy.

The complex interrelationship of romantic love (the rose) cankered by the "invisible worm" that appears to be airborne, like a disease, and which also has sexual and physical connotations, and the physicality of the "bed/ of crimson joy", both literally and metaphorically, overlain with the "dark, secret love"—the opposite of innocent or open, celebratory love—is a destroyer, at the very heart of love/beauty. Part of the compression of the metaphor into a powerful symbol comes from the sparing use of words, thus opening up the possibilities of interpretation: there are fewer words to

54   *Imagery in Poetry*

contextualize or pin down the meaning. Here symbol is multi-levelled in its meaning and multi-faceted (not all aspects of its meaning are compatible). It is multimodal in the sense of implied multimodality.

Lastly, metonymy is a side-by-side relationship: more a matter of association and contiguity than of analogy or implied reference: "Downing Street did not comment" rather than "The Prime Minister and his/her press office did not comment".

What Is the Function of Imagery in a Poem?

It should be acknowledged, from the outset, that the everyday language from which poetry takes its resources is itself imbued with imagery. It is hard to hold a routine conversation without resorting to imagery. Even a seemingly innocuous statement such as "I'm going down town this afternoon" has more than a literal sense: the preposition 'down' suggests something different to a New Yorker (down in the sense of 'south' on a map, to those in the northern hemisphere) than to a dialect speaker in England (down in the sense of 'down to the centre'). Each of these usages reveals a metaphorical and spatial/visual architecture to the imagination that unconsciously informs the statement. So, first and foremost, imagery is there in the weft and weave of the language itself.

When the language is selected for a poem, there could be a similarly unconscious reference to imagery. Gary Snyder's flat, Buddhist diction often appears simply to *describe* and that description itself has significance because it is saturated with a Buddhist aesthetic. The ordinary is resonant with the extraordinary simply by virtue of the ideology of Buddhism being embodied in things.

More commonly, once an image is set within a poem, it is endowed with more significance than the words around it because it provides the multi-levelled suggestions of meaning and the types of ambiguity that are associated with poetry. It looks out beyond the words of the poem to a set of ideas and associations that are brought back into the mix of the poem.

As an example, take this simple poem about listening to a trio play Bach:

Bach in California

This is a room in Berkeley,
where three musicians are playing
Bach sonatas for viola and flute.
Outside, the noise of planes,
the unorganized racket of freeway traffic
coming over the bridge. Suddenly,
mind's flux falls into a pattern:
there must be two million lights
illuminating the Bay tonight—

Imagery in Poetry 55

this brilliant nothing. Then
Bach's clarity cuts through like ice.
I want to go up there and crash the keys.

On one level, this is a simple description of a reaction to listening to Bach sonatas in an urban environment. The opening lines are purely descriptive. They set the scene. Instead of imagery, there is a different poetic process taking place: one of the comparison of sounds. Inside, there is the order and beauty of Bach's music and outside the contrasting "noise" and "racket" of planes and cars. With the "suddenly" at the end of a line, however, the comparative scene-setting description shifts to another level, effected by the phrase "mind's flux". The mind is not easily envisaged. By yoking it together with 'flux' (from the Latin *fluere*—to flow) and perhaps by association with the physical and applied mathematical senses of flux (a vector field) what seemed flowing and chaotic "falls into a pattern" and is grounded. The colon points towards how the mind's pattern is forming: as "two million lights" illuminating not only the San Francisco Bay Area but also the 'mind'. In a sense, there is an overlay of the mind onto the Bay Area—a few keywords of imagery have created this multi-levelled overlay. The poem then returns (again with an end-of-line articulation) to the room and to Bach's music. The only simile of the poem is introduced: "Bach's clarity cuts through *like ice*". Are the referents here ice on the Bay (unlikely), ice in a drink (more likely, and suggestive of the pleasurable shock of the chill) or, more generally, ice's properties as pure, transparent, solid water—a kind of physical transformation/miracle? This could have been the end of the poem, but the final line brings something else: a desire to counter and re-balance the cool order and harmony of Bach with chaos ("crash" possibly being a reference back to the traffic coming over the bridge and thus endowing the bridge with significance beyond its literal sense, and into that of bridging between two worlds/states of consciousness) with an act of disruption, violence and/or sheer exuberance.

Ut Pictura Poesis

Horace's (1965) *On the Art of Poetry* gives a practical guide to poets (and dramatic poets) as to what to do and what not to do: be succinct, elegant, proportionate and decorous. The key phrase that has come down from the guide is *ut pictura poesis* ("as is painting, so is poetry") and is used to convey a certain classical take on imagery in poetry—*viz* that its function is to *depict,* to *imitate.* The analogy is that both art forms frame their subject and convey its essence: one in paint, the other in words. Horace, already cited in Chapter 1, suggests something else with regard to perspective:

A poem is like a painting: the closer you stand to this one the more it will impress you, whereas you have to stand a good distance from that

56 *Imagery in Poetry*

one; this one demands a rather dark corner, but that one needs to be seen in full light, and will stand up to the keen-eyed scrutiny of the art-critic; this one pleased you the first time you saw it, but that one will go on giving you pleasure however often it is looked at.

(1965, 91–2)

It could be said, in response to Horace's guidance on the craft of poetry, that the framing of the subject is a key first move and that it is the author's responsibility as well as that of the audience to conceive of the frame and the 'distance' it and the subject require. Thereafter, the poem acts like a picture, giving an insight, through selection of aspects of what is 'seen' and through words, which because of their abstract nature, operate in more multi-levelled and resonant ways than painting, even if they lack the tangible lines, colours and affordances of paintings.

Images within poems are combined. Rarely is a single image presented. The combination makes for the particular networked significance of the words. So *ut pictura poesis*, although it suggests the close analogy of painting, imagery and poetry tells only part of the story of what poems can do.

To summarize this and previous section, and to answer the question, "What is the function of imagery in a poem?", the combination of still images in a poem provides a network of association beyond the literal meaning of the words. Words that are naturally imagistic within the language are mined for their range of meaning; those meanings are combined with other such meanings from the other words in the composition. Sometimes the image is so striking or dominant that it moves the imagination beyond the confines of the poem, almost into another dimension, as in Keats's 'On First Looking into Chapman's Homer':

> Much have I travell'd in the realms of gold,
> And many goodly states and kingdoms seen;
> Round many western islands have I been
> Which bards in fealty to Apollo hold.
> Oft of one wide expanse had I been told
> That deep-brow'd Homer ruled as his demesne;
> Yet did I never breathe its pure serene
> Till I heard Chapman speak out loud and bold:
> Then felt I like some watcher of the skies
> When a new planet swims into his ken;
> Or like stout Cortez when with eagle eyes
> He star'd at the Pacific—and all his men
> Look'd at each other with a wild surmise—
> Silent, upon a peak in Darien.

The final line transports the imagination to Central America and the isthmus between the Atlantic and the Pacific, thus moving from the Mediterranean and "western islands" to a whole new expanse of ocean—an analogy with reading Chapman's translation of Homer. The function of imagery in this poem, and more generally, is to provide another level of reference in order to bring richness and meaning to the ostensible and initial level of reflection.

Imagism

The Imagist movement was a logical conclusion to the debate between fancy and imagination in the eighteenth and nineteenth centuries which couched fancy as an inferior operation of the imagination, providing decorative images for ideas and concepts that appeared to be informed by 'taste' and propriety. Imagination, on the other hand, was a more integrative operation of the mind, fusing feeling and thought. In discussing Wordsworth's writing in *Biographia Literaria* (1971: 231), Coleridge writes:

> It was not however the freedom from false taste, whether as to common defects, or to those more properly his own, which made so unusual an impression on my feelings immediately, and subsequently on my judgement. It was the union of deep feeling with profound thought; the fine balance of truth in observing, with the imaginative faculty in modifying the objects observed; and above all the original gift of spreading the tone, the *atmosphere*, and with it the depth and height of the ideal world around forms, incidents and situations.

The secondary imagination, for Coleridge,

> dissolves, diffuses, dissipates, in order to recreate; or where this process is rendered impossible, yet still at all events it struggles to idealize and to unify. It is essentially *vital*, even as all objects (*as* objects) are essentially fixed and dead.
>
> (1971: 246)

As such, the secondary imagination was only different in degree from the primary imagination, "the living Power and prime Agent of all human Perception" (ibid.). The centrality of the imagination to human consciousness led, via several turns in the Romantic movement in the nineteenth century to the Imagist movement with its tenets to concentrate on the image. One of these turns was a re-affirmation of the Romantic tenet of the centrality of the individual and of the individual's perceptions and experience; another was a resistance to sentimentality. The first of these could lead to gushing expression—the antidote to which was the encouragement to look at the thing, not the feeling. Hence the second turn, away from the sentimentality of Swinburne and other late-nineteenth-century English poets. Part of the inspiration for Imagism came from the French poets, especially Laforgue and the Symbolistes whose free verse rhythms as well as arresting

58   *Imagery in Poetry*

juxtaposition of seemingly unconnected images (cf. the metaphysical poets of the seventeenth century) set a new direction. It was as if a new, hard classicism was founded on the image used to generate an intuitive (thought and feeling combined) response rather than a merely intellectual one.

One of the principles of the movement was to "present an image": "We are not a school of painters, but we believe that poetry should render particulars exactly and not deal in vague generalities, however magnificent and sonorous". In other words, the image was used to speak for itself. The generation of images and the juxtaposition of images was seen by the Imagists as a direct and creative function of the poet: images that might later be incorporated in prose as figures of speech. This is a different line from *ut pictura poesis*, in which poetry approximated the depictive nature of painting. Rather, in Imagist poetry, the image does all the work, presenting the reader with resonant and suggestive imagery to evoke emotional and/or intellectual responses. For example,

Catédrale de Quimper

I passed through it
as one would pass through
a shopping precinct:
postcards? candles? souvenirs?

The difference?
It was dark, cavernous.
The connection?
People drifting, window-shopping.

Conveniently,
one didn't have to
pass the altar
to get through it.

And yet its spire
can be seen for miles
"dominating the surrounding
countryside".

Its best function now
as a beacon
guiding you to the next
Hotel des Voyageurs.

Although there is narrative and a persona, the emphasis is on simply recording detail. And yet there are two functions that provide significance and reference outside the images themselves. One is the analogy between the

Imagery in Poetry   59

shopping precinct and the cathedral. The other is the value judgement implied in "conveniently" and "its best function now". The conclusion is not stated, but implied. The rest of the work is undertaken by the imagery.

One of the criticisms levelled against Imagism was that, because of its concentration on and dependence on images, it could only focus on small themes. It is true that most Imagist poems are short, but like Blake's 'Sick Rose', imagery can become symbolic and thus multi-levelled in its significance when historical and/or cultural dimensions are invoked. Pure Imagism would eschew such multi-levelled referencing; on the other hand, the very nature of language is referential. It is not the words themselves that are signified, but the ideas and emotional complexes that they refer to. On the positive side, there is a virtue in smallness. Like other art forms that concentrate on miniature or small works—such as bonsai, netsuke, haiku in Japanese culture—there is *resonance* in the compact composition. What Imagism also did to counter the criticism that it could only contain small themes was to use polyptical or multi-panelled forms to not only juxtapose images within short sections but also juxtapose the sections themselves. In the work of Pound, Eliot and H. D. can be seen as the use of film-like sequences of short sections, with each section being driven by images. The sequences themselves (see, for example, 'Hugh Selwyn Mauberley', 'The Love Song of J. Alfred Prufrock' and H. D.'s war trilogy) cannot be described as narrative sequences. They are collage-like and thus build up multi-levelled significance not through symbolism, but through juxtaposition of images and image clusters. It is a different poetic from narrative poetry, from poetry as the expression of feeling or from image as embellishment.

Implicit and Explicit Imagery

According to the thesis of the current book, imagery which is implicit operates largely within the network of imagery within the poem, adding to a tissue of internal references that help to unify the work. Imagery which is explicit refers outside the poem to other modes (largely visual). The two types of imagery are ends of a spectrum rather than binary opposites. Images can function both internally and externally, both implicitly and explicitly. These images, by their very nature, are multimodal: they sit within the poem as words, possibly performed in speech. But they refer to the visual and aural worlds, and to other worlds of multimodal resource, such as gesture, touch and movement.

The poem is a particularly rich frame within which to convey such implicit and explicit multimodality. Again, what seems internal goes on within the frame (the white space on the page, the performance introduced and ended by silence), and what seems external goes on outside the frame. Readers and listeners bring their own frames of reference, their own associations to bear on the interpretation of the words in the poem. Take the poem cited earlier, 'Catédrale de Quimper': to a Christian, the poem might seem heretical, or at least narrowly secular in its sensibility. To an agnostic or atheist

60 *Imagery in Poetry*

tourism office worker, the poem might seem bafflingly negative. The frames each person brings to a reading of the poem will determine their response and which modes they are prepared to admit to the experience. Someone who does not like poetry will not even read or listen to it. They will see the frame as impenetrable and not worth engaging with. The language within the frame operates in a way they do not operate, and the imagistic connections both within and beyond the poem will be of no significance. On the other hand, someone with a more open mind, who does not read poetry, will see the work as a straight depiction of a cathedral—rather like an extract from a travelogue—and compare the description to their own experience in 'real life'.

It is the contention of the present book, however, that any seemingly monomodal work, such as a poem, is actually, in its composition and in its reception, *multimodal*. In the composition, the writer has selected a mode to work in, and consciously kept out the other modes, using his/her chosen mode (words, in this case) to do all the work of communication. As Horace, Aristotle and others have written, the craft of gaining command of this selective monomodal form is onerous and demanding. In terms of reception, the reader/listener brings frames of reference from reading and experience to bear on the interpretation. Such reception does not necessarily use the same modes of reference as the speaker/writer, so the poem is a seemingly monomodal vehicle through which the terms of engagement between speaker and audience, writer and reader, are negotiated.

Moving Imagery

In multimodal terms, moving imagery combines two modes: the still image and movement. Poetry can evoke moving images, again implicitly or explicitly. It is rarely accompanied by an explicit moving image (film, video, animation) but when it is—as with Selina Nwulu's 'A Strange Kind of Beauty', discussed elsewhere in this book, or performances and recorded performances of poetry—it can be doubly powerful because of the physical dimension to communication and meaning.[1]

Burn suggests that film and video could be seen multimodally in terms of orchestrating modes (functions) and contributory modes (functions). He argues that the multimodal perspective can offer "new ways to think about the combination of sign systems to be found in such cultural forms as narrative film, television, animation, moving image art installations and machinima" (2013b: 1). He also extends the discussion of framing, used elsewhere in the present book and in Andrews (2011, 2014), to include the temporal as well as the spatial. The link with the discussion of Imagism and its implications is further enriched by this perception of spatial and temporal framing. Imagism embodies its intellectual and emotional complexes in images in the way that (say) a photographer captures and frames an image. A filmmaker puts together sequences of images in time through the processes of juxtaposition and editing. It is no coincidence that not only the larger works that derived from Imagism, such as 'The Waste Land', were edited to remove narrative links and concentrate on the imagery, but also that smaller Imagist poems sometimes underwent the same process, as in the suggestion by Pound to Harold Monro that a draft of a poem could be cut from 97 to 56 words.

Figure 4.1, after Burn, suggests a multimodal taxonomy for poetry:

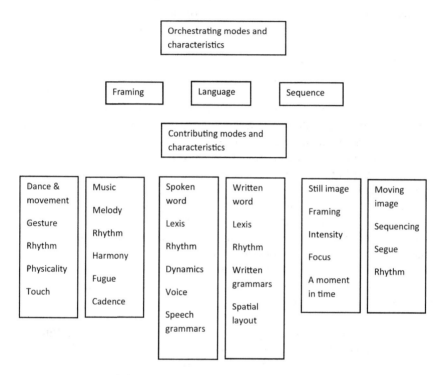

Figure 4.1 Multimodal Poetics

What this table suggests is that the composing process in poetry consists of a range of possibilities, with elements being combined, selected and left out in order to create a vehicle for communication. Equally, in reading/listening and interpreting terms, the range of possibilities is re-invoked and selections made to filter the experience. Thus the poem represents a vehicle of potential: so much the more because of its brevity, compression and resonance, but also because of the multiple layers of meaning and the co-reference that it affords.

In the model of multimodal poetics, it can be seen that the overarching orchestrating modes and characteristics are language, framing and sequence ('words in space and time'). At the core of the model is language, in spoken and written modes. This centrality does not imply that they are the only carriers of meaning; rather than in a model of multimodal poetics, they

62   *Imagery in Poetry*

have a direct line to the orchestrating modes that are the consideration of this particular book. Their depiction *on the same level* as the other contributing modes (and their affordances) suggests that the other modes are not subsidiary, but operate alongside and are juxtaposed with the central modes of written and spoken language. Poetry, it is argued, provides an intensification of the relationship of words in space and time that allows us to focus in the present book on a particular art form in poetics: one which has proved, because of its framing and foregrounding of rhythm (time relations), to be an appropriate test case for the wider theory of poetics.

There is no significance in the proximity of the other contributory modes to those of the linguistic ones. Dance and movement, music, image and moving image all stand in potential and actual juxtaposition to words. All will be present to some degree in the composition of a poem, whether implicitly or explicitly.

Because of the temporal nature of rhythm, all modes include reference to it, except that of the still image, which could represent the capturing (framing) of a moment in time. Even so, there is implied rhythmicity in a still image (what came before and after it, what visual elements are excluded as well as included and how is the image edited?) which may be more evident in a painting than a photograph.

In a different way, editing, which has been assumed to relate principally to moving image and specifically to film, is also a function that could apply across the modes. Words, dance moves, musical compositions and still images can all be edited for sharper, more focused, communication.

Burn (2013b) reiterates that such a model is an attempt to see how the modes work together in a multimodal framework, not to disaggregate them. Such a combination of modes

> can be thought of as a fugue: the modes working as voices [literally and/or metaphorically] which build a theme, the relationship between them structured as a form of counterpoint. This polyphonic structure allows for the modes to develop their own contours, contribute their own colouring, yet contribute to an overall coherence. The fugue metaphor also suggests sequential structures such as exposition, statement of theme, coda and so on, which apply well to the temporal aspects of the kineikonic.
>
> (2013b: 8–9)

Imagery in Fugue

Fugue, in however small a poetic work, is an enduring metaphor for understanding how poems and literary genres work. Fugue, as a musical form, is built on imitative counterpoint with a number of voices. Its multi-vocal nature suggests to poetry and poetics a Bakhtinian heteroglossia: that literature is not the result of a single authorial voice expressing itself in a Romantic universe, but of a dialogue between contemporary voices with those of

Imagery in Poetry 63

the past. Furthermore, these contemporary voices are in counterpoint to previous voices and utterances, whether spoken and/or written.

In terms of poems, themes (if they exist) are stated implicitly or explicitly and developed through repetition, variation and formal or informal rhythmic structuring. In large-scale works (e.g. 'Paradise Lost', 'Leaves of Grass', 'The Waste Land', 'The Cantos', 'Paterson') the overall structure "is an alternation of expositions and episodes" (Apel 1970: 335) with the episodes being "somewhat freer and 'lighter in weight'" (ibid.). There is also a difference between Milton and Whitman on the one hand, and Eliot, Pound and Williams on the other: the former is more likely to undertake exposition ("Of man's first disobedience and the fruit/of that forbidden tree [. . .] sing, heavenly muse") and the latter a more elliptical approach ("April is the cruellest month.").

In both Milton and in the twentieth century, and whether the exposition is explicit or not, imagery operates in large-scale fugal structures in a multi-levelled way (the same is true of Shakespeare's plays). Milton provides architectural (and therefore relatively static) infrastructure for the developing imagery of 'Paradise Lost'; the infrastructure for Eliot, Pound and Williams is relatively more organic, fluid or fragmented. In both cases, the imagery is pervasive, resonant and creates, despite the dissonance that operates in all the aforementioned poems—a harmonic integrating unity to the respective poems.

In smaller works, it can be seen how the constituent elements of the poem work together like different voices, still in counterpoint to previous utterances and in relation to each other, to provide a resonant network of associations that generate the 'meanings' of the poem. Such generation of meaning is often sparked by tension between different images, or between images and explicitly stated themes.

Such fugal interplay can be demonstrated in the following poem:

Skyros

A vertical life.
From the gods,
down through the windings streets
and labyrinthine alleys

each turn gives a short view.
You only see a few yards at a time.
In a side street
at the entrance to a church

a man is flat on the ground
on his way in or out.
Family and friends surround him.
Another died the next day.

64   *Imagery in Poetry*

Round the next corner, bougainvillea
oleander and rosemary spill over
the white walls. Heat shimmers
from rooftops.

Then a glimpse of the sea and sky
In variations of blue.
Inscriptions made on water by boats.
No clear signature, but

a café hangs from a cliff,
houses teeter on the edge;
and a sense of the line
between life and death is ever present.

In this poem, the theme is stated at the end. The rest of the poem has been working towards it through the juxtaposition of colour, through the shifting horizons of the short views of the twisting streets and the longer views to the horizon, by the 'vertical' difference of the gods and people and by the implied contrast between life and death, and the fine line between the two. In a more Buddhist, Imagist-like rendition, the last two lines could be omitted. Such explicit stating of an emergent theme could be seen as unnecessary. However, the "sense of the line" is important to the poem as a whole, not only thematically but also formally. The lines of the poem alternate between short ("A vertical life") and longer, run-on statements that through enjambement take up as many as three or four lines. The form is that of tight, unrhymed quatrains that give both a frame for the utterance and a fluidity between each line and each stanza. There is no adherence to the syntax of the sentence, but rhythmic alternation between truncated statements ("A vertical life"—perhaps in itself a half-stated theme?) and fully fledged sentences ("Family and friends surround him.").

Finally, what of the other modes at play? The visual is invoked. There is movement on the walk and its turns through the village or town. There is both stasis and movement. The voices are multiple: that of the narrator and 'you', the addressee. The poem is heteroglossic, with some reference to its historical antecedents this place ("the gods"). It is built on imagery which in turn is juxtaposed within the poem and looks outward to other reference banks of the visual. And it operates in a sound world when read out loud as well as in print on a page.

Note

1 See the record of the seminar on multimodality and the moving image at https://mode.ioe.ac.uk/2014/06/11/multimodality-and-the-moving-image/ and Burn (2013c).

5   The Framing of a Poem

Introduction

Framing theory (see Bateson 1972, *Steps to an Ecology of Mind* and Andrews 2011, *Re-framing Literacy*[1]) is largely unexplored in poetics, poetry and multimodality. Yet poetry is the most obviously framed kind of literature, especially as it appears in printed form on the page. This chapter looks at the form and shape of poems, how they all are defined partly by the white space that surrounds them and what such framing means for the way in which they could be read. The suggestion is that the framing of poems on a page gives them the aura of a sacred text that must be read with reverence and awe. However, much poetry works against this association, preferring to operate in a more worldly fashion. The chapter explores both the highly framed poem and the types that question and/or break the frame. It also addresses the relationship between framing and multimodality—what is inside/outside the chosen 'frame'? Why? What kinds of meanings are suggested by what is 'inside'?

George Herbert's 'Easter Wings'

On the multimodal spectrum, poems that have an explicit visual dimension in terms of their layout on the page are at the extreme edge of multimodality in a seemingly monomodal vein. An example is George Herbert's 'Easter Wings':

Lord, who createst man in wealth and store,
Though foolishly he lost the same,
Decaying more and more,
Till he became
Most poore:
With thee
O let me rise
As larks, harmoniously,
And sing this day thy victories:
Then shall the fall further the flight in me.

66 *The Framing of a Poem*

> My tender age in sorrow did beginne:
> And still with sicknesses and shame
> Thou didst so punish sinne,
> That I became
> Most thinne.
> With thee
> Let me combine,
> And feel this day thy victorie:
> For, if I imp[2] my wing on thine,
> Affliction shall advance the flight in me.

The visual dimension of this two-stanza poem is best seen if the page is turned 90 degrees to reveal more clearly (especially if the page is held at a distance so that the words are illegible) two sets of angel-like wings. Part of the conceit of the poem is its witty use of the angelic wing formation to cast the words of the poem; another part is the movement towards the central pivotal lines in each stanza ("Most poore:/ With thee" and "Most thinne:/ With thee"). The metaphysical movement from "man" in the first line of the poem to "let me rise" in line seven, followed by the rest of the poem in a more personal vein, is also characteristic of the age. Furthermore, in visual terms, there is symmetry not only within each stanza but also between the two stanzas/sets of wings. Much of the effect of the poem, then, is conveyed through its visual properties, especially when they combine with the verbal to generate new and more complex meanings. It is not too fanciful to suggest that the *movement* in each stanza towards the pivotal point is reflective of the fall of mankind, and the second half of each stanza, as the lines lengthen, is suggestive of the flight of the soul and its taking up by God. To add to the multimodal resonance of the poem, the characteristic physicality of the metaphysical imagination is there too: "I became/Most thinne." The poem *embodies* its expression.

John Donne's 'A Valediction: Forbidding Mourning'

The visual dimension is still evident in a poem collected in the same year (1633) by John Donne: 'A Valediction: Forbidding Mourning'. Here the first visual impression is of regular stanzas, but set in a distinctive typographic pattern:

> As virtuous men passe mildly away,
>   And whisper to their soules, to goe,
> Whilst some of their sad friends doe say,
>   The breath goes now, and some say, no:
>
> So let us melt, and make no noise,
>   No teare-floods, nor sign-tempests move,
> T'were prophanation of our joyes
>   To tell the layetie of our love.

The effect of the stanzaic regularity and the typographic layout of the lines in each stanza is to set up a framework for the poem in which each stanza is discrete. The argument of the poem is set out in a series of propositions, stanza by stanza. The full stop at the end of each stanza reinforces their discrete nature. The reader is asked to pause before the next stage of the argument: the visual space between the stanzas acts like a pause in music. At the stanza level, what difference would it make if the lines of each stanza were all aligned left and lines two and four were not indented? There would be more of a narrative drive and less of an argumentative one. There is *almost* a counterpointed rhythm within each stanza, with the first half-beat of lines two and four missing in each case. It is likely, however, that this shadow of counterpoint would not be heard if the lines were not indented visually. The poem continues:

> Moving of th'earth brings harmes and feares,
>   Men reckon what it did and meant,
> But trepidation of the spheares,
>   Though greater farre, is innocent.
>
> Dull sublunary lovers love
>   (Whose souls is sense) cannot admit
> Absence, because it doth remove
>   Those things which elemented it. [. . .]

and ends:

> If they [our two soules] be two, they are two so
>   As stiffe twin compasses are two,
> Thy soule the fixt foot, makes no show
>   To move, but doth, if th'other doe.
>
> And though it in the center sit,
>   Yet when the other far doth rome,
> It leanes, and hearkens after it,
>   And growes erect, as that come home.
>
> Such wilt thou be to mee, who must
>   Like th'other foot, obliquely runne;
> Thy firmness makes my circle just,
>   And makes me end, where I begunne.

In addition to the explicitly visual elements that have been discussed so far in the poem, the extended analogy of the set of compasses refers us back to the discussion in Chapter 4 about verbal imagery in poetry. Here, again in typical metaphysical style, the image is a mundane one: a set of compasses. But the concepts of love and absence, loyalty and humility are conjoined in a brilliant image that itself provides the principal imaginative locus of the final section

68   *The Framing of a Poem*

of the poem, hard on the heels of another that is more 'poetic' ("like gold to aiery thinnesse beat"). In this case, the visual image of the compasses—the 'vehicle' or 'figure' or 'source' (the object to which the attributes of love are attached)—is almost as powerful as the 'tenor' or 'ground' or 'target' to which it refers. Such power of the image is also the case in poems in which there is a particularly strong evocation of an image: in Blake's 'Sick Rose' or 'Poison Tree', for example. In these cases, the resonance of the image appears to take over the senses, almost to the exclusion of the referent.

Framing

The poems considered so far in this chapter are both highly framed. Concentration of the analysis has so far focused on the 'shape' of the poem themselves and their internal dynamics. What has been taken for granted in the discussion so far is that these are highly wrought examples of a genre—poetry—that always consciously frames itself on a page or in performance. Its highly framed nature makes for an intensity of intention, and an intensity of reception: the reader is expected to surround the poem with empty space, silence, reverence, and thus pay a higher degree of attention to the words than with everyday prose or literary prose. To demonstrate the nature of framing in poetry, here is an example of a poem from the late seventeenth century (1684) by Aprha Behn, 'Love Arm'd':

> Love in Fantastique Triumph satt,
> Whilst Bleeding Hearts around him flow'd,
> For whom Fresh paines he did Create,
> And strange Tryranick power he show'd;
> For thy Bright Eyes he took his fire,
> Which round about, in sport he hurl'd;
> But 'twas from mine he took desire,
> Enough to undo the Amorous World.
>
> From me he took his sighs and tears,
> From thee his Pride and Crueltie;
> From me his Languishments and Feares,
> And every Killing Dart from thee;
> Thus thou and I, the God have arm'd,
> And set him up a Deuity;
> But my poor Heart alone is harm'd,
> Whilst thine the Victor is, and free.

Even on this page of an academic book, framed by commentary and analysis, the true nature of the poem is not evident. It needs more white space around it. It is diminished in its present context. In a modern poetry publication, it would have a page to itself; if read at a poetry reading, it would be framed by silence. Even if the poet read it at such an occasion and was introducing the poem to provide autobiographical or some other contextual

The Framing of a Poem 69

setting, there would be a pause before the recitation of the poem because the poem is framed as an artwork and as separate from everyday discourse.

Poems are robust because they retain their form in different contexts, and even when they are encroached upon by other kinds of written or spoken language. The poet whose work is close to the demotic of everyday speech still wants to frame his or her poem by white space and/or silence to signify that the genre is different and that it must be attended to more intensely.

In the case of the poem by Aphra Behn, the opening four lines are distinctly poetic in that they use personification ("Love in Fantastique Triumph"), verbs that all come at the end of lines and clauses ("satt, flow'd, Create, show'd") and in their rhythmic regularity (basically iambic tetrameter, with variations), which is reinforced by end rhymes in an ABAB pattern ("satt, flow'd, Create, show'd" again). These devices are not exclusive to poetry, but in combination, they set the language apart from everyday discourse in speech or prose. So, too, at a higher level, the two eight-line stanzas, each of which is divided into two quatrains of the ABAB pattern, are separated by a space. There is symmetry in the musicality of the poem, indicated on the score of the page by regularity, variation and spacing.

Attention to the white space on the page or the silence framing the performance of a poem is important, because it is in this marginal space that the framing suggests the reader/viewer must not only attend with concentration but also provide some of the emotional, spiritual and intellectual resources that help to generate meaning in combination with the text on the page/in the air. Into this space is brought our own experiences: personal, linguistic, cultural and, therefore, social and political, as well as an 'ear' for musical pattern and knowledge of poetry and other literary forms. But, crucially for the purposes of the emerging argument of the present book, what is brought is not only our five senses but also a multimodal imagination.

The multimodal imagination enables the manoeuvring of a response to a poem until sense can be made of it. In other words, the reader brings what he or she can to the poem in order to make some kind of meaning. Because poetry, through its suggestive nature, leaves interpretation more open that with pinned-down prose, there is more 'white space' to inhabit. The imagination is multimodal in that it is composed of more than mere imagery. It can bring to bear the modes and dimensions of sound, still and moving images, verbal resonance and physicality, as appropriate. By 'as appropriate' is meant that the highly wrought verbal construct of a poem may evoke and call into play particular other modes. Rather than always being a multisensory, multimodal experience, the poem may evoke a particular mode: visual or aural or physical, in still or moving form.

Robert Lowell's 'The Heavenly Rain'

Lowell's unrhymed sonnet sequence, published as *Notebook* (1970) and reworked in *History* (1973), includes a poem, 'The Heavenly Rain'. The first point to note is that the unrhymed sonnet is still a recognizable sonnet: its 14 lines stand on the page with a title and in a squarish shape. Although

70　*The Framing of a Poem*

there is less internal cohesion than with the more highly wrought, rhymed poems that have been discussed so far in this chapter, the poems are still highly framed and surrounded, in print, by 'white space'.

The version in *Notebook*:

> Man is the root of everything he builds;
> no nature, except the human, loves New York—
> the clerk won't prove Aseity's existence
> running from helpless cause to helpless cause . . .
> The rain falls down from heaven, and heaven keeps
> her noble distance, the dancer, seen not heard.
> The rain falls down, the soil swims up to breathe,
> the squatter sumac, shafted in cement,
> flirts its wet leaves to heaven like the Firebird.
> Two girls clasp hands in a clamshell courtyard to watch
> the weed of the sumac aging visibly;
> the girls age not, are always young as last week,
> wish all rains one rain—this, that will not wash
> the fallen leaf, turned scarlet, back to green.

The multimodality of the form and the space is immediately evident when the full poem is looked at. Again, the white space defines this text as a poem. Within the genus of 'poem', the form is that of a sonnet. Within the form of 'sonnet', it is an unrhymed version. Furthermore, the sonnet is part of a long sequence of unrhymed sonnets. Unrhymed does not mean 'unmusical'. As suggested in Andrews (2016), free verse operates according to rhythms that are not based on metres and that are more like accretive jazz rhythms. Rhyme simply points up the rhythmic markers in metrical verse, as well as adding a sonorousness to the musicality of the poem. In the unrhymed sonnet, and in the example noted earlier, the 'music' (in multimodal terms, the sound dimension) is different. The poem consists of four sentences which sit in dynamic relation to the standard length of line (hard to quantify, but an average of seven or so words per line). These sentences are punctuated as in conversational prose, except that the language is compressed, imagistic, formal at times ("the girls age not"), informal at others ("this, that will not wash"), relaxed and imperious/humble in tone at the same time.

What Happens in Terms of the Imagery?

Although ostensibly this is a poem of abstract propositions ("Man is the root of everything he builds"), the complex cross-imagery of natural forms ("root", "the squatter sumac, shafted in cement", rain, the sumac's "wet leaves" and the generalized "fallen leaf, turned scarlet") with man-made built forms ("shafted in cement", "a clamshell courtyard", New York) is where the paradoxical heart of the poem lies, as in the first line. These

The Framing of a Poem   71

are visual images and provide the emotional, cultural nexus of the poem. But they are more than visual: they are architectural. The verbal construct of the poem allows reference to the literal and the metaphoric/symbolic. What is evoked and imagined, as the poem is read or listened to, is the cityscape of New York within which the "two girls clasp hands". On first reading, it might be imagined that these were two Asian-origin girls, by association with the sumac, but they need not be. The sumac "flirts its wet leaves to heaven like the Firebird", also invoking Russian fairy tales (and perhaps, through the capitalization of Firebird, referring to Stravinsky's breakthrough ballet—a further musical/choreographic and thus multimodal allusion). So the cultural range of references gives the poem a New York/Asian/Russian feel, although its application is global and of general application to mankind.

The poem was revised for inclusion in *History*:

> Man at the root of everything he builds;
> no nature, except the human, loves New York—
> the clerk won't prove Aseity's existence
> busing from helpless cause to helpless cause . . .
> The rain falls down from heaven, and heaven keeps
> her noble distance, the dancer is seen not heard.
> The rain falls, and the soil swims up to breathe;
> a squatter sumac shafted in cement
> flirts wet leaves skyward like the Firebird.
> Two girls clasp hands in a clamshell courtyard, watch
> the weed of the sumac failing visibly;
> the girls age not, are always last year's girls
> waiting for tomorrow's storm to wash
> the fallen leaf, turned scarlet, back to green.

The same comments as for the original version apply. But in this later version, there are a number of changes that, although seemingly small, are significant in a compressed form like the sonnet. The first line is different: instead of the imperious statement "man is the root of everything he builds", there is the more elliptical "man *at* the root of everything he builds", with an implied main verb. The replacement of "running from helpless cause" in line 4 to "busing from helpless cause" in the later version is one of a number of changes which somehow take the eye off the focus of the intensity of the original: "busing" seems as arbitrary as "training" or "taxiing" across a city, whereas "running" more acutely captures the futility of the clerk's existence as a human being. The shift from "the dancer, seen not heard" to "the dancer is seen not heard" also diminishes the rhythmic focus on the dancer (the comma acknowledges the focus on the noun), which in the first version prefigures more strongly the dancers in the Firebird. Similarly, the inclusion of "and" in the following line in the second version loses the rhythmic

72 The Framing of a Poem

undulation of the first version, with its "The rain falls down, the soil swims up to breathe". To revise this line to "the rain falls, and the soil swims up to breathe" is to lose that up-and-down motion as well as to wrench the syntax more towards the conventional syntax of everyday discourse.

What does the replacement of the definite article "the" in "the squatter sumac" with an indefinite "a" do to the poem? It makes the reference to the location more specific, but at the same time loses the generality of the sumac as a symbol for organic growth in a built environment. The revision of "to heaven" to "skyward" also dissipates the overall effect of the poem, with the heavenly dimension set up in line 5 losing its focus in the vaguer "skyward". Like the "and" in line 7, "skyward" seems redundant, vague, inappropriate: not the precise invocation of "heaven" that is so powerfully resonant in the poem and which provides a higher level of reference, a more generative, expansive kind of imaginary multimodality than the more limited "skyward".

The two girls "clasp hands in a clamshell courtyard to watch/the weed of the sumac aging visibly" in the first version. In the second, they "clasp hands in a clamshell courtyard, watch/the weed of the sumac failing visibly". In the first version, the girls are there "to watch", in other words 'in order to watch'. In the second version, the watching is simply consequent on their being in the courtyard. The replacement of "aging" with "failing" loses the contrast with the girls' youth and their apparent agelessness. It more obviously makes reference to the fall, but unnecessarily as references to the fall/Fall pervade the poem. The final three lines also reveal a diminution in effect. The second version is more accessible, but loses the rich ambiguity of "are always young as last week" (that could be another set of girls, but could also be the same ageless girls); it loses the fact that they "wish all rains one rain" and thus the universality of the reference; it loses the deictic "this, that" which functions to keep the reader guessing and to makes his/her own referents (is it the clerks, the girls?); it loses the rhythmic imprint/shape of the last three lines.

What is the overall effect of the revision in terms of multimodality and poetics? There is a loss of focus, internal cohesion and range. The positioning of the images—halfway between the actual world and the heavenly world in the first version, but oddly and arbitrarily specific in the second version ("busing")—makes the balance of the poem, and its evocation of two worlds, a significant feature that cannot be lost. Poetry, at its best, walks the line between levels of significance, setting up creative ambiguities in order to capture paradox and complexity. We can acknowledge what is lost in the second version by a comparison of the two versions, as noted earlier, and thus makes it possible to see that multimodality operates constantly within a poem because the framing of the construct allows multi-level referencing. To move from one level to another requires an act of the imagination. Whereas the vehicle/mode of the operation is ostensibly verbal, the other modes that have to come into play to contribute to the meaning are sonic/

The Framing of a Poem   73

musical and visual (both still and moving images), aided by the framing of the words as a poem and sonnet in the first place. The wider significance of the way that Lowell's words work within an unrhymed sonnet is to suggest that a multimodal poetic must acknowledge that words gain more multimodal power when they cohere within a framed artwork. The intensity of the creation (dissipated in the second version) evokes the other modes in a decorous and balanced way so that, in spite of the fact that the expression is cast in words, there is a delicate balance of modes in operation throughout, maximizing the intensity of meaning. Such a balance is different from that of sensory experience in the 'real' world, where the balance of relatively normal conscious preserves a harmonious relationship between the modes. In the world of art, the balance is achieved through artifice, but makes the reader/audience experience via reflection the integrated nature of everyday perception. In this way, a new aesthetic that is similar to the Augustan/ classical notion of imitation can be formulated, but one which is reframed in the light of multimodality, cognitive poetics and a sense of holistic balance. Such an aesthetic conception means that 'art for art's sake' cannot be a basis on which to build a new aesthetic theory; rather, the theory must be built on a socially and politically informed theory of meaning-making that is grounded in social semiotics and/or contemporary rhetoric.

Framing in Free Verse

Lowell's sonnets are unrhymed and ametrical, but they are clearly sonnets. What happens to the concepts of framing and multimodality when a poem moves beyond recognizable generic form and takes on free verse characteristics? Many of the qualities of formal, metrical verse are retained: the words have rhythm; they are surrounded by white space on the page; the words, in themselves, can generate multi-levelled meanings and a wide range of associations that are contained and influenced by the other words in the composition.

But there are differences too. In a previous chapter, 'Bach in California' was discussed in terms of its imagery. Here it can be compared in terms of framing to a very different free verse poem:

This Is the Age of the Typewriter

This is the age of the typewriter.
It began in 1922 and is just about to end.
It makes handwriting look like scribbling.
It is one of the few 20th century forms of order.
It gave unity to 'The Waste Land' and to the bank statement.
It is not yet fitted with silencers.
It gave rise to the concrete poem.
It fats nicely on a briefcage.

74   *The Framing of a Poem*

It is such maller than it used to be.
Everyome shuold gave one.
Than the reboltuion on connumicatoin woll habe raelly takn plase.
Forgxhetting dreghfwoul kj suhfpq.
But it is already too late, because the age of voice is about to st

In both poems (they are recognizably poems), the affordances of poetry are at play: the evocation of multi-levelled experience through imagery; the concentration on the words within the frame, making for greater intensity of resonance and reception; the musicality; the dependence of acknowledging that the line is the unit of rhythm. The first one, 'Bach in California', does not fall into any recognizable poetic genre. Its twelve lines are unrhymed, ametrical. It constitutes the evocation of an occasion and a moment. The nominal length of line, established at the start, allows for the creation of the line as unit of rhythm, with variations incorporated for specific effects: for example "suddenly" and "then" both signal a pause at the end of lines before the acceleration in the following line. The rhythms follow those of everyday written syntax and of the 'normal' patterns of written grammar, thus approximating and suggesting (because the grammars of writing and speech are different) speech. There is a clear 'sense of an ending' in the final line, so the poem is framed both rhythmically and semantically.

The second poem, 'This Is the Age of the Typewriter' works to a different internal cohesion: one of repetition. It is as if the typewriter itself has dictated the form: each line ending with a full stop, considerable variation in the length of lines, less of a-rhythmical approximation of the voice and more of a staccato pattern and a more 'automated' feel. The form that is 'borrowed' by the poem for artistic purposes is that of a list. The breakdown in sense in the last few lines is then punctuated by a line space (perhaps a mistake of the typewriter, or a slip of the hand?) which creates an effect like that of the "suddenly" and "then" placings in the first poem: a pause, followed by a conclusive, climactic line.

This latter poem, in more ways than one, touches upon the question of whether the typewriter, and its successor, the word processor, have shaped the meanings of poems as well as the format. This is a question of medium rather than mode, although there is a degree to which the printed word has affected the nature of poetry in relation to spoken or handwritten modes. The effect has been to move poetry away from narrative/epic mode to lyric, with the spatial dimension of the printed word allowing precise calculations of timing, rhythm and sense.

These internal cohesive devices tighten the poem, give it 'unity' and define its borders in relation to the world beyond the poem, signified by the immediate white space that surrounds it. There are thus a series of frames at play: that around the edge of the poem itself, the white space that signifies a liminal 'space' between the artefact and the rest of the word of semiotic signification and interpretation and the particular cultural and historical framings that societies and individuals bring to the interpretation of poetic texts.

Frame Breaking

All artworks break from their frames in one sense: they signify beyond it, using the frame to touch it, permeate it or break it. Such transgression of the frame takes place in all the arts: in theatre, via the actors placing themselves in the audience or inviting the audience onstage; in film, for example, in Woody Allen's *The Purple Rose of Cairo*, when a character seemingly steps out of the film into the cinema; or in painting, when the artwork spills across the frame, as in some of the work of Howard Hodgkin. In poetry, the act of frame transgression is less common, because the very nature of the poem is to contain and to increase compression and explosiveness.

It is more common to experience frame breaking in literature more generally and thus in poetics. Charlotte Bronte's "reader, I married him" (from *Jane Eyre*) is a direct address to the reader, as if the author had turned away from the composition of the novel for a moment to make the reader aware of an intervening author. Such mediation between the reader and the artwork is more possible in drama and fiction because of the ostensible fictionality of those genres. Poetry does not operate so obviously in the fictional world, so its framings are different.

The very discussion of framing in relation to poetry and other art forms—including the literary—is a multimodal act in itself because the original practice of framing belongs to the visual arts. The term 'frame' is also used to describe the still images that make up a moving image series in analogue film. Thus framing is inherently multimodal in its application and range of reference.

Notes

1 Bateson, Gregory (1972) 'A theory of play and fantasy' in *Steps to an Ecology of Mind*, Northvale, NJ: Jason Aronson and Andrews, Richard (2011) *Re-framing Literacy*. New York: Routledge.
2 Imp: strengthen by grafting.

6   The Basis of a New Poetics

Introduction

Multimodality manifests itself in most contemporary communication. Even where there appears to be only one mode in operation, there are other modes at play. Examples abound, and multimodality has become accepted as the principal means of communication. It is worth reminding ourselves, however, that pedagogies for teaching the different modes (writing, speech, still images, moving images, movement (e.g. athletics or dance), gesture) see them as separate systems. It is as if each mode were not connected to others and as if the internal logic and patterns of each mode were sufficient, and indeed *only necessary*, to teach that particular mode. Multimodality argues, however, that although the internal systemic patterning of each mode is crucial to learn, actual meaning is generated by the combination of more than one mode. If an understanding of how poetry works is required—and by wider implication, poetics—there must be an understanding that not only are poems implicitly multimodal but also explicitly multimodal. Furthermore, poetry is made from the elements of everyday communication. It is no longer of interest to write in, or compose or read a limited, refined poetic diction.

A Brief History of Literary Stylistics

Literary stylistics ('poetics' tends to be reserved from the wider category that addresses genres and text-types as well as the minutiae of literary devices) has a long history, going back at least to Aristotle's *Poetics*, as discussed in Chapter 1. As Scott (2014) points out, Aristotle moved on from Plato's discourse on literary mimesis and poetic inspiration to provide the first categorization and classification of literary discourse, at least as far as the narratology of tragedy and epic were concerned. Scott suggests that this manual, which influenced literary study through the Renaissance, was as much a manual of composition as of analysis. Like the current book, its intention was and is to help the makers of texts rather than merely their readers.

Russian formalism, with its focus on poetic language, was a natural descendant of the *Poetics*. Its emphasis on poetic language—a language that

The Basis of a New Poetics 77

drew attention to itself in 'performance', and thus was like a stained-glass window as opposed to a transparent pane of glass—was adopted by Britton in the language in education movement of the late 1960s and early '70s in England and the USA. For both Russian formalism and Britton, 'poetic' meant more than a kind of language confined to poetry. Rather, it referred to any kind of language in the wider set of discourses in the world that had these qualities. In 'drawing attention to itself', the suggestion is of narcissism. But poetry, too, can operate through a transparent glass; its character as *poetry* is the result primarily of its framing and rhythm, and secondarily and optionally of its compression. Furthermore, the applicability of poetic language in Russian formalism to everyday functions, and vice versa, is echoed in the current chapter in the move towards a multimodal poetics that is open to all functions and which, in turn, embraces all kinds of discourse in its poetic expressiveness. Scott's discussion of Bakhtin's 'dialogized heteroglossia', while accepted as a natural development of literary stylistics, is not so relevant to a discussion of multimodal poetics, other than in its conviction that there is more than one voice in operation in the creation and reception of literary texts—even, it must be emphasized, of the seemingly singular lyric voice.

The contribution of narratology—seen by Scott as another strand deriving from Aristotle and Russian formalism—to multimodal poetics is explored in Chapter 8 on the imaginative and fictive dimensions of poetics.

Word and Image

There is nothing new about the combination of word and image. Graphic artists work at the interface of word and image, along with logos and icons; children's book designers, authors and artists work together to create engaging texts for young people; medieval scribes and illustrators work together on 'illuminated' manuscripts; many fine artists use words in their artworks; cartoonists almost always use word and image to convey their humour; *Word and Image: A Journal of Verbal/Visual Enquiry* has been published regularly since 1943. No longer is it accepted to think that in the dynamic relationship between word and image, the verbal has primacy. Although the phrase is more often seen as 'word and image' rather than the alphabetically more logical 'image and word' (the reason for the sequence is probably more rhythmical than alphabetic or hierarchical), the two modes work alongside each other, each bringing their different affordances to bear on the act of communication. Sometimes word dominates and at other times the visual. At times, they are so balanced that the composition and the response can foreground either mode.

In a weekend in York in April 2016, I picked up some free materials that demonstrate different degrees of multimodality in graphic design (Figure 6.1).

This catalogue of rare and out of print books "focuses on the structure and components of all types of buildings. It includes books, original drawings and some trade catalogues all themed around this fundamental subject"

78 *The Basis of a New Poetics*

BUILD

ASPECTS OF CONSTRUCTION
CATALOGUE 13
JANETTE RAY BOOKSELLERS

Figure 6.1 'Build: Aspects of Construction, Catalogue 13, Janette Ray Booksellers'

(Ray, n.d.: 2). The cover is bold, using a move from left-ranged lettering in the title and sub-title of the catalogue to right ranged for the catalogue number and the bookseller's name. The balancing of the left- and right-ranged text could be interpreted as suggestive of building. What is incontrovertible is the use of lettering in itself to convey as strong visual message.

The inaugural brochure for the Centre of Ceramic Art in York uses a wider range of modes. First, it depicts the ceramics (Figure 6.2). Second, the colour photograph of the ceramic ware is used as the background to the words and graphics: the acronym for the Centre of Ceramic Art, CoCA, takes centre stage, the lettering bleeding off the page, suggesting CoCA is bigger than the framed front cover itself. The CoCA graphic is complemented by the full title of the centre at the top of the page and the logo at the top right. The remaining lettering is informational ('Opening Summer 2015' and 'August 2015–February 2016') and also positions the new centre within York Art Gallery, which is itself part of York Museums Trust. So there is a good deal of information on this front cover, but the information is not just verbal and abstracted; it is also multimodal, with the visual, photographed tactile and verbal modes working in combination, and with colour highlighting the messages that come across. There is a depth to the composition, requiring the eye to move from the foreground to the background, across the page from top to bottom and to take in the different kinds of symbol: purely verbal, acronymic, iconic and visual. The experience is more complex (and more simple) than that: a brochure in the hands suggests the tactile experience of print on a good quality card and paper, all in turn suggesting newness, quality and aestheticism.

The free map, 'Art in York' is a foldout with six square panels on each side (Figure 6.3). The key item—the map itself—takes up four panels on one side. Like most maps, it has its own 'key' of symbols. It is diagrammatic, showing

Figure 6.2 Centre of Ceramic Art Brochure: Cover

only the roads, rivers and main landmarks, as well as the walls of the city and the galleries that are listed by number. Maps are interesting documents in multimodal terms. This one is relatively simple. It uses lines, shading, words and numerals on a white background to orient the reader and to contextualize and locate a selection of the galleries in the city. It assumes knowledge of

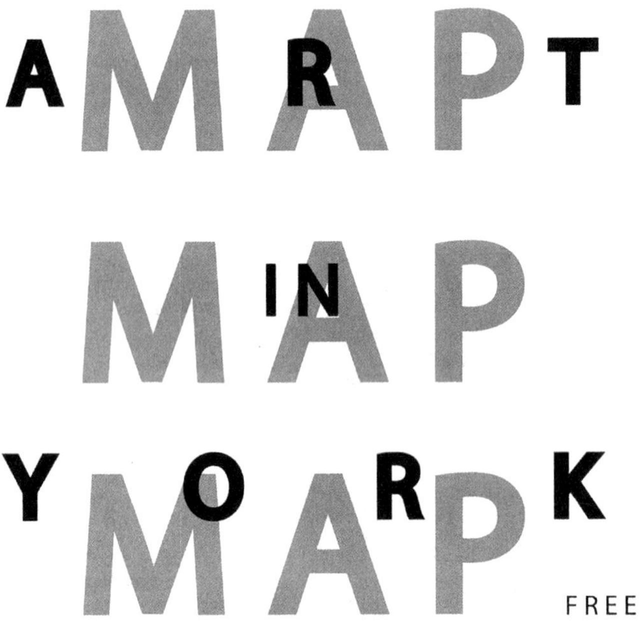

80 *The Basis of a New Poetics*

A **M** **R** **A** **P** **T**

M **I** **A** **N** **P**

Y **M** **O** **A** **R** **P** **K**

FREE

Figure 6.3 Art in York

the cardinal points (the top of the page, as usual, is north). Its art provenance uses a *sans serif* typeface for the names of streets and eschews the apostrophe. The icons in the key are simple and effective. In effect, it is a map that should be overlaid on other, more detailed maps, as it assumes much about the geography of the city. But it is effective because it is selective.

On the same side is a continuation of the list of galleries, each described in a short paragraph and with key informational details included (opening times, contact details). The numbers of the galleries also act as a marker, a bullet point, to indicate a new gallery entry.

It is the other side of the foldout that is even more interesting in multi-modal terms. Because of the printing constraints and nature of this particular foldout, the alignment of the square pages is more complex and the full range of colour printing is used. There are six panels: three are devoted to the list of galleries, as on the other side of the foldout. The other three contain a) the title page in which the title, 'Art in York' is overlaid in black on larger but more subdued ochre lettering which simply says 'map' and that the map is free; b) a page of logos of the contributing galleries and organizations that have made the compilation of the map possible, plus a brief verbal acknowledgement to "kiosk projects and Lotte Inch Gallery for their hard work and organization"; and c) four small advertisements for related activities and organizations.

Cookbooks

It is not just in the ostensible arts that word and image are combined. Whereas cookbooks used to consist primarily of verbal text with an occasional illustration, they now contain high-quality photography. Indeed, food photography is a sub-genre of photography itself. Even in the 1970s, Friedlander's *Cookbook for the New Age: Earth Water Fire Air* (1972), the contiguity of image and word was used to send out not only a recipe but also the sense of a lifestyle (Figure 6.4).

The recipe is straightforward: title, number of servings, preparation time and a list of ingredients, followed by a numbered sequence/procedure. Within its white space, it is instantly recognizable as a text-type of a recipe. On the opposite page is a black-and-white photograph, bled to the edges of the page, embodying some of the mystery of the book as a whole in its contrast of light and dark, the knife and board contrasting also with the chopped carrots. The earthiness of the ideology is mirrored in the unpeeled carrots, the cracked chopping board, the well-used knife. In terms of the double-page spread, there is a white page with plenty of white space contrasted with a darker page. The written recipe both contrasts and complements the photograph. The reader is asked to 'read' the written script to know how to make the soup; it's literal and practical. The photograph is 'read' differently: as a mystical complement to the recipe, to help create a state of being where appreciation of the ingredients and their oneness with the tools (think *Zen and the Art of Motorcycle Maintenance*, Pirsig 1974) are essential to the spirit of the book and its ideological approach.

Journalism

Newspapers have held photographs, cartoons, advertisements and other visual material for nearly 150 years. The earliest appearance of a half-tone photograph is in the *New York Daily Graphic* from December 1873 (Figure 6.5).

Colour photography is now commonplace in newspapers, as evidenced in a feature from the *International New York Times* of 8 May 2016, 'The shirt collar': the light-hearted, fashion-as-social-semiotic article à la Roland Barthes' *Mythologies* is the main text, even though the image of the shirt in question takes the masthead position in the overall composition. What draws the eye to the article is the image of a Brooks Brothers classic blue button-down Oxford shirt, floating above the text. Stage by stage, the eye is drawn to the bold title, then to the light-grey sentence of the sub-title and finally to the written text of the article itself:

> The most profound recent development in men's clothing concerns the millimetric adjustment of a garment first sold in 1900. In January [2016], Brooks Brothers issued a re-design of its oxford-cloth button-down, the shirt known commonly, and not quite insufferably, as an OCBD.

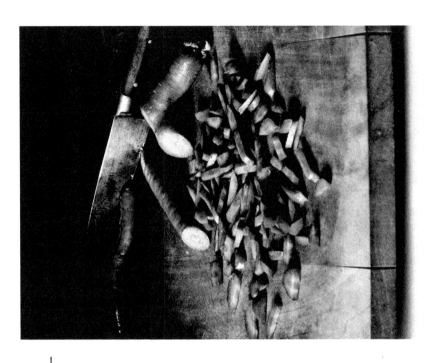

SWEET CREAM OF CARROT SOUP

servings: 4   preparation time: 50 minutes

1 pound carrots, chopped
4 cups water or vegetable broth
salt and pepper to taste
1 teaspoon honey
1 egg yolk
4 tablespoons light sweet cream
1 tablespoon butter

1. Bring carrots and water or broth to a boil. Cover pot, lower heat, and simmer for approximately ½ hour.
2. When carrots are tender, remove them from water and purée either in a food mill or blender. Return carrots to water and bring to a boil.
3. Add seasoning and honey.
4. Beat egg yolk and cream together in a small bowl.
5. Remove soup from heat and slowly stir in egg mixture and butter. Heat through but do not boil. Serve hot or cold.

Figure 6.4 Sweet Cream of Carrot Soup

Figure 6.5 Text and Image From 1873 Newspaper

    The upgrade to mother-of-pearl buttons, the addition of side gussets to the shirttails, even the disappearance of the breast pocket—these tweaks are no big deal, unless you are an emeritus professor wondering where now to stick his reading glasses. The removal of the collar's interior lining, however, constitutes a major moment in the history of minutiae, as it re-instates a first-rate collar roll.

The article goes on to suggest that the 'newly refreshed' style brings back a softer look to formal men's clothing and that the shirt suggests the nonchalance of a true preppy. Ms Birnbach, editor of *The Official Preppy Handbook*, is quoted at the end of the article as saying "Nonchalance is

84 The Basis of a New Poetics

everything to a preppy [. . .] It's a virtue, a value, a trope and an aesthetic. As far as studied nonchalance is concerned, that's how you learn".

A Visual Artist Uses Words

Linda Combi's work as a visual artist uses words in different ways: sometimes to complement the visual mode, sometimes to inspire it and sometimes, as in cartoon-like works, to work in close dynamic with the visual.

In 'Herb Garden Melody', for example, the list of herbs, as they often appear in cookbooks, herbals, poems, plays and songs, is given primary visual representation (Figure 6.6).

The central panel of verbal terms appears in no particular order, but is framed as a vertical panel. The lettering is highly visual, breaking the conventions of upper and lower case. Some of the letters are filled in. The panel

Figure 6.6 Linda Combi, 'Herb Garden Melody'

is overlaid, and/or underlaid, with washes of colour; each item separated by a visual dot (as opposed to a mark of punctuation, although the effect is of visual punctuation); and the panel is further framed by the edges of the work, through which a hand, a cat and, possibly, a bee and butterfly transgress. It's a work in which the meanings are multi-layered, evocative and highly framed, and in which the verbal and visual modes not only work in combination with each other but also take on some of each other's characteristics. If the words were extracted, they could stand as a free verse poem. With the layering, they operate additionally in the visual world.

In 'Mosque', verbal language fulfils a different function (Figure 6.7).

This time, the words are (literally) peripheral: they appear on the edge of the work. From one perspective, the visual work illustrates the words and from another, the centrality of the visuals in their colourful, geometric and curvy collage-like relationship determine the way the work is looked at,

Figure 6.7 Linda Combi, 'Mosque'

86 *The Basis of a New Poetics*

and how the words are seen as mere annotations. The list-like compression of the words is descriptive, poetic, explosive and dance-like.

In a different way, the political cartoon provides a popular genre in which word and image combine. In this genre, the visual element makes little sense without the words. The words appear as speech bubbles, as title or as commentary, but they are equally central to the composition as the drawings. The following cartoon/artwork by Linda Combi captures all these elements, although as artwork, it carries a further frame of the aesthetic (Figure 6.8).

Figure 6.8 Linda Combi, 'Politics and Rhetoric'

The Basis of a New Poetics 87

The cartoon, depicting the prime minister, frames the act of rhetoric within a media context and then again as artwork (and invisible frame).

Moving more towards a composition in which the verbal mode begins to dominate is the following artwork, 'Flexible Language' (Figure 6.9).

In this work, language (verbal language) is not only the ostensible subject, as represented in the title. It is also the demonstrable subject of debate and contention within the work. It is as if language is made into art, as it is in the work of a number of other artists and in the field of typography.

Figure 6.9 Linda Combi, 'Flexible Language'

88 *The Basis of a New Poetics*

Furthermore, street artists are depicted as sending a message, but also playing with verbal language. It is interesting that the term 'language', primarily associated with words, is used as a metaphor for a number of different other modes: the visual, dance languages, the language of sculpture and the language of dress. In these senses, 'language' is a placeholder for 'semiotic system'.

As a final example on a spectrum from the visual/verbal to the verbal/visual, Linda Combi's 'Shipping Forecast' builds around an existing text-type or largely spoken genre: the shipping forecast on the BBC (Figure 6.10).

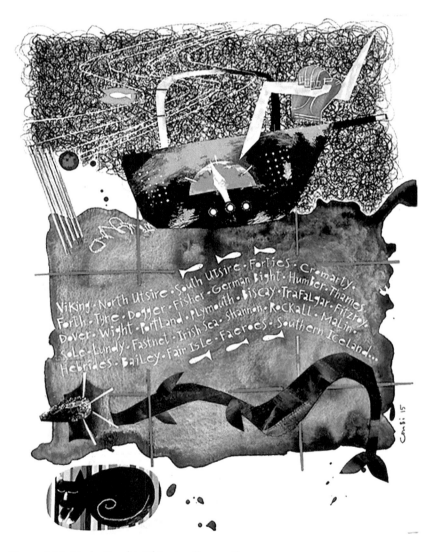

Figure 6.10 Linda Combi, 'Shipping Forecast'

The shipping forecast was discussed in the precursor to the present volume, *A Prosody of Free Verse: Explorations in Rhythm* (Andrews 2016) in terms of its potential and actual use as a free verse poem. The forecast itself takes the form of a clockwise journey around the shores of the UK, from Viking and North Utsire/South Utsire in the north and north-east, to Faroes and South-east/Southern Iceland in the north-west. The forecast itself is rarely seen in print: there will be a script in the BBC studio, and shipping may transduct/record the forecast in print form. In Linda's artwork, as in the many poems that the forecast has inspired, the list is given print form because of its sonorous, rhythmic and, thus, 'poetic' qualities. It serves as the centrepiece and stimulus for a brilliantly visual depiction of the weather offshore. The associations need not be explained, but the rich symbolism of the elements is captured in the visuals, thus adding a dimension to the original verbal stimulus.

Linda Combi's work captures the energy and dynamism, the beauty and humour of multimodality. It is multi-layered (literally and metaphorically) and creative in its combination of modes. What does it, along with the other examples of the relationship between the verbal and the visual, have to offer an emerging theory of poetics? This question will be discussed at the end of the chapter.

Poetry, Poetics and the Everyday

It is not only multimodality per se that is relevant to an emerging theory of poetics but also the fact that everyday communication takes multimodal form. Unless poetry works to a narrow, selected diction, it is open—as in Selina Nwulu's poem discussed in Chapter 2—to everyday discourse: vernacular, colloquial and unlimited in its range of vocabulary and style. Part of the move to give poetry a more demotic range is to take it off the pedestal of the 'highest art form' and make it accessible to writers/composers and readers. This popularization of poetry is not a dumbing down, but rather a democratization of language that is highly compressed, explosive, highly framed and choreographic.

The reason for discussing a range of examples of the multimodal in action is twofold: both to demonstrate the ubiquity of multimodality in contemporary communication and to make such forms available to poetry and poetics.

Digitization and the emergence of the worldwide web and Internet have made multimodal communication possible for a large number of the world's population. Mobile phone use, as one vehicle for the composition and receiving of calls and multimodal 'data', has increased exponentially. By 2015, over 50 per cent of the world's population were on the Internet.[1] The projected number of mobile phone uses by 2019 is over 5 billion[2] of a total world population of 7.4 billion in 2016.[3] Whereas telephone calls are seemingly monomodal in that the communication is restricted to voices, to watch someone on the phone is to see them gesture as if the interlocutor is

90   *The Basis of a New Poetics*

in the same room. The imagination is at work, even if the channels of communication are restricted. But social media, web-based messaging systems, such as WhatsApp and computer interfaces, make possible the combination of word (moving) image and sound.

Conventional literary stylistics/poetics has concentrated on the internal dynamics, rules and features of verbal language: principally in printed, written form, but also, to a lesser extent, in spoken verbal form. The present book attempts to widen the range of poetics to include a multimodal and digitized range. It has tended to ignore those poems that return to the natural speaking voice to find their inspiration: the colloquial voice and voices of the street, of everyday discourse. These voices are often deployed as an antidote to an over-formalization of poetic language. A good example of such a reaction is captured by Davie in *The Purity of Diction in English Verse* (1952), where he concentrates on the late Augustan poets of the second half of the eighteenth century. Their refinement of the language to a poetic diction that is used to express niceties of thought in a restricted code provided part of the abreaction of the Romantic poets such as Blake (through simplicity, although he still uses some of the archaisms of the poetic diction) and more so in the work of Wordsworth and Coleridge in the preface to *Lyrical Ballads*. Again, the manifestation of the common language of everyday discourse is not as clear-cut as might be imagined; it is still laced with literary diction, and the inventiveness is in a simplicity (and deepening) of sensibility and a narrative celebration of primitive or ancient historical (Romance) traditions. Keats is another example of a Romantic poet ploughing new ground in terms of sensibility, but with some of the opaque and elaborate poetic diction of previous traditions, as in this stanza from 'The Eve of St Agnes' (Buxton Forman 1917: 221):

> A casement high and triple-arch'd there was.
> All garlanded with carven imag'ries
> Of fruits, and flowers, and bunches of knot-grass,
> And diamonded with panes of quaint device,
> Innumerable of stains and splendid dyes,
> As are the tiger-moth's deep-damask'd wings;
> And in the midst, 'mong thousand heraldries,
> And twilight saints, and dim emblazonings,
> A shielded scutcheon blush'd with blood of queens and kings.

The language is rich and sensuous, conveying a sensibility more highly attuned to feeling than in Augustan or late Augustan poetry. At the same time, the language is syntactically Latinate ("A casement high and triple-arch'd there was") and archaically compressed ("arch'd", "imag'ries", "'mong", "blush'd"), even though we would not have pronounced the elided syllables in everyday discourse nor in the preservation of the rhythm of the poem. It is poetically archaic in other ways: in its use of "*all* garlanded", "midst"

The Basis of a New Poetics   91

as well as in its celebration of ancient terms such as "carven" and "scutcheon". Part of this intense evocation of the Romantic past is the highly inventive creation of neologisms such as "diamonded" and "emblazonings", the whole "blush'd with the blood of queens and kings": a sensual, physical touch to link death with love and life.

The case of Keats and his sensuous archaisms takes us back to a central question posed by Scott (2014) as to whether literary language can be defined in any universal sense. The consensus among stylisticians is that it cannot, that literature draws on any kind of language and is free to do so. Instead, Scott concludes,

> A universal characteristic of literary language (although not of course exclusive to it) can be found in its function of creating worlds through mimesis and diegesis [a narrative or plot]. These worlds are created through the interaction of two distinct (though inextricably linked) aspects of narrative (and I include poetry here): the discourse and the fabula. The discourse exploits mimetic and diegetic aspects of narrative discourse the more effectively to represent, or mediate, the fabula.
>
> (Scott 2014)

In depending on mimesis and diegesis, Scott is remaining firmly within the Aristotelian conception of poetics with its categorization and classification of types of narrative in epic and tragedy. Plot does not operate in the novels of Virginia Woolf nor in most poetry via these categories. Nor, to take the opposite position, does it operate solely through the lyricism of the supposed individual voice. Rather, it operates according to rhythmic principles within a highly framed and suggestive space; it is more akin to music than to the everyday world or its mimetic versions in the possible worlds of narrative (except, of course, in narrative verse). But in the case of poetry, the exceptions prove the rule.

However, we can use the notion of distance from the real world in the theory of possible words (see Pavel 1986) to suggest that there are degrees of opacity and transparency in poetic language, just as there are degrees of distance in narrative worlds from the 'real world'. On the spectrum of opacity and transparency, there are interesting aspects of multimodality to address. Is it the case that, in a more opaque stained-glass window version of poetic language, the poem is trying to do the work of other modes more than in translucent and transparent poetic language? In the latter case, if the window is translucently clear, is the effort of communication mainly on the topic of the poem, as in the best journalism (which does not draw attention to itself)? These questions are the kind that can and should be asked of multimodal poetics, and they come back to a new spectrum: not that of the mimetic, but of the implicit and explicit, which was explored in Chapter 1. Whereas the implicit-explicit multimodal spectrum does not map entirely on to the spectrum of opacity and transparency, it has

92 *The Basis of a New Poetics*

parallels. These, and the relationship with the fictional, will be explored *passim* and in Chapter 8.

Multimodal Poetics

In summary, as far as the present chapter is concerned, but only as a marker for further discussion, the following principles of multimodal poetics can be established.

First, it can be said that each mode embodies the potential signification of the others. A word suggests an image. An image suggests a word. And, referring to other modes, speech/song are referenced, as are moving image, movement, gesture and other modes of meaning-making. It could be said that although there are 'special relationships' among this set of modes of communication, all are able to relate to and invoke each other.

Second, when two or more modes are in explicit relationship with each other, one is likely to be dominant or foregrounded. This rule does not always apply, and the relationship can change (for example, in a film) during the course of the framed work. The rule does not apply to cartoons, where in most cases there is a balanced and reciprocal agreement between words and images.

Third, the 'meanings' are generated by each of the modes by themselves, but also by interaction/tension with other modes (like sparks) and/or in the spaces between modes. Abstract meanings, which may be suggested by metaphorical association, can hover above or below the work itself.

Fourth, the actual presence of other modes can extend, affect or constrain the affordances of each mode.

In all cases, the presence of visible or invisible framing provides a way of containing, preserving, delimiting and conveying the communication within conventional social and social/aesthetic frames (that can also be transgressed or broken), as well as referring outside the conventional frames.

Notes

1 http://dazeinfo.com/2015/05/27/internet-mobile-phone-users-worldwide-2000-2015-report/, accessed 13 May 2016.
2 www.statista.com/statistics/274774/forecast-of-mobile-phone-users-worldwide/, accessed 13 May 2016.
3 www.worldometers.info/world-population/, accessed 13 May 2016.

7 Implications for Poetics

Introduction

The argument and aperture of the book now widens to include a discussion of poetics. If Aristotle were writing today, what kind of *Poetics* would he write? The suggestion, as outlined in this chapter, is that it would be less focused on drama and narrative (important though they continue to be) than on the collage-like combinations of contemporary art and of performance, both of which can use a range of media and a number of different modes to convey meaning. A twenty-first-century poetics, then, would need to take into account that a single narrative direction is not the sole determinant of poetics, but that a more kaleidoscopic approach is more appropriate. What is retained from classical poetics, however, is the same commitment to linking poetics and rhetoric—or, to put it more simply, the fact that every composed artwork is at the same time informed by political and economic choice: what are the available materials, and what can be said in the particular societal and international context—and how?

Edwin Morgan's *Instamatic Poems*

A good way to start the discussion of what a new poetics might look like is via the example of Edwin Morgan's *Instamatic Poems* (1972). Morgan was an experimental poet, particularly interested in *form* and in the affordances and limitations of words. The *Instamatic Poems* (the word 'instamatic' refers to the 1963 Kodak easy-to-load-and-use camera which made everyday affordable use possible) are snapshots of moments in the early 1970s. The touristic nature of the snapshot is given ironic treatment by Morgan who describes, in words, the shots that are often surreal and/or grimly realistic. 'Glasgow 5 March 1971' describes a violent robbery; another poem with the same title describes a knife being thrown in the Central Police Court; 'Germany December 1970' describes a macabre inflatable safety airbag test in an old Mercedes. An example is 'Bangaon India July 1971':

> A grey-haired man half-runs,
> carrying his white-haired mother on his back

94   *Implications for Poetics*

> along a dusty road from East Pakistan.
> She is a hundred years old.
> What they own
> fills a knotted cloth at his hip.
> Even to them
> the hands of the dying are stretched out
> from both sides of the road.

The free verse nature of the rhythm is not at issue here. What is significant about this collection of poems is the transduction from the mode of still image, in the medium of photography, into words. All art transducts, with the help of framing. It takes perceptions, feelings, insights and other kinds of experience and shapes it into words, images, movements, sound or a combination of these. Some of Howard Hodgkin's abstract paintings (which paint over their frames) are the result of prolonged reflection and memory or of the experience of a place or relationship over a period of time. When, as in Morgan's case, a still image is appropriated into words, transduction (translation between modes) is taking place. From an aesthetic perspective, one could argue as to whether such transduction is a re-creation, imitation, commentary of one mode or another and/or complementary work. From a multimodal poetics perspective, it could be any or all of these. In a sense, it does not matter anymore whether art in relation to 'life', and one art form in relation to another, is informed by any one aesthetic theory. Multimodal poetics asks a more inclusive and more difficult question: what modal complexity is accounted for in 'everyday life'? What are the possibilities and implications of modal transduction between 'life' and 'art', and between the arts themselves?

A more pragmatic way to look at the example from Edwin Morgan (although there are no instamatic photographs to compare with the poems) is to ask, what is gained and what is lost in transduction from photography to poetry, and vice versa? Photographs capture a moment in time. They are heavily framed, both in the initial framing of the shot by the photographer and in any subsequent editing by the photographer or picture editor. They capture—whether in colour or black and white—the immediate context of the main focus. They are two-dimensional in space; there is a matter of the unity and cohesion of the photograph itself, as well as the issue of what is in inside and outside the frame and what these two elements 'say' to each other. The poem, on the other hand, is a verbal construct. It carries the abstraction that words carry; it leaves more room for interpretation and imagination. It appears visually as a single viewable entity, but it also operates in time and in sequence: the words are arranged by the poet in a particular syntactic order, but also in rhythmic shape, driven by the line as unit of rhythm within a free verse format. It can be read aloud, as well as read silently, and thus is transductible in itself from the medium of print to voice.

Rather than consider what is 'lost' and 'gained', a better way to look at such transduction is to define the affordances of each mode (and each mode carried in a particular medium). In the case of *Instamatic Poems*, there is conscious reference by Morgan to the fact that these poems are to be read with the idea of an instamatic photograph behind them (informing our reading of them). The poems are all in the present tense. They 'borrow' from photography the sense of a moment captured, of immediacy, of realism, or, at least, of closeness to the real world. At the same time, they have the sequential argument of words in a particular order. There is also the cumulative effect of a series or collection of poems, and the analogy with a collection of photographs is clear. They can be arranged in chronological order ('Glasgow October 1971' before 'Bradford June 1972') or not. In short, Morgan is using the analogy with photography to deepen the resonance and referentiality of the poems.

What is also evident is the ludic nature of the multimodal shift. Modal play of this kind is a way of generating a further level and further kind of meaning. It is not parasitic, but rather another dimension of how meaning is made in the world by framing and re-framing the available resources.

Multimodal Perspectives

Kress (2010) gives a comprehensive account of multimodality as a social semiotic approach to contemporary communication. Various elements of the multimodal approach have implications for poetry and poetics. But first, it is important to consider what is distinctive about poetry and its nature as a genre or meta-genre.

Poetry is highly framed; it is meant to be read slowly; it can be performed quickly, but in general, readers and listeners are asked to attend to the words that make up the poem. There is a high degree of aestheticism about the poem. Its framing suggests what is inside the frame is worth saying and worth attending to carefully. What is inside the frame is also highly wrought and deliberate—a form for capturing emotions, feelings, thoughts, reflections, spiritual and/or political musings or exhortations. Many people find this high degree of framing off-putting. It suggests preciousness; it is often delivered in a voice that is 'distant', hieratic, Oracle-like. At its worst, it can be self-serving, lachrymose and self-absorbed. It seems to purport to be important—more important than everyday discourse or prose, or indeed any other form of words. Although various definitions of poetry have tried to capture its essence and distinctiveness—'emotion recollected in tranquility', 'the best thoughts in the best order', 'explosive compression' and 'a dance in words'—the most accurately descriptive definition is 'writing that does not go up to the right-hand edge of the page'.

That formal definition of the arrangement of the words on the page attempts to describe what poems are formally, rather than what their function is, or what processes are at play in poetic composition. It is a good

96 Implications for Poetics

starting point for an exploration of what a theory of poetry informed by multimodality might look like and from there what a new multimodal poetics might contain.

In considering what a multimodal perspective on the *written* poem could offer, it can first be discussed what the white space around the poetic lines *signifies*. It could be said that this white space acts as the ground of the poem. Each line ends before the right-hand edge of the page. Even if the poetic lines run over to the next 'line' of the page, there is still a sense that the poetic text is not delimited by the page. Therefore, the white space or ground of the poem partly contributes to its meaning: by defining the poetic line as a unit of meaning and presenting the ground of the poem as a visual white space that suggests other modes. Such use of white space around a poem helps to preserve its distinctiveness, its otherness, its aspic-like qualities. But it also invites the reader to supply imaginative dimensions that are less evident in other genres.

Regarding the *spoken* or *performed* poem, multimodality plays a different role. To begin with, the act of speaking, reciting or performing poetry is already, ostensibly, more multimodal. Speech/voice, gesture and physicality are (potentially) present. The experience is more obviously three-dimensional. The variables are more numerous in delivery, but interestingly, the meanings are more limited in a collective audience than in the mind of a single reader.

Kress lays down a challenge to the domination of words (2010: 17) that is highly relevant to a contemporary poetics: "How do we now think about *imagination*, when much of our thinking has been shaped and dominated by the possibilities offered in linguistic modes? What of creativity?". The issue of imagery and of the imagination have already been partially explored in Chapter 4, but the assumption is that the imagination is a distinctly linguistic and literary construct that uses words and their associations to project visual, architectural, sonic and gestural worlds, often in combination. Because words are in themselves abstractions, their combination in poems that are at once highly framed but loosely associative suggests that they act like finely tuned mathematical equations at a level that is not quite as abstract as equations, but which retains links to the real world. Thus language operates with its feet on the ground and its head in the clouds, suggestive at many levels. At each of these levels, words can suggest images, three-dimensional constructions, sounds, gestures and other modes of representation and reference.

Creativity (in poetry) thus inheres in the bringing together of modal elements that spark each other to suggest rich possibilities of meaning. It is a collage-like activity. The metaphor is co-construction of meaning through sequences and arrangements of words that evoke other modes of communication and reference rather than of a 'fountain' of expression or the single imprint of a singular 'voice' that is the expression of a distinctive soul, self or spirit.

Multimodal poetics, then, is not a classical (highly scientific, bent on categorization), nor a Romantic (based on expressiveness) conception of poetics, but one based on the combination of one or more modes to suggest other modes of reference. It is multivalent, bridging text on a page and in the delivery of speech/voice, linking poetry to song, poetry to visual collage and poetry to gesture and rhetoric. Essentially, like multimodality based on a theory of social semiotics, it is concerned with making meaning through the deployment of modal resources with frames which, by their very nature, carry aesthetic weight. The attention is drawn to the particular combinations that are presented, with the expectation that such careful attention will reveal richer textures of meaning (inter-relational, intermodal meanings) than in everyday discourse. It is the beginning of a theory of poetics that sees concentration of modal resources within a frame as a means of generating high intensity meaning.

The Social Dimension of Poetry and Poetics

Multimodality is grounded in social semiotic theory. Such theory suggests that meaningful signs (and sign systems) are generated socially; that is to say, they only make sense in social context, whether they are produced by an actor/rhetor or received by an audience/reader (who themselves are actors in the acts of communication). The emphasis is not so much on system as on agency and participation in a dialogic meaning-making activity. And because social relations are informed by politics and power relations, multimodal meaning generation is political as well as social.

What are the implications of the socio-political dimension for poetry? First, that the individual 'voice' of the Romantic conception of poetry is self-delusory. It emanates from the notion that the self is self-contained, generative, self-sufficient, free, creative and independent, as well as, above all (literally), the passage to a different plane of being. Much derives from this Romantic conception: the cult of the author, the obsession with celebrities, the convention that the book, for example, is the result of a single author's work rather than a collaboration with editors, designers and printers, with reference to other books/voices that have preceded it.

Second, that poetic creation, however isolated the poet might be in the moment(s) of creation, is essentially social. The poet seeks solitude to write/compose. He/she is part of a number of social networks. The very act of self-isolation is a socio-political act in that it is asking for space to bring a number of thoughts/feelings together and then return them, in due course, to family, friends and/or wider audiences. The different rhetorical contexts for composing can be demonstrated in this two-part poem. The first part was written soon after the birth of a new baby in the family; the second part (and thus the whole) was commissioned for a christening.

98   *Implications for Poetics*

Poem for Emily

I

Born on the first day of spring, her eyes
are adjusting from darkness to light.
Already she is reading the curtain's patterns,
the shapes of letters, the synaesthetic buzz.

She's the answer to the equation: A + Z = E.
She's a small bumble bee
at the pollen of every aquilegia, every blossom in the garden.
Life vibrates; she is at the quivering edge of experience.

One day she will walk the garden paths
that we have all walked. For the moment, she's translucent,
distinguishing day from night, wakefulness from sleep
as in the creation, on the first day of Genesis.

II

Now, at the tips of her fingertips
are the colours and shapes of her letters and toys.
One day she's at Mini-Mozart, the next
she's swimming in her element.

She's on the verge of words.
Meaning comes slowly into focus.
She's beginning to read
her parents' faces: the first narrative.

She's the light at the centre of this day;
like pre-Copernicans, we orbit around her.
Following her small bright star,
let's hang on to the coat tails of her comet

as she finds her way across the firmament:
stellar, beautiful, illuminating
and, in the grand scheme of things,
still quite small.

The first part is more meditative. There was little conception of audience in
its composition. (A+Z = E is an equation using the letters of the parents and
the baby.) It was not meant to be read aloud, but to be a tribute that captured an early state of being and development, like a photograph that serves

Implications for Poetics 99

as a record for the archives: a point of reference, of departure. And yet, even with such a meditative, seemingly a-social poetic conception, future audiences are imagined.

The second part is more outward looking, more occasional. It was commissioned for an occasion: the christening of Emily when she was about 5 months old. Writing this second part was difficult, because the occasional tone and celebration had to be grafted onto the first, meditative, inward part. So the "now" at the start of the second section marks a pivotal shift from the first part. Not only is the baby becoming more social but also the tenor of the section is more social. It's political, too, in that a gathering of 50 or so people is a result of socio-political networks, resources, ritual, collective will power and intention. Invitations are issued; calendars adjusted; long journeys made; gifts thought about, purchased and given; and so on. The second part is addressed to the people at the christening ("let's hang on to the coat tails of her comet") rather than forming part of a short series of inward reflections.

Further analysis could examine the form of the poem in terms of its socio-political poetic. Although, in its early draft of the first section, the four-line unrhymed stanza emerged organically from notes on a page, its establishment as the framework within which the poem develops is a conscious formal choice from a range of possible forms and genres. Why did the initial notes shape themselves in poetic form? What social expectations of what is being said informed the very quick move to a four-line stanza? Why does it take unrhymed form?

The answer to the first question is that there is a rhythmic imperative (and a desire for intensity of expression) behind the two contiguous statements that make up the first stanza. Once this pattern is set, the further stanzas follow it. Similarly, once the group of three unrhymed quatrains had been established for the first part, the second started out to mirror that framework, except that there was more to say, more expansiveness was needed for the performed, occasional nature of the second part—and so it works out to be four quatrains rather than three. Not a symmetrical balance between the sections, but a sense that the second one is more airy, more generous and more developmental.

The social expectations that inform the choice of quatrains come partly from literary history. The unrhymed tercet or quatrain is the default form of much of Heaney's middle period and allows a conversational yet tightly economical voice to express itself, echoing previous uses of the form. But the unrhymed quatrain also allows space. It's a generous form, allowing much white space around it for visual and aural resonance.

Why the unrhymed form? The lack of rhyme de-emphasizes any sense of regular beat that rhyme always reinforces. It makes the expression more everyday, prosaic and understated. In socio-political terms, the effect is to say, "This poem is offered as part of an ongoing dialogue for the day, with reference to the biblical/ritual/Christian context as well as to the social and developmental occasion".

100   *Implications for Poetics*

The framing of the poem in its socio-political context was further defined by the occasion of the reading itself. People were gathered outside the back of a house. Drinks had been served after the return from the church christening; people had talked with each other, re-establishing the human dimension after the highly formal/ritual of the christening; it was a moment before serious eating took place. A bell or gong was sounded to draw attention. The reading given. Then it was over—a few moments in time and part of the flow of social engagement for the day.

What has happened to the poem as a whole, with its two originally different parts now melded into a single entity? Since the occasion of the reading, one of two people asked for copies. The parents were given a copy. No further appearance of the poem has occurred before its inclusion in print in this chapter. It is likely to make no further public appearance, other than (perhaps) in a private collection some years or decades down the line.

Dynamic Multimodal Poetics

A general principle of multimodality is that the relationship between modes is dynamic. That is to say, one mode plays alongside or against another in the creation of meaningful communication. Sometimes one mode will be dominant and the other supporting or contrasting; at other times, the modes will be equal in weight and the tension/complementarity will be more evident, more alive.

If general principle is applied to poetry and poetics, the conventional printed poem on a page can be seen as a highly selective composition on white (paper, screen) ground. The words on the page seem static. They are 'fixed' to ensure preservation of a feeling/thought complex. Around the fixed imprint is what has already been categorized as white space. This 'ground' gives space for the imagination, for soundscapes, for other modal resources to come into play. These other (invisible) modes, including associative visual, spatial, gestural and aural 'imaginations' help to create the meaning that is perceived/conveyed in the dialogic interaction with the text. In turn, what such dynamic multimodality suggests about the printed poem on the page is that it is, in itself, but a snapshot of a dynamic interrelationship between words and other modes. In other words, it is dynamic, contained within a frame and, at the same time, with rich potential for complex meaning via interaction with other modes.

If the poem is spoken, recited or sung, or performed in any other way, the other modes come more readily into view. A poet or reader may use gesture, modulation of voice, expressiveness (including facial expression), movement, sound/music to 'deliver' the poem. The very physical presence of the poet him/herself brings resonance, added layers of meaning and human contact to the communication, whether the performance is live or on audio and/or film. The audience is more aware of life history behind the poem when the work is spoken. Often the poet introduces the poem with a short anecdote; the selection and sequence is varied according to the occasion and the audience; within the mode of the spoken poem, the genres and modulations can change to vary the experience.

In summary, then, there are a number of rhetorical choices to be made in poetics.

These are as follows:

- What do I/we want to 'say'?
- In which principal mode shall I/we say it?
- If this mode is the verbal, am I/are we using the spoken or written version?
- What kind of framing is being used?
- Specifically, is there a conventional genre being selected, or is this a hybrid?
- What degree of association and engagement do I/we expect?
- How implicit/explicit are the other modes that are brought into play?

The rhetorical choices make for a specific form of communication within a specific socio-political context.

One could say that the conception of an audience, so typical of rhetoric, is hardly at play in the composition of poetry. A lyric poet, for example, has little conception of *to whom* or *for whom* he or she is writing. The work is composed, and all the attention appears to be on personal expressiveness and on the framing and composition of the words within the frame.

There are two dimensions whereby this Romantic conception of making poetry can be varied and challenged. One is to suggest that the notion of the single author can be varied by more than one composer: expression can be collective, as in a Greek chorus, or an author can compose individually and his or her editor operate additionally to give the work better shape, form and economy. The second dimension is that of the implied audience. Whether the audience is imagined in the act of composition or not, it is always there. It could be as minimal as the audience within the composer's own mind; it could be a small set of friends and/or family, or it could be a larger, more extensive audience that cannot be exactly imagined. In ostensibly political poetry, there is often a specific audience that is addressed, either to express a collective sentiment or to protest a state of affairs. The socio-political context is always there in some degree.

So dynamic multimodal poetics takes into account not only the dynamism that is evident within the frame but also the relationship with an implied or actual audience. Hence poetry and poetics is rhetorical, and multimodality forms a critical sub-section of rhetoric in any composition.

The Elements of a New Poetics

Literary poetics has customarily been classificatory. Its plethora of terms and devices has been a guide for literary critics and readers who wish to know how a literary effect is achieved. Multimodal poetics is different.

102 *Implications for Poetics*

Instead, it uses a limited number of 'elements' and looks at the relationships between them, within an overall theory of rhetoric and rhetorical choice. Because these relationships are dynamic, there is little point in accounting for every possible arrangement. The advantage of such a poetic is that it is simpler in terms of analysis, but it is also more useful in terms of productive composition.

At one level, the elements are modal: words (in spoken or written form), images (still or moving), gestures and movement (including the physical dimension), sounds and other signs.

At another, more specific level, are genres: poetry, drama, narrative fiction and documentary. Even at the level of genres (e.g. narrative fiction), there is hybridity. Not all narratives are fictions, and not all fictions are narratives.

At a yet more specific level are sub-genres or forms: the sonnet, the comedy or tragedy or 'kitchen-sink' drama, the historical novel or short story or the travelogue or recipe.

Consideration of media can be discounted from this poetic. Whether a poem or novel is carried by electronic means, or via a printed book or on film is largely irrelevant to consideration of multimodal poetics, except where the medium has affordances which affect the mode, genre and form. For example, white space around a poem can be the ground of a page in a book, the blank space on an electronic screen, the silent space on a film or the white wall of a gallery. Although the media are different, the ground is the same.

Let us demonstrate these rhetorical choices, and multimodal dynamism, in the composition of part of Milton's *Samson Agonistes*. Samson in captivity, and blind, bewails his lot:

> Scarce half I seem to live, dead more than half.
> O dark, dark, dark, amid the blaze of noon,
> Irrecoverably dark, total eclipse
> Without all hope of day!
> O first-created beam, and thou great Word,
> 'Let there be light, and light was over all,'
> Why am I thus bereaved thy prime decree?
> The Sun to me is dark
> And silent as the Moon,
> When she deserts the night,
> Hid in her vacant interlunar cave.
>   (Lines 79–89)

The mode is verbal, the genre poetic and the sub-genre dramatic, tragic poem. The white space around the words makes it clear that this particular poem does not follow strict hexametrical rhythm, nor does it rhyme. It moves not in stanzas or verse paragraphs, but in dramatic exchange and dialogue. Milton himself is at pains to explain the rhetorical choices he has

Implications for Poetics 103

made in the composition of the work. He does so in an introduction to the poem called 'Of That Sort of Dramatic Poem Called Tragedy'. The ostensible starting point for a discourse on the rhetoric of choice is tragedy: "The gravest, moralest, and most profitable of all other poems" (1911: 353). His litany of previous writers of tragedy, in a number of different genres, is mentioned

> to vindicate Tragedy from the small esteem, or rather infamy, which in the account of many it undergoes at this day, with other common interludes; happening through the poet's error of intermixing comic stuff with tragic sadness and gravity, or introducing trivial and vulgar persons.
>
> (1911: 353)

Milton goes on to justify the use of chorus in the poem, citing the practice of epistles at the start of poems in 'the ancient manner'. The use of the chorus "is here introduced after the Greek manner, not ancient only, but modern, and still in use among the Italians" (ibid.)

There is then a detailed account of the measure of the verse. At one level, this is blank hexameter bordering on free verse. As far as the chorus is concerned, Milton uses the classical categories:

> The measure of verse used in the Chorus is of all sorts, called by the Greek *Monostrophic*, or rather *Apolelymemon*, without regard had to Strophe, Antistrophe, or Epode—which were a kind of stanzas framed only for the music, then used with a Chorus that sung; not essential to the poem, and therefore not material [. . .] Division into act and scene, referring chiefly to the stage (to which this work never was intended), is here omitted.
>
> (1911: 353–4)

Already, the elements of a modern multimodal poetics are evident in Milton's justifications for his rhetorical choices: part of the socio-political and aesthetic function of the poem is to restore tragedy to its classical high seriousness, devoid of Elizabethan and Jacobean levity. The chorus is a tribute to classical precedent (in line with practice of Aeschylus, Sophocles and Euripides, "the three tragic poets unequalled yet by any" (1911: 354)), and the use of the unity of time (the action takes place in a single day). And yet intermixing is evident in the use of the unsung chorus and the omission of acts and scenes.

As far as implied multimodality goes, the poem is rich. As well as Samson, the 'persons' in the drama include Manoa, his father; Dalila, his wife; Harapha of Gath, a rival; and a public officer, messenger and the Chorus of Danites. Each of these comes 'onstage' to dialogue with Samson. At the end, the audience hears the clamour offstage as Samson brings down the temple

104 *Implications for Poetics*

on himself and on the Philistines. There is soliloquy, argument, a sense of location, the wider geographical and political context.

Thus Milton chooses the form that suits his intent. At the same time, he is restoring tragedy to its true high state—a literary political act in itself. The drama is interior, unstaged and monolithic. But this is dialogic writing in more than one sense: it contains interchange between the characters and comments on the previous generations' practices (including Shakespeare's) in mixing comedy with tragedy.

8 A Further Look at the Imaginative and Fictive

Introduction

One of the most problematic splits in the study of language and discourse is that between documentary or 'non-fiction' texts on the one hand, and fictive texts on the other. The problems are several: how can the two types be distinguished when there is often blurring of the boundaries between them? Why is 'non-fiction' given an umbrella-like *negative* term, as if it needed to be defined *in relation to* fiction? How to account for literary forms that are not fictive, like the lyric or much of poetry? Or for literary forms, like realistic drama, where the action may be more 'real' than life itself? What is the relationship of the imagination, and how does it operate, in documentary as well as fictional modes? The basic argument in this chapter draws on Pavel's 1986 book, *Fictional Worlds*, but re-interprets it in the light of contemporary multimodality theory and reflections on space and time in fiction and 'non-fiction'.

A Rhetorical Take on Fiction and Non-fiction

Poetics in the broader sense includes literary genres such as the novel, short story and dramatic works. In that sense, it might be cast as a late development of twentieth-century literary stylistics, returning to the broader classical meanings of poetics. Literary stylistics—a fusion of linguistics and literary study—is a creation underneath the broader umbrella and longer history of poetics. The categories are problematic in a number of ways.

First, 'poetics' suggest the edifice of theory about literature is based solely on poetry. This is not the case. The specific focus on poetry in the present book is simply to provide a starting point and an empirical basis for the exploration of multimodality in relation to poetics. There will need to be further research on the way that multimodality brings a different theoretical perspective to bear on the novel, short story and other literary genres.

Second, the binary distinction between 'fiction' and 'non-fiction' is unhelpful. It appears to be based on the notion that there is reality which 'non-fiction' addresses and an unreality which 'fiction' explores. It can be surmised

106 *Further Look at the Imaginative and Fictive*

from the borders between these two categories that much fiction contains non-fictional elements, and vice versa. The categories are not watertight. A concrete example would be Robert Pirsig's *Zen and the Art of Motorcycle Maintenance* (1974): part fiction, part autobiography, part travelogue, part philosophical treatise, part motorcycle manual. In another example of the sagacity of fiction, the first lines of Jane Austen's *Pride and Prejudice*—"It is a truth universally acknowledged, that a single man in possession of a good fortune, must be in want of a wife"—might as well be the start of a guide on marriage etiquette or a sociological study as be the start of a novel (Austen's wit suggests it might be all three).

Third, 'non-fiction' is a negative category. The works within this category are defined by what they are *not*. Such categorization appears to give fiction the prime place, with all other documentary genres relegated to a broad negative space. Instead, 'non-fiction' could be conceived as 'documentary', with its various sub-fields defined as they are now: cookery, travel, autobiography, reference, etc.

Fourth, why is 'fiction' dominated by the novel? In the pages of review supplements and literary reviews, and in bookshops, novels take priority. Is it that, since the seventeenth century, the novel has emerged as the principal vehicle for fictive representation because of its affordances: its ability to carry a narrative, its relative (light) density compared to poetry or plays or its 'readability'? These affordances will be explored in the course of this chapter, relating them to the broader theme of poetics and the narrower genre of poetry.

All the aforementioned issues are raised by seeing fiction and non-fiction within a rhetorical framework. Rhetoric, sometimes conceived as political literary criticism, is best defined in the contemporary context not as the 'art of persuasion' but as the 'arts of discourse'. That means that whether the discourse operates in the fictive or 'real' world, it is subject to the same overarching theory of rhetoric. Rhetoric asks questions that define a text: who is 'speaking' to whom? About what? What modes and forms are chosen for the communication and why? What media are used to convey the communication? Each act of communication involves choices such as these, and the resources to make such choices are politically distributed and informed. Not only is discourse in all its manifestations (from everyday discourse to formal art forms) embraced by rhetoric; there is also an art to the choosing and shaping of those acts of communication. Sometimes, as in Pirsig's book, the genres are hybrid.

Poetics, with its particular focus on literary creation, production, reception and analysis, is therefore best seen a sub-section of contemporary rhetoric. By 'contemporary' is meant a rhetoric that is not bound by ancient classical contexts of the public forum or persuasion, nor by medieval and Renaissance manuals of literary tropes and devices, but by the range of social (and therefore political) modes, media and genres of everyday communication as well as of specialist art forms.

Is Poetry Fiction or Non-fiction?

Before continuing the discussion of the nature of fiction and its relation to poetics and multimodality, what is the position of poetry within the broader categories of literature from one perspective, and the fiction/documentary categories from another? In every bookshop I have visited, poetry is categorized under literature but has a separate section from 'fiction' (novels and to a lesser extent, short stories) and drama. The section is always smaller than for fiction.

It seems odd to think of poetry as non-fiction or documentary. Tony Harrison's *V* (1985) might fit that documentary category in its autobiographical, social commentary style. Much classical verse (Dryden, Pope and their contemporaries) operates in this way. A very different example, from the Romantic tradition, is *The Prelude* with its strong autobiographical line. This dimension of poetry does not exclude the lyric mode, with its close association with song. And yet poetry tends to be seen, at least in the West, as belonging to the Romantic or late-Romantic lyric tradition: relatively short, personal, expressive, integrating the imagination and defined by its rhythmic foregrounding.

To what extent is poetry 'fictional'? Lyricism is not easily couched with the fictional, as it is seen as emanating from the heart/soul/intellect of the writer. It therefore is afforded an inner reality that is not a projection into the lives of others (as is prose fiction) but has a force and intensity of its own. There are exceptions to this generalization, most notably in the modernist works discussed earlier in the book (Chapter 4), in the classical and neo-classical works referred to earlier and in the poetry of worldwide cultures, where not all works operate within the Romantic, expressive and 'Western' tradition.

The Limits of Narrative

Narrative poetry does not sit easily within the expressive, lyric tradition. It is there in ballads, in some large-scale works (see Chapter 4, where most of the twentieth century and longer contemporary poems discussed do not have a strong narrative line) and in some autobiographical work. Narrative seems to have been appropriated by the novel and the short story. Narrative is not only the domain of the fictive; it is there in everyday accounts of experience, in making sense of disparate experience, in political argumentation and in history, as framing the past, understanding the present (as part of an ongoing narrative) and shaping the future.

Key to the development of argument in this chapter, and within the context of the book as a whole on multimodality and poetics, is the role played by fiction and, to a lesser extent, by narrative. Pavel (1986), in *Fictional Worlds*, sets his theoretical exploration of fiction in a wider frame than formalist poetics (stylistics) by including perspectives from modal logic and aesthetics. He attempts to "pave the way for a theory sensitive to the nature

108 *Further Look at the Imaginative and Fictive*

and function of imaginary worlds, the representational force of fiction, and the links between literature and other cultural systems" (1986: vii).

Fundamental to the conception of fictions being the representation of 'worlds' (with narrative as a rhetorical meta-genre often used to structure that world in relation to time) is the philosophy of modal logic and possible world semantics. In the creation of possible worlds, Pavel argues that narrative has been relied upon too heavily to carry the burden of the created worlds, that over-dependence on plot has minimized mimesis (imitation) and reference (to non-narrative aspects of a created world) and such over-dependence has suggested that "relations between literary texts and reality were merely aftereffects of a referential illusion, spontaneously projected by narrative syntax" (1986: 5–6). The close association between narrative and text has further limited the wider referential aspects of fictional worlds. In the present book, the disaggregation of narrative, poetics and text is an important post-structuralist move to enable us to see that poems, for example, are more than words on a page: they inhabit, like all art forms, a multimodal space that is framed for us to consider and (possibly) contribute to.

Thus narrative poems are not the main focus on the present book, and narrative studies more generally are not employed to make sense of a contemporary poetics. One of the general principles of narrative—*post hoc ergo propter hoc*—implies a causality, both in narrative and argument, that does not apply to the complex, multi-panelled and multimodal world of poetry and the non-narrative sections of contemporary poetics. Narrative *poems* are fewer and farther between. Narrative, as a vehicle of communication, while vibrant in everyday discourse and in the novel and short story, has partly been appropriated by politicians who try to link narrative to power and thus to propound the stronger political narrative. Because these political 'narratives' are often not supported by (or even eschew) evidence, they lose the validity that narratives in public discourse can carry. Instead, they take their place in a post-truth world where narratives compete without a foundation in anything more solid than ideologies or personal, power-based conviction.

Possible Worlds

Pavel's contribution to literary theory is based on a discussion of modal logic in relation to segregationalist notions that "there is no universe of discourse outside the real world" (1986: 13). The present discussion, however, does not engage with the philosophical debates about the relation of real worlds to possible worlds, nor with the derivation of some aspects of Pavel's argument from speech-act theory. It simply accepts that the real world as experienced and perceived is one version of a range of possible worlds that could have obtained, that not everyone sees the 'real world' with the same eyes and that poetics need to free itself from an over-dependence on narrative theory in order to be seen as part of the wider picture of rhetorical framing and choice. It also argues that multimodal choices are central to the

Further Look at the Imaginative and Fictive 109

shaping and reception of literary works (with a focus on poetry), and that even where it appears that one mode is used, there are other modes at play, implicitly or explicitly. Modes, therefore, are one dimension of the rhetorical choices that are available to the rhetor/creator/audience.

Rhetorically, Pavel sees the real world as one of a number of possible worlds arrayed on an inclusive spectrum. Realist literature would be close to the assumed real world: "Not merely a set of stylistic and narrative conventions, but a fundamental attitude toward the relationship between the actual world and the truth of literary texts" (1986: 46). Fantasy literature would be further away on the spectrum, but would be no less a commentary on the assumed real world through its framing of fantasy. It represents a different degree of possibility. In such conceptions of possible worlds, it is the internal cohesion and thus the believability of such worlds in relation to the experienced and perceived real worlds that is the issue, rather than too binary a distinction between the real world and the excesses of fiction. The internal aesthetics of such fictional worlds leads us to the realm of design, cohesion and (indeed) narrative coherence that makes a fictional novel or story compelling.

These possible worlds do not, however, exist in a parallel universe or space. They are involved through language and other modes in the chemistry between the reader/audience and the affordances of the text. What the reader brings to the work is almost as important as what the work itself offers. The framings, through previous reading and other life experience, determine the nature of the experience in reading a novel or a poem. More accurate is to say that fictional worlds offer *hypotheses* about the world that can only be tested by comparison with other fictional constructs, or be measuring the degree to which they can be configured in relation to the real worlds of their audiences. None of this hypothesizing would be possible without the operation of the imagination on the part of the creator/rhetor and the audience.

What Kinds of Possible Worlds Does Poetry Inhabit?

Most contemporary poetry does not reach epic proportions. It is more modest: not necessarily in theme, but in scale. If Pavel's notion that fiction inhabits possible worlds is accepted as a hypothesis, what kinds of possible worlds does poetry inhabit? More specific notions of the borders of fictional worlds, and their distance from the 'real' world, do not seem to apply to poetry. Instead, poems delineate a more personal, individualistic space that is tightly framed. They might say much within that tight frame by virtue of the compression that is taking place, both in their creation and reception (the unpacking of compression).

A key difference between prose and poetry is that poems tend to operate in the present. They have different relations to time than prose fiction. Whereas prose fiction arranges time (most of it is written in the past tense), poetry concentrates on time in order to eliminate it in a perpetual present.

110 *Further Look at the Imaginative and Fictive*

This does not mean that all poetry is written in the present tense, but that past and present tenses are fused in an evocation of the present. The difference is subtle. Both genres create possible worlds that sit alongside the real world in an imaginative space/parallel world, but the possible worlds of prose fiction are set in the past tense because they need to handle and arrange time (past, present, future). Poetry, on the other hand, fuses past, present and future into the present.

In terms of space and spatial location, prose fiction depicts geographical worlds with boundaries, distance from the real world and size as constituent and defining features. Poetry, because it works on a smaller canvas and is more highly framed, creates windows into possible worlds that are not so separate from the author. To continue the metaphor, the poet is both inside the window looking out and outside the window looking in.

Take the following two poems as examples. Both were written during stays in the Adirondack Mountains of upstate New York. One takes the perspective from Vermont, looking west towards the Adirondacks; the other is more domestic and smaller in subject, and based on the closing of a camp after a summer season.

A Pale View of the Hills

From Vermont looking west
over Lake Champlain

the Adirondacks fade into the distance,
each ridge a paler version of itself.

First, the foothills of the valley:
farms, fields and barns.

Then the dark green silhouette
of the mountains;

next, a dusty green
and the tops of trees edging the sky.

Then a greyer line
before a signature trace.

Finally, the last ridge of hills, indistinguishable
from the late summer sky.

Closing

All the tables, chairs and stools come in from the porch.
The pipes are cleared, for fear they'll freeze in the winter.
Taps are turned off; the carpets rolled. In the drawers

Further Look at the Imaginative and Fictive **111**

sit the valuables: a plate from Brittany, ornate candlesticks,
Buddhas, netsuke, an African mask. The Adirondack chairs
are stored under the house where no one sits. Propane
is turned off at every tap, the electricity's off, the grill is cleaned
and put in the garage. Windows are nailed, the hummingbird feeder
brought in so they'll forage on berries, later-flowering shrubs.
The fire grate is cleared of ash, and we pour it, cold, into the forest.
The flowers that decorated the porch are dumped. Logs are stacked,
the kayak and row-boat upturned and stacked for the season.
We leave moss on the tree stumps in the hope new life will start;
and in the mountains all around, the green turns gradually to gold.

Putting aside issues of form and rhythm, the first poem takes a particular perspective, like that of a painter. The writer (invisible, not named) is looking west. He/she alludes to the title of a Kazuo Ishiguro novel (1982) to depict distance. There's hardly a main verb in the poem ("fade"), so the depiction is not dynamic. There is no movement in time; the scene is static. What the poem tries to do is capture a moment.

The second poem is more of a domestic, inside/outside composition. Again, while putting aside questions of form and rhythm (it's an unrhymed sonnet), there is nevertheless a reference to previous poems in that format. It depicts a moment in time between past (the summer) and the future (fall/autumn), and is composed in the present tense, also to capture a moment. Like the first poem, it is descriptive, but in a more active way: there is movement and action. The writer is more conscious of his/her joint work ("we pour it, cold, into the forest" and "we leave moss on the tree stumps"), and so the authorial voice as well as actions convey presence. Despite the capturing of a moment between two seasons, the poem is about the here and now.

Both depict possible worlds, but these worlds are closer to the real world because of their detail, focus and perspective. They do not purport to create a world into which the reader might walk, nor a territory with boundaries in which the imagination might wander. Strangely, prose fiction is more welcoming and more inviting to the reader because it allows such space to move; poetry seems, on the whole, more personal and individualistic to the writer; therefore, the reader has to make more of an effort to enter that world. It could also be added that the window through which the poet looks is more like stained glass than entirely transparent because the language itself that is used draws attention to itself through its compression and framing. In prose, the windows, if there are any, are more transparent—the language is looked through in order to see into the worlds it depicts.

A further distinctive feature of the poem as opposed to the prose fiction is that it is always possible to see the edge of the poem when reading it. The reader is more conscious of form. In a novel, part of the pleasure is immersion in a possible world—a suspension of disbelief, being caught up in a narrative that, until he or she reaches the end, the reader cannot know its outcome. A second reading of a novel is different from the first because in the second we know the ending, the outcome. The 'experienced' reader,

112 *Further Look at the Imaginative and Fictive*

therefore, reads with the knowledge of how the constituent parts of the novel fit together: how this character relates to that one, how the events unfold towards a conclusion and how time is managed. A second reading of a poem is different: there is a gradual deepening of understanding of how the words of the poem relate to each other, how the frame of the poem shapes interpretation and how the metaphorical levels relate to each other.

In both cases of prose fiction and poetry, there is a gradual understanding and appreciation of how the worlds depicted relate to our own worlds.

Borders

Pavel (1986) explores the borders of fiction, positioning myth at one end of a spectrum of distance from the real world and the frontiers of fiction inhabiting a space in between the two. As suggested earlier, the borders of poems are more immediately evident. In print, they are defined by the white space that surrounds the poem; in performance, they are defined by the silence that frames the reading. Crossing these borders in poetry is important to the argument of the present book, because not only do experience and the lenses of the reader play a part in the creation of meanings in a poem but also the modes of communication (image, moving image, gesture, speech, movement) are pressing in on the edge of the poem. The same may be the case with prose fiction—there is silence and emptiness at the edges of a work of fiction and other modes press in—but the reader is less immediately conscious of these beyond-the-frame elements than when reading poetry. In theatrical drama, the edges of the stage and the role played by intermediaries, such as choruses or narrators, fulfils the same functions of marking the interface between the action of the play and the experience of the audience. Again, transgression of the border is sometimes actual (as when the actors move into the audience's space, or a member of the audience is invited onto the stage) as well as imagined.

It could be said that the defined edges of poems and their more highly framed nature makes for a different kind of world of reference than with novels, short stories or plays. Combined with the resonant *presence* of the poem, as discussed earlier, the reference is more multi-levelled and 'vertical' than horizontal and placed in time. It is as if the words on the page or in the air evoke associations and suggestions that are combined both in the actual text and in the minds/imaginations/sensibilities of readers and listeners. Suggestion and inference is more likely than explicit exposition. The reader has less to go on: there are fewer words, so more space for inference. Crucially, inference is encouraged: the poet does not try to pin down the range of reference in the same way that a novelist wishes to define the relations between elements in his/her novel. With longer poems, structuration plays a role in juxtaposing one section in relation to others so that the poem becomes more like a novel with its chapters or a play with its scenes.

Further Look at the Imaginative and Fictive   113

At the same time, once the language of poems is encountered, the reader is not asked to suspend disbelief in quite the same way as when we read a novel or watch a production in a theatre. The personal nature of poetry invites him or her to inhabit its worlds with the author. There is nothing like horror movies or detective plots in poetry, not least because both of those genres depend heavily on fantasy and plot. The challenge is different in poetry: it is to empathize and to enter the world of the poem as ourselves rather than as a fictional self. In that sense, it could be said that departure to another world is not so much the domain of poetry as it is of prose fiction or drama. Pavel (1986: 89) outlines what he sees as the process with fiction:

> The principle of minimal departure is precisely a way of not acknowledging the consequences of the leap [. . .] In order to make fiction function smoothly, the reader and the author must pretend that there was no suspension of disbelief, that travel to a fictional land did not occur [. . .] Therefore travel to fictional lands does not necessarily entail a weakening of the usual methods of inference, common-sense knowledge, and habitual emotions [. . .] The impersonated fictional ego examines the territories and events around him with the same curiosity and eagerness to check the interplay between sameness and difference, as does any traveller in foreign lands.

With post-Romantic contemporary poetry, travel is not so much a willing suspension of disbelief as an engagement with the framing and expression of the poet, and a willingness to believe. The belief is predicated on an engagement with the language and conscious framing rather than with any journey involving narrative or dramatic sequencing and tension.

The Size of Poetic Worlds

Whereas fictional worlds must eventually have a limit so that they do not transgress into the realm of maximal possible worlds (*War and Peace* or the works of Elena Ferrante cannot go on *ad infinitum*), poetic worlds that are not mythical (*The Odyssey*) or huge in theme (*Paradise Lost, The Prelude,* Ezra Pound's *The Cantos*) have more modest scale. With the exception of political poetry, which often speaks directly, without metaphor, most poetic worlds are one step removed from the actual world and smaller in size. This does not mean that a very short poem cannot contain multitudes, or that a longer poem is necessarily larger in theme and scope. It simply suggests that poetry, by nature of its compact form, compression and clear edges, works in smaller packages.

A short story is, as well as being shorter than a novella or novel, driven by a single theme. Longer works of fiction can be more heterogenous. Poetry too can be heterogenous as well as homogenous, as it works to both unify

114 *Further Look at the Imaginative and Fictive*

and contain difference, but it does so on a smaller, more compact scale. The difference between poetry and the novel could be characterized in musical terms: poems are like chamber works, and novels more like orchestral works.

Poems have a greater degree of relative intensity because of their compression of words into a tightly edited frame. An expectation of intensity is brought to bear in reading to or listening to a poem. It could be said that whereas a novel or play has a number of moves and turning points within it that are part of the fabric of such compositions, in poems, the moves are between words, phrases or lines and strophes/verse paragraphs (dependent on the type of poem).

Incompleteness

What is true of fictions—that they are necessarily finite and incomplete (Pavel 1986: 107ff.)—is also true of poems, but perhaps to a greater extent in the poetic mode. This means that the reader/listener has to do more work to meet the demands of the poet than a reader of a novel has to do to meet the demands of a novelist. The novelist provides more detail, more internal referencing and more spacious prose. It would be wrong to go as far as to say that the reading of a novel is a more passive experience than that of a poem, but the relaxed engagement that many readers of novels enjoy is not to be underestimated. Reading and engaging with poems involves an empathetic leap as well as an imaginative one.

The incompleteness of the worlds of poems—their tight, formal edges, their limited range—requires the reader/listener to undertake the completion.

The Economics of Attention and of the Imaginary

Both Lanham (2006) and Pavel (1986) use the term 'economy' to address the ecology of ideas and practices that constitute attention and of the imaginary in the late twentieth and early twenty-first centuries.

Lanham (2006) in *The Economics of Attention* builds on his earlier work on rhetoric in the digital age to ask not only what is new about the digital expressive space—and what is not new—as words move from the printed page to the electronic screen but also a wider question: what is the nature of the economics of attention in the information age? For now, it is pertinent to questions of the place and nature of poetry and poetics, and in particular in relation to the function of the imagination. Attention, according to Lanham, "is the commodity in short supply" (2006: xi), and because "the devices that regulate attention are stylistic devices" attracting attention is what style is all about. As a fellow rhetorician, I cannot but agree with the shift of the arts and humanities and social sciences to the centre of such an economy, with intellectual property, for example, a more valuable commodity than 'stuff'; but as far as the present book goes, with its focus on multimodality, poetry and poetics, I would take a more limited and more pragmatic view: that attention is apportioned as much by cognitive concentration as by style and modes of communication. However, Lanham's tenet is that "in the digital writing space, words no longer have it all their own way. They have to compete with moving images and sounds" (Lanham 2006: xii), which leads to "a new theory of communication".

Pavel (1986: 136) is clear that "fictional texts employ the same referential and modal mechanisms as non-fictional use of language, and that the logic of such texts is better understood when considered in relation to other cultural phenomena". This line has been taken in the present chapter and in the book as a whole, which questions the dividing line between fiction and its negative shadow, 'non-fiction'. As far as poetry is concerned, there has been further critique of its fictional identity, with suggestions that not only does the fiction/non-fiction binary split not apply to poetry but also that poetry operates in a more compressed, more dynamic and more 'vertical' way. However, like fictional texts, poetry is better understood "when considered in relation to other cultural phenomena"—both modal and more broadly cultural.

The verticality of poetry is based on the assumption that "virtually every object belonging to the literal world has a place in the ontological framework of a secondary, symbolic world" (Pavel 1986: 138). The secondary symbolic world is not necessarily a sacred one, but is operated via metaphor, metonymy and symbolism. An image in poetry both is, and is not, part of the literal world. Even written language itself, however 'literal' in its descriptions, is a second order symbolic system based on speech, according to Vygotsky. A ladder (sic) of the operation of metaphor could be drawn as follows:

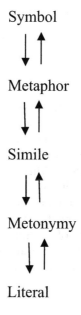

116 *Further Look at the Imaginative and Fictive*

Such a two-way ladder of imagistic abstraction would apply to speech as well as to writing and therefore to spoken poems as well as to printed ones. The ladder simply shows the degrees of abstraction, generality and significance of the image borrowed from the literal world, and used to express complexes of perception, intellect and feeling from the immaterial world. In turn, the immaterial world of symbolic and metaphoric reference informs, from an ontological perspective, 'the metaphors we live by', the value systems that shape our social and individual actions and choices in the world.

Key to Pavel's conception of the economy of the imaginary are the principles of distance and relevance (1986: 145). The vertical ladder can be extended to create a greater distance between the world of symbol and the literal world. To change the metaphor (and return to the horizontal), the topographical and geographical distance between literal and poetic (for the first time I replace 'fictional' with 'poetic') worlds is measured as if in another territory and other land. Pavel notes (1986: 145):

> Creation of distance could well be assumed to be the most general aim of imaginary activity: the journey epitomizes the basic operation of the imagination, be it realized in dreams, ritual trance, poetic rapture, imaginary worlds, or merely the confrontation of the unusual and the memorable. The requirement of relevance makes for a connection to actuality—both to individual and social experience—and therefore meaningful engagement with the imaginary. Literal worlds are compared to imaginary ones. Distance is the more salient principle with regard to fiction and poetry, and to poetics in general, as it maps out distant other worlds that both are modelled on the real world and reflect back upon it, or closer imaginative worlds that are more mimetic "in order to gather relevant information or just for the pleasure of recognition".
>
> (1986: 148)

Dialogism

Whereas Bakhtin's (1981) collection of four essays, *The Dialogic Imagination*, consists of four treatises on the novel, its title reveals its application to a new, more socially grounded stylistics: one which takes into account "the social life of discourse outside the artist's study, discourse in the open spaces of public squares, streets, cities and villages, of social groups, generations and epochs" (1981: 259) rather than the dry after-the-event taxonomies of "abstract linguistic discourse" (ibid.) There is no reason that such a new, socially grounded stylistics could not apply to poetry as well to novelistic prose and thus to poetics (literary stylistics) more generally. Bakhtin thus situates his theory of novelistic prose within an overarching theory of rhetoric, and "once rhetorical discourse is brought into the study with all its living diversity, it cannot fail to have a deeply revolutionizing influence on linguistics and on the philosophy of language" (1981: 268–9).

Further Look at the Imaginative and Fictive   117

The importance of Bakhtin's conception of a theory of poetics grounded in rhetoric will be explored further in the final chapter.

For the moment, within the limits of the present chapter, the distinction between the poetic genres and the novel is worth pursuing. From a Bakhtinian perspective, the centrifugal, decentralizing spirit of the novel, with its openness to heteroglossia and a diversity of voices, is contrasted to the "unifying, centralizing, centripetal forces of verbal-ideological life" (1981: 272–3) in poetry. The distinction is an interesting one, but in simplifying the poetic mode in order to make the point about the dialogic, heteroglossic nature of the novel, it misses the fact that poetry, too, uses dialogism, both within the formal structure of the poem and in the poet 'speaking' to the audience or reader and in poets responding to the work of previous poets (Raleigh and Marlowe come to mind, but there are also correspondences and dialogues extending over centuries and cultures). The difference is that the compressed, 'vertical' nature of poetry as it plays along the metaphorical spectrum is not the same as the expansive, 'horizontal' nature of the novel with its uses of narrative as a principal structuring device. It would not be fair to say that poetry has a unifying tendency and the novel the opposite. Both, as art forms, have both. Poetry, perhaps because of its compactness and compression, has explosive referentiality, largely through suggestion; novelistic prose is more explicit in its range of reference. The fundamental misconception, perhaps used for rhetorical purposes of the argument, is to associate poetic genres too closely with literary stylistics and to see the novel as a liberating force much more closely related to the demotic dialogism of everyday discourse. There is no doubting Bakhtin's antipathy to stylistics:

> Stylistics locks every stylistic phenomenon into the monologic context of a given self-sufficient and hermetic utterance, imprisoning it, as it were, in the dungeon of a single context; it is not able to exchange messages with other utterances; it is not able to realize its own stylistic implications in a relationship with them; it is obliged to exhaust itself in its own single hermetic context.
>
> (1981: 274)

But there is also no doubting that poetry can accommodate the dialogic word, and thus the dialogic imagination. In many cultures, that dialogic relationship is explicit as poetry functions like speech, with question-and-answer enshrined in its form, but that relationship is implicit in all but the most hermetically sealed, obscure and impenetrable poetry. Furthermore, as discussed in relation to framing earlier, the highly framed nature of the poem is not to seal it off from external, everyday dialogic discourse, but to invite transgression of the frame. Bakhtin's criticism of poetic discourse could be levelled at those poets who seek to 'purify the dialect of the tribe' or work with a limited diction (cf. Davie's (1952) study of late eighteenth-century poetry, *The Purity of Diction in English Verse*), but not at those who use the

118 *Further Look at the Imaginative and Fictive*

full range of vocabulary, dialect and everyday language, as most poets do. It is therefore just as applicable to poetry as to novelistic prose to say "as a living, socio-ideological concrete thing, as heteroglot opinion, language, for the individual consciousness, lies on the borderline between oneself and the other. The word in language is half someone else's" (1981: 293).

Poetry can also operate in the 'horizontal' as well as the 'vertical' dimensions, as defined earlier. It can be social as well as symbolic, heteroglossic as well as unitary, centrifugal as well as centripetal and dialogic as well as (seemingly) monologic. In particular, Bakhtin's notion that rhythm—when foregrounded, one of the defining features of the poetic repertoire—

> destroys in embryo those social worlds of speech and of persons that are potentially embedded in the word [. . .] puts definite limits on them, does not let unfold or materialize [and] serves to strengthen and concentrate even further the unity and hermetic quality of the surface of poetic style, and of the unitary language that this style posits appears to be based on a limited sense of the range of poetry.

This chapter has explored a number of aspects of the nature of the poem in relation to the fiction/non-fiction distinction, in relation to narrative prose, in relation to axes of verticality and horizontality in the construction and resonance of literary works and in relation to conceptions of possible worlds and the function and range of the imagination. In doing so, it has drawn primarily on the work of Pavel and secondarily on Bakhtin in order to position a new approach to poetry within literary theory and contemporary poetics. It has hinted that any new theory of the relationship of multimodality, poetry and poetics must situate itself within a broader and generous conception of rhetoric, and, in particular, to ensure that poetry does not lose touch with the range and richness of everyday discourse.

9 What Part Do Rhetoric and Politics Play in the Relationship between Multimodality and Poetics?

Introduction

This chapter draws out some of the points that have been made throughout the book and charts the relationships between multimodality, poetics and rhetoric. It argues that the poetic is always political and thus rhetorical. But it also suggests that the aesthetic dimension to dialogue, public communication, personal and private communication (indeed the whole 'universe of discourse') has been largely unexplored in multimodality studies to date. The rhetorical can be aesthetic and/or poetic as well as public. The chapter thus works towards a model of communication in which poetics and rhetoric are not seen as opposite poles, but as two dimensions of communicative action. To illustrate some of the points in the chapter, reference is made to the work of John Berger and to the work of the Belarus Free Theatre, suggesting that the work of radical art thinkers and practitioners has much to tell us about the relationship of the arts to contemporary rhetoric.

John Berger

In the 1970s, the British Broadcasting Corporation worked with John Berger to produce *Ways of Seeing*, a groundbreaking, radical look at visual and verbal encoding and perception. The television production was followed up by a book of the same title (Berger 1972), re-issued in 2008. More recently, his work was celebrated at the Sainsbury Centre for Visual Arts at the University of East Anglia, Norwich, in an exhibition entitled 'Looking Beyond: Conversations between John Berger and John Christie'. This exhibition (Berger and Christie 2016b) was itself based on a book, *Lapwing and Fox: Conversations between John Berger and John Christie* (Berger and Christie 2016a). The project, including the exhibition, book, letters, films and other modes and media, draws on the earlier work on ways of seeing.

Ways of Seeing, although attributed to Berger, is "a book made by John Berger, Sven Blomberg, Chris Fox, Michael Dibb, Richard Hollis". Its acknowledgement recognizes the collaborative nature of most artistic

120   *What Part Do Rhetoric and Politics Play?*

production. Its 'Note to the Reader' sets out some of the parameters and inspiration behind the conception:

> The form of the book is as much to do with our purpose as the arguments contained within it [. . .] The book consists of seven numbered essays. They can be read in any order. Four of the essays use words and images, three of them use only images [. . .] Sometimes in the pictorial essays no information at all is given about the images reproduced because it seemed to us that such information might distract from the points being made [. . .] Our principal aim has been to start a process of questioning.
>
> (1972: 5)

One of the key ideas in the book is that "the reciprocal nature of vision is more fundamental than that of spoken dialogue"; in other words, it is a dialogic, chosen, explanatory process. Similarly, but also differently, words operate dialogically, even when they appear to be monologically enshrined in print.

Another way in which politics and rhetoric can affect ways of looking is by exclusion, by 'cultural mystification': "the art of the past is being mystified because a privileged minority is striving to invent a history which can retrospectively justify the role of the ruling classes" (1972: 11). Such cultural mystification and distancing is effected by the creation of a 'club', a strata of society that 'appreciates' high art and sees it almost as a possession. For some, it is literally a possession; for others, it is 'possessed' by forming part of the cultural capital that is visited, looked at and talked about. In such cases, it is not so much the actual looking at the art, but the fact of being about to go and look at it or having looked at it that counts.

Yet another aspect of the political/rhetorical context in which art is seen has been brought about by reproduction. Berger writes eloquently and perceptively about how the camera, then mass reproduction, have changed the way that original artworks are looked at. My own experience of this transformation is having first encountered pre-Raphaelite art in slideshows, with the light from the projector lending a luminescence to the works. Such illumination of colour and presence was disappointed when I subsequently visited the original paintings (smaller, darker, duller) in a gallery. As Berger says of the original of Leonardo's cartoon of 'The Virgin and Child with St Anne and St John the Baptist' in the National Gallery, London,

> It hangs in a room by itself. The room is like a chapel. The drawing is behind bullet-proof perspex. It has acquired a new kind of impressiveness. Not because of what it shows—not because of the meaning of its image. It has become impressive, mysterious, because of its market value.
>
> (1972: 23)

What Part Do Rhetoric and Politics Play? 121

Berger's perceptions about how paintings are seen prefigure multimodality, although like much of the discourse in the 1970s and 1980s, they couch the argument in terms of media rather than modes. (One of the breakthroughs of multimodality literature in the 1990s was to separate media of production from the modes of communication, thus enabling a richer analysis and understanding of their relationship.) Berger's understanding that paintings hang in a gallery and are usually surrounded by words, which can change the meaning of the way a painting is looked at, is prescient; so too the positioning of reproductions of paintings in relation to all kinds of verbal print and oral language(s):

> A reproduction, as well as making reference to the image of its original, becomes itself the reference point for other images. The meaning of the image is changed according to what one sees immediately beside it or what comes immediately [before or] after it. Such authority as it retains, is distributed over the whole context in which it appears.
>
> (1972: 29)

The implication here is that the aesthetic via which art forms are interpreted is framed socially, politically and rhetorically. The viewer cannot look with 'an innocent eye' at paintings or poems or any other form of art because of their contiguity to other forms and to phenomena that are not highly framed, like social schemata, as well as to immediate, contiguous and historical experience. See also Benjamin (1970), referenced by Berger (1972: 34).

In a sense, part of Berger's perspective is to look outside the frame of the artwork as well as inside it. He would see a purely internal consideration as formal, exclusive and not with full consideration as to how the formalities of internal composition work. That is to say, internal formal relations are always informed by external rhetorical, political and social concerns. Both Benjamin and Berger bring a critique of fast capitalism to the interpretation of images, seeing them as not only juxtaposed with the modes and media of expression but also in relation to the identity as material objects and to the wider political and socio-economic influences of choice, resource and representation.

More Recent Work

Lapwing and Fox: Conversations between John Berger and John Christie (Berger and Christie 2016a) is the book upon which the exhibition at the Sainsbury Centre for Visual Arts was based in late 2016. Previous collaborations include a four-part BBC television series based on Berger's book with Jean Mohr, *Another Way of Telling* (1995); *Pages of the Wound: Poems, Drawings, Photographs 1956–94* (Berger 1996); and *I Send You This Cadmium Red: A Correspondence between John Berger and John Christie*

122   *What Part Do Rhetoric and Politics Play?*

(Berger and Christie 1999). Christie is a painter, photographer, filmmaker, writer and publisher, and used to working in a range of, and across, modes. Berger's own eclecticism in this regard is well known: he is an art critic, novelist, poet, essayist and artist. It is inevitable, then, that a collaboration between these two multi-faceted and multi-talented 'makers' should result in a series of works that explore the interfaces of different modes of communication and different art forms.

Contiguity is key to the relationships between modes. In *Lapwing and Fox* (2016a: 144–5), there is a double spread that seems almost incidental to the book as a whole. It is not titled, but referred to obliquely on one of the following pages and is not significant to the actual juxtaposition of the three 'texts'. The printed text is by Gael Turnbull and is sent by John Christie to John Berger along with a print of black and red blocks of colour and a short letter. For the purposes of the present book, the focus is first on the text/poem:

> The density of certain stars is so slight
> that on earth they would be an almost perfect vacuum
> and yet their presence can be clearly perceived
> without the aid of any instrument
> from the other side of the universe
> with one glance of the human eye.

This 'poem', sent to John Christie "30-odd years ago" (Berger and Christie 2016a: 151), is more like a found poem or a piece of text (prose) that has been re-set and becomes a poem by virtue of its line-stopped arrangement on the page. The black-and-red print that accompanies it is the same shape—rectangular—and yet sets up, within the frame of its own mode of communication, a contrast and complementarity between the two colours, just as in the 'poem' there is an implied contract between darkness and light (neither of the terms is mentioned). The handwritten note/letter adds context, setting the gift of the card (and book) in place and time. Again, the formal rectangular shape of the created work is mirrored in the note/letter, as if the artist and composer (Christie) is conscious of the two other works (print, poem) that he is accompanying with the note/letter (Figure 9.1).

From a different modal perspective, Berger writes in a letter to Christie a passage of description (Berger and Christie 2016a: 171) that captures gesture, image, choreography in what he calls 'inaudible music'. This is a multimodal, poetic, photographic/filmic imagination at work via the mode of words in the media of a handwritten letter and (in the book) printed version:

> Eight o'clock on a summer evening in a metro train heading for a Parisian suburb. There are no empty seats but the standing passengers are

What Part Do Rhetoric and Politics Play? 123

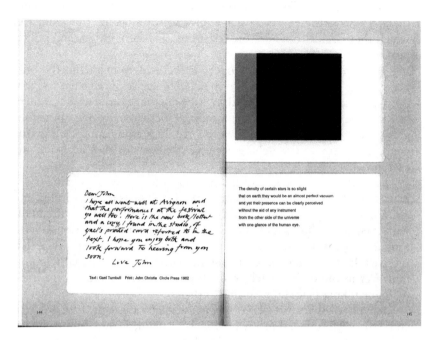

Figure 9.1 John Christie and Gael Turnbull, 'Poem, Print, Note'

not crammed together. Four men in their mid-twenties are standing in a group near the sliding doors on the right-hand side of the coach. The doors don't open when the train is running in this direction.

One of the groups is black, two are white and the fourth is perhaps Maghribian. I'm standing quite a distance away from them. What first caught my attention was their very visible connivance and the intensity of their conversation and story-telling.

The four are casually but scrupulously dressed. What they look like, their appearances, would seem to matter to them even more than to most men of their age. Everything about them is alert, nothing is hangdog. The Maghribian is wearing loose blue shorts and spotless Nikes. The black has combed meshes, the colour of sandalwood, in his thick black hair. All four are virile and masculine.

The train stops and a few passengers get out. I can move a little closer to the quartet.

Each intervenes frequently in the recital of each of the others. There are no monologues but equally nothing seems to be an interruption. Their fingers, very mobile, are often near their faces. Suddenly it dawns on me that they are stone deaf. It was their fluency which prevented me from realising this before.

124 *What Part Do Rhetoric and Politics Play?*

Another station. They find four seats together. I stand close behind them. They continue to behave as if they were alone. Yet the manner in which they decide to ignore the rest of us, is a form of tact and politeness, not of indifference.

I glance up and down the coach. It seems as though I'm the only person who has noticed them. In the metro, one seldom listens to what other passengers are saying. And so if the language being used is a silent one there is nothing remarkable to notice. Occasionally one of the four grunts with laughter. Their story-telling, their commentary on events continues. I am now watching them as curiously as they are watching each other.

They share a vocabulary of gestural signs to replace a vocabulary of pronounced words, and this vocabulary of theirs has its own syntax and grammar, mostly established by timing. Their gestural signals are made with their hands, faces and bodies which take over the function of both tongue and ear, of one organ that articulates and one the other that receives. In any sustained dialogue anywhere both are equally important. Yet in the entire coach, probably in the entire train, there is no dialogue taking place comparable to theirs.

Each physical feature with which the quartet gestures in order to converse—eye, upper lip, lower lip, teeth, chin, brow, thumb, finger, wrist, shoulder—each feature has for them the range of a musical instrument or of a voice, with its specific notes, chords, trills and degrees of insistence and hesitancy. Watching them with one's eyes is like listening with one's ears to a jam session.

Yet in my ears there is only the sound of the train which is slowing down for the next stop. Several passengers are getting to their feet. I could sit but prefer to stay where I am. The quartet are of course aware of my presence. One of them gives me a smile, not of welcome, but of acquiescence.

Intercepting their myriad exchanges, to which I can give no name, following their responses back and forth whilst remaining ignorant about what they refer to, swinging to the rhythm, carried forward by their expectancy, I have the sensation of being surrounded by a song, a song born of their solitude, a song in a foreign language. A song with no sound.

Why is this passage such a telling one in terms of the themes of the present book, and how does it relate to the previous example of the Turnbull/Christie work?

First, it is clearly multimodal. An observer looks, listens and, later, records in writing. The quartet shares 'a vocabulary of gestural signs' which is different from and yet conveys speech. There is a physicality to the communication that is observed and indeed in the seeming non-communication in the rest of the carriage. There is also the semiotics of fashion, noted in the third paragraph. The whole scene is moving along on a Paris metro train in place and time—a different sort of multimodal transport ('multimodality' is also used as a term in haulage to refer to different modes of transport).

Second, there is an aesthetic dimension to the scene. It is like a film ("I can move a little closer to the quartet")—a highly framed piece of reportage. It is like music ("A song with no sound"). It has rhythm (their communication is "mostly established by timing"). Indeed, timing and rhythm are essential to the making of meaning in a social context, and in the particular time and place of this encounter.

Third, in formal terms, there is a parallel with the work of Turnbull and Christie that is discussed above. As its simplest, it could be said to be rect-angular. In other words, each paragraph, whether set in shorter lines in the printed version in the book (p. 171) or in longer lines as set out earlier, takes an oblong, horizontal shape. Such framing is partly to do with the photographic, serial and cinematic style of the writing. But it is also poetic. The passage could be characterized as a prose poem in two senses: one, as a 'poetic' subject (a lyric moment in time), and two, as a rhythmic composi-tion. There is an intensity to the writing, a sharp focus, that foregrounds the imagery and demands our close attention.

In another passage in the book, Berger is more consciously poetic (although the writing is still in prose), largely through his concentration on the nature of angels in a humanist world (Berger and Christie 2016a: 265):

[Angels'] promises are wordless and physical. Some can be seen, some can be touched, others can be heard, some can be tasted. Some are no more than messages in the pulse.

The taste of chocolate. The width of her hips. The splashing of water. The length of the daughter's drenched hair. The way he laughed when he woke up in the morning. The gulls above the lake. The dog with its tongue hanging out in the heat. The tattoo he made such a thing of. Such messages are wordless yet they are shareable with a few others who are in the know. They are all messages about a remembered expec-tancy, about an open but not guaranteed promise concerning life, about an expectancy which, when refound on a sunny afternoon on vacation, acquired a physical presence—like the presence of an angel.

At the core of this extract of prose, the poetic suggests itself as more than to do with the topic. It is a concentration on the images that embody the angelic touch. There is no reflection at the core: merely a sensation "in the pulse". The rest is prosaic reflection on the experience.

Lapwing and Fox, as a book of shared correspondence and images, pro-vided the basis and inspiration for an exhibition, *Looking Beyond*,[1] curated by postgraduate Museum Studies students at the University of East Anglia

126 *What Part Do Rhetoric and Politics Play?*

(UEA). Like the book, the exhibition was grounded in the Sainsbury Centre for Visual Arts and acted as a portal or guide to looking at the exhibits in the permanent collection. It included video footage, artefacts, paintings, written correspondence, photographs and pasted postcards. Further information and comment on the exhibition was provided by various digital social media (Twitter, Instagram, Facebook) in written and image modes. A blog was composed, again consisting of words and images. The blog notes that *I Send You This Cadmium Red* (2000), while originally a book illustrated with paint splashes, photographs and collages, had also been re-imagined as a stage play. In response to the exhibition, invitations were to reframe experiences in image and/or word. The fact that one can respond to an artwork in a different mode means that not only is dialogism at play (the work is one 'utterance' that invites another) but that a multimodal awareness allows or affords a range of different responses, in different modes.

Berger's Contribution

John Berger's contribution is to have helped us to think about looking and seeing, to understand that seeing depends on habit and convention, and is shaped not just by personal experience but also by social and political framing. The political act of looking is a concept that, until his work was released, may not have established itself as a possibility in the world of art history and appreciation, and more importantly, in the nature of the everyday act of looking.

The socio-political framing of his work, eschewing hierarchy, snobbery and convention, does not diminish a sense of the here and now, and of the present. One could say that poetry is the art of the present, and in the act of composition, it *tries to capture a moment*. Lyric poetry is certainly close to that presence, and even narrative and epic poetry compresses time into a living presence so that the action of plot (clear selections and arrangements in time) can be seen and experienced in the present. In the act of reading or listening to poetry, too, the sense of suspended time is evident. Each word, although one follows another in time, seems part of a unified and focused present. Although there are plenty of examples that could counter this claim, it is generally true that narrative fiction works in and with the past. Very few novels or short stories use the present tense. The tendency is to use the past tense, and occasionally to use the present and future, so that time is seen as a key consideration in the unfolding of the narrative: the stories are told as if they happen in a parallel fictional world, and as a novel or short story is read, the reader is transported into that parallel possible world. But in order to sustain a narrative (plot) over some length, the supporting structures of time are used.

If poetry operates mostly in the present, there is (or should be) a sense of newness in its composition and reception. That is why reading and re-reading a poem is common practice. Each reading feels like a renewal, with

What Part Do Rhetoric and Politics Play? 127

different layers or nuances of meaning revealed. In short stories and novels, such renewal can also take place (to read the same novel three times in one's life comes with the experience you bring to that novel as 'frame'), but the genres/text-types are still set in time, as they are in film and other time-based arts. The making of something new in poetry brings with it another feature: the conflation of time and layers of meaning. Such conflation reduces hierarchy and can be radical in its physical grounding of ideas in imagery and symbolism. It is close to the 'real world' as well as an artistic construct that lifts one away from the world into reflection, contemplation and meditation.

There are implications for poetics from such a conception of poetry. These are explored more fully in Chapters 10 and 12 in terms of literary theory and ideas about the application of multimodal perspectives. For now, it is worth noting Berger's observation that reflecting on looking and seeing has inspired him "to do something on paper, or in three dimensions" (Dvorák 2016). In other words, he is a natural multimodalist who not only wishes to explore the meaning of visual art forms in terms of their significance to a humanist culture and to human experience but also their suggestiveness in terms of other modes of expression that can be generated by them. It is no surprise then, that he should work in such a wide range of forms: drawing, photography, poetry, novel, short story, play and documentary; always linked closely to his physical experience of looking, seeing and working on the land; and being transported in media as wide-ranging as films, books and exhibitions—and, it should be added, translated into a number of languages.

The Case of Film

The film *The Seasons in Quincy: Four Portraits of John Berger* (Derek Jarman Lab 2016) raises issues about the relation of multimodality to media, as flagged in Chapter 1. The film is a tribute to the many faceted contribution of Berger to thinking about still and moving images, and their relation to politics, power and social interaction. The four portraits are four separate short films: one by Tilda Swinton about her emotional, intellectual and professional kinship with Berger; one by young French filmmakers about animals and their relation to humans; one focussing on a round-table discussion about perception in relation to Berger's work; and one about children, community, place and their 'vertical' layering and significance as opposed to the thinly spread ubiquity afforded by Internet, with its tendency to pitch forward its users into the immediate future (the next click, the next piece of information/data) rather than inhering in the present. One of the contributors to the third film makes a concise insight into Berger's contribution: that it celebrates the physical and sensual and at the same time is never nostalgic. That sense of multi-sensory, multimodal *presence* and attentiveness is a core quality of his work.

Two further questions are raised by this film: what does it say about narrative? And what does it say about the relation of multimodality to media?

128   *What Part Do Rhetoric and Politics Play?*

The structural framework for the film is less of an internal matter than one determined by the title: the seasons. The first film takes place in winter, and the sequence moves through to autumn in Quincy. There is sequence but not much narrative: the juxtapositional nature of filmic composition backgrounds narrative in favour of 'portrait'. If there is a narrative, it is one of renewal and of cyclical regeneration. Indeed, sustained narration is not a characteristic of Berger's prose, poetry or photographic collaborations: these are more like windows to enable new ways of seeing, new ways of looking at things from a social, political and neo-Marxist perspective. Finally, what does a film like this say about the relation of multimodality to media? The medium is film. Film, however, has a number of affordances: it captures sequences of moments in time and puts them alongside other sequences; it adds music to create mood; it moves between close-up and panorama; it frames its subjects. As a medium, it is open to a number of modes working together to convey 'what it wants to say': still and moving image, sound, voice, spoken language, a two-dimensional account of physical presence. As a medium, it has the affordance of being able to compose and recompose/rearrange time.

The Belarus Free Theatre

In October 2016, the Belarus Free Theatre played *Tomorrow I Was Always a Lion* at the Arcola in Dalston, London. Belarus Free Theatre (BFT) is a radical theatre company, exiled from Belarus and based in London. It is independent, committed to producing socially and politically relevant material, and fiercely critical of any aspects of repression or restraint. At the same time, it operates according to high aesthetic principles to create works of art that speak directly to its audiences. See www.belarusfreetheatre.com/ for more details.

Its production of *Tomorrow I was Always a Lion* was based on a memoir of a recovery from schizophrenia by the Norwegian Arnhild Lauveng. It is a study of the nature of psychosis, with its principal focus being the understanding of that state. Testament to its power were not only the standing ovation at the end of the performance I saw but also the discussion afterwards, with psychiatrists and 'service users' (patients) debating the exact pitch of the play, and the extent to which it shed light on the life of those suffering from schizophrenia. A trailer for the production is available at www.arcolatheatre.com/event/tomorrow-i-was-always-a-lion/.

What struck me in terms of the poetics of performance was the following: the original book *I morgen var jeg alltid en løve* was based on a series of experiences. The book, once translated into English (See Lauveng 2013, *The Road Back from Schizophrenia: A Memoir*) and possibly into Belarusian and/or Russian too, was read by the director, the creative team and the actors. Then they worked together to create a 'devised piece'—that is to say, a piece of drama in which they worked from their own responses

What Part Do Rhetoric and Politics Play?   129

to the book, suggesting possibilities as to how elements of it could be lifted from the page. The development and rehearsal process took some weeks. Once the scenes had been created, it was sequenced and transducted into a script. The script, as in all theatre, formed the basis for the production and then the performances. In the performance I saw, a number of modes and media were used to create the 90-minute production: principally, the actors onstage, using their voices, singing, moving and interacting with each other; back projection of live video feeds (with the cameras encased in books—a mock-up of the book *Tomorrow I Was Always a Lion*); some pre-recorded film; and music and other sounds from offstage. This particular performance was also streamed live to Belarus and around the world.

These transitions from mode to mode need to be explicated in more depth. Let us say that before Arnhild Lauveng wrote the book, the experience of schizophrenia, and in particular the institutional experience of someone who had been held down with forced restraint during an episode, had not been fully articulated. It may have been spoken about, but the book enshrines the experience in print. The book, then, provides the starting point for this particular multimodal excursion.

The act of translation is one aspect of transduction (the translation from one mode to another), but moving from one language to another is an act, not only of linguistic transference but also of bringing cultural, political and linguistic frames of reference to a text which is then re-made in a different language. There is a spectrum of translating approaches, from the so-called 'literal' translation at one end, to a more freely interpretive style of translation at the other (usually an attempt to 'make it new' and accessible in a different culture, and from the target culture's perspective). It cannot be said that such translations from printed verbal mode to another printed verbal mode are multimodal as such, but significant transformations take place.

Once the book was in the hands of the director and actors, significant modal transitions began to take place. The director, his creative team and the actors brought to the experience of reading the book a different set of experiences and expectations. These might be called different frames of reference. Most of the participants knew someone among their family or friends who had experienced bipolar or schizophrenic states. These frames were tested by the book and by collaborative exploration of it: not only in talk but also in action. So, for example, actors were asked to take one part of the book that struck them and to represent it to the team to bring out laughter, whether hysterical or incongruous or genuinely comical. Ideas were assessed, rejected or taken up, developed and shaped into the devised play that was, in due course, performed. The play, as it took shape, must have been like the creation of a string of beads, held together by a common thread, but with distinct 'scenes', each of which shed light on a particular stage in the development of and recovery from schizophrenic states. Each scene, then, will have been partly created through the physical enactment of the ideas on the page.

130   *What Part Do Rhetoric and Politics Play?*

When the scenes were arrayed in sequence to tell the story of Arnhild's development, they moved into rehearsal and production. The decision to use live video feed, thus creating a backdrop to the action, and at the same time providing close-ups of aspects of the actors' facial expressions or of other parts of their bodies (feet, hands) that were expressing some detailed, specific moment of significance in the play, added a further modal dimension to the play. The decision the audience takes, as it watches and listens to the action, is where to focus the attention. You move from video projection to action on the stage, from one part of the stage to another and from listening to voice, offstage sound and onstage video. Sometimes one mode comes to the fore; at other times, the attention is scattered and diffuse (replicating the experience of unsteady mental states).

There was more to the physical movement on the stage between the five actors in this production. At times, the movement becomes choreography; in other words, there is a deliberateness to the relative positioning and movement between the actors. At other times, the movement is 'purely physical' and does not suggest choreographic design. Sometimes the actors were autonomous and separate; at other times, they interacted closely, even to the extent of fierce physical engagement (for example, in holding down restraints on the actor-as-patient, or in more sensitive and tender moments, such as helping an actor-patient to take a bath).

The whole multimodal performance, combining spoken words, printed words, film, sounds, movement and other modes, took place in the intimate context of a radical theatre space in north-east London. The Arcola is noted for its streetwise and experimental productions. The audience comes with expectations of experiencing something arresting in a small space; usually the audience is 'open' to such experimentation. The play itself, framed by the conventions of theatre (the play starts and finishes within a limited period of time; the entrance to the theatre is via a door that gives onto a framed acting space surrounded on three sides by seats; there is suspension of disbelief during the performance; lighting helps to mark the beginning and end of the performance; there is the convention of applause at the end when the actors move from their roles to become actors again and then into 'people' again in the bar afterwards). To an extent, the conventions of theatre are fixed: the medium of theatre, with its framed spaces and conventions, is largely invariable, although there are elements that can be varied: the audience can sit on one, two, three or four sides of the stage; theatres can be outside as well as inside buildings; the frame that separates the actors from the audience can be breached, and so on. When the play moved to South-East London, to the Albany in Deptford, the framing of the theatrical space was different, requiring a re-thinking of the relationship with the audience.

To complete the circle of multimodal creation, the play was talked about afterwards, first in a post-show discussion and then informally in the bar, and beyond. The audience was invited to complete and send in a postcard to the East London National Health Service Trust, urging it to cease facedown

The Relation of Rhetoric to Poetics

restraint practices. The play was reviewed in magazines, newspapers and online. It remains archived on YouTube or in other filmic depositories. Gradually, it will fade from memory and dissipate its power and communicability. It will be forgotten as an artwork, but may have direct and indirect effects on health care for bipolar and schizophrenic patients.

The Relation of Rhetoric to Poetics

What part do rhetoric and politics play in the relationships between multimodality and poetics? The examples discussed earlier illustrate different approaches to the movement between modes of communication/expression and refer to the different range of modes in play in each case.

What do they have in common? First, all display an interest and engagement with the physical. Berger's deliberations on-screen, and his interest in human form, reveal a strong sense of physicality in all his work. Such a sense means that words on a page, or an image or the relationship between them cannot be fully understood and appreciated without being felt on the blood and through their physical presence. Shcherdan's work for the BFT could be called physical theatre, in its storytelling through physical movement and gesture; its devised origins; its multimodal crossover between film, drama, speech and movement; and its invocation to the audience to act and to engage with the real world through the artifice of the play.

Second, both examples see language as tied to action and politics. The framed artwork has a direct relationship to the referents it depicts. It is not operating in a vacuum, or in a socially elite space. Rather, it has often taken the form of protest because it wishes to engage directly with the political process, which in part determines how the arts are seen. Conventional ways of seeing are questioned; Marxist or neo-Marxist perspectives question the actual construction and perception of social experience.

Third, contemporary rhetoric itself is closely related to politics and social action, whether it be a private rhetorical world (it can never be entirely monologic), or social action on a global scale. To see language and other modes of communication as rhetorical is to see them enacting something in the world within a socio-political sphere rather than to be mere words on a page or an image in a painting or photography exhibition.

Even the uttering of a word or two in a fleeting conversation is rhetorical and takes its place in the socio-political domain. When more than a word or two—perhaps an image, some printed words, spoken words, moving image and physical movement—are combined in a composition such as a play, the extra layers of framing make for a highly concentrated comment on aspects of living in the contemporary world. Even time is compressed or expanded in a two-hour play onstage, or in a novel that has the sweep of hundreds of years or the depiction of a single moment. The compression of time, from the classical duration of a day compacted into the performance of an hour or two, or the history of a social movement compacted into a 90-minute

132 *What Part Do Rhetoric and Politics Play?*

film, requires rhetorical choices about selection. The act of editing—so crucial to filmmaking, but evident in writing too through the editing of a poem, play or story—is a key feature in the armoury of the writer or filmmaker or director, as the composition that goes on is deliberate, shaping time and space and human relationships through tropes and juxtapositions that generate sparks of enlightenment. That is why it is hard to see any theory of literary composition maintaining a position of pure introspection or mono-logic limitedness.

Note

1 *Looking Beyond: Conversations Between John Berger and John Christie*, 7 May–27 November 2016, Sainsbury Centre for Visual Arts, University of East Anglia.

10 A New Approach to Literary Study?

Introduction

A multimodal perspective suggests that even in seeming monomodal literary texts, there is more than one mode at play. Conventionally, literary stylistics was the sub-discipline which dealt with form, style and language, almost totally from a linguistic perspective. A new approach to literary study has to take into account other implied and explicit modes in the composition and interpretation of texts. The implications for language-only approaches to text are clear: there is more going on in such texts than the purely linguistic and its referents. Even the 'purely linguistic' has a visual identity when it is printed on a page and when it is spoken or performed; there are questions of context, of the resonance of the speaker, of gesture and audience, as well as other factors in communication. The study of literature (and the making of literature) is thus seen as a choice among a range of possible modal choices—but one which carries legacies of the modes that are often 'excluded' from the work in question.

Literary Stylistics

Literary stylistics has inhabited a space between literature on the one hand and linguistics on the other. Conventionally, as a sub-category of applied linguistics, it uses linguistic knowledge, categorization and methods to shed light on literary texts and their effects. The advantage of the liminal space it inhabits is that it has not been erected into a discipline, although it has formed the theme of many an academic book series. Writing from 2017, its history as a sub-category of applied linguistics in the practice of interpreting literary texts can reasonably be dated in the Anglo-American tradition from the 1940s (for example, Grierson 1949)—a history of some 70 years, marked by key writers such as Jakobsen (e.g. 1960) and Widdowson (e.g. 1975), although with precursors in Russian formalism, the Prague School and followers of Saussure in the first part of the twentieth century. A sub-sub-category of the field is that bound by an interest in poetic prosodies, which reached intensity in the 1920s in the wake of free verse practice

134 *A New Approach to Literary Study?*

and theories—themselves dating back to the *vers libre* and *vers libéré* of late nineteenth century French poets (see Andrews 2016).

Conventionally, then, literary stylistics has preoccupied itself with linguistic features in the service of literary effect. It could be said that its preoccupation is with linguistic style *within* the genre (as text-type) and within the formal sense of the poem or other literary work. As such, it has not been so interested in the poem within a historical and/or social and/or political context, nor in the reader (and thus not in reader response), nor in any contextual features outside the limits of the frame of the poem itself or outside literary contexts. It has hardly been aware of framing theory and thus is less aware of the interface at the liminal edge of the poem or literary work. Although stylistics might be said to have derived ultimately, in Western theory, from Aristotelian poetics and rhetoric, it has inclined to poetics. As such, in estimating and analyzing effects of literary work, it is not so much interested in the actual effects on readers as on the implied technical effects that are embodied and analyzable within the literary work itself. At its most limited, stylistics is interested in literary style at the surface level; in its more generous formulations, stylistics is interested in poetic and literary genres (as text-types, not as social acts).

The limitations of literary stylistics are captured in this statement from Verdonk's *Stylistics* (2002), where he suggests,

> If you have become familiar with the stylistic conventions of [poems], you will know that the language of poetry has the following characteristics: its meaning is often ambiguous and elusive; it may flout the conventional rules of grammar; it has a particular sound structure; it is spatially arranged in metrical lines and stanzas; it often reveals foregrounded patterns in its sounds, vocabulary, grammar, or syntax[;] and last but not least, it frequently contains indirect references to other texts.
> (2002: 11)

Here is a strophe from the beginning of Pound's 'Canto XLIX' (Pound 1964: 255) that has almost none of these characteristics:

> For the seven lakes, and by no man these verses:
> Rain; empty river; a voyage,
> Fire from frozen cloud, heavy rain in the twilight
> Under the cabin roof was one lantern.
> The reeds are heavy; bent;
> And the bamboos speak as if weeping.

The language is distinctly poetic, but there is little ambiguity here; it only flouts conventional grammatical usage in being in note-like form; it has no specific sound structure; it does not follow metrical line and stanza shape and includes no reference, other than perhaps by translation or reference to classical Chinese poetry, to any other texts. Much Eastern European poetry

A New Approach to Literary Study? 135

of the mid-twentieth century, to give another example, is un-elliptical, direct, easily intelligible, un-literary and not interested in its own soundscape.

The implication is that literary stylistics is a 'Western' phenomenon designed for Western poetics. It is inward looking, both culturally and formally. As Verdonk would have it, "poetry is detached from the ordinary contexts of social life. [It] does not make direct reference to the world of phenomena but provides a representation of it through its peculiar and unconventional uses of language" (2002: 12). Such a definition would be appropriate for a poetry of diction, such as late eighteenth-century triumphs of style over substance, but such a definition is not appropriate to the range, both verbal and multimodal and of poetry in the twenty-first century.

My argument, then, is that although formal stylistics has shed a more focused light on how language operates to create (assumed) literary effect, it is caught within a classical rhetorical tradition of seeing literature as 'persuasion'. It is one-way, author and text centred; it takes insufficient notice of its readers and what they bring to interpretation, and it is narrowly unaware of the wider 'contexts' which actually play directly into the literary work. These contexts are seen as outside the work itself. A more dialogic, multimodal stylistics will draw as much on rhetoric as on poetics, will be concerned with all three aspects of communication (text at the centre of rhetor, audience and meaning) and will be applicable to a wider cultural range than the supposed literary western tradition of lyric, personal and individualized poems designed for 'cherishing private souls' (Barnes and Barnes 1983).

Contextualized Stylistics

Halliday's systemic functional grammar (see, for example, Halliday 1994) offered hope to literary stylistics in that it set literary texts within the social and cultural nexus. The emphasis on context, in all its complexity, afforded consideration of cultural, social, political, literary and other worlds that impacted on the making of and reading of literary texts. Not only has Halliday prepared the ground for the development of multimodality (backed by social semiotic theory) but also his work has made possible the more general investigation of multimodality and poetics attempted in the present book.

Contextualized stylistics, however, ventured carefully beyond the tight focus of formal stylistics in order to shed light back on the text itself. An example is Knottenbelt (2000), 'a study in sound sense', which explores the rhythms of John Donne's poetry to suggest that there is a rugged speaking voice behind the disruption in metrical balance of the poems. There is reference to "Donne's rhythm and thought [being] manifest in the unsettling connotations of words, in [his] appreciation of them as paradigms of the criss-cross nature of the human individual in the midst of life" (2000: 120). Oddly, though, the sense that there is presence beyond the tight frame of the poem that affects the arrangements of the words (and vice versa) is nebulous: "the criss-cross nature of the human individual in the midst of life" is a vague and weak referent. The strength in the analysis is in identifying the

136 *A New Approach to Literary Study?*

lineaments of thought in the syntax and rhythm of Donne's poetry—and so the reader is brought back to the text itself. The problem is that 'thought' cannot be characterized or captured other than through the words of the text. Knottenbelt's contextualized stylistic analysis gets more interesting when he tracks the social, theological and religious issues affecting Donne as a thinker and poet. It is the specific contexts and their relations to the words on the page that is telling. These specific contexts help Knottenbelt to suggest that Donne's sensibility is attuned to music (particularly harmony), image (particularly the metaphysical image), the auditory imagination (the spiritual dimension) and a prevalent physicality, as though words themselves were embodiments of experience and thought. In these senses, contextualized stylistics begins to suggest multimodal poetics.

Widdowson's essay in the same volume (Widdowson 2000) suggests, provocatively, that "we do not *need* the language any more" (2000: 231) if contexts are fully provided in, for example, the staging of a Shakespeare play. He recites the assumption that Shakespeare's theatre was a linguistic one in which the audience had to imagine darkness, battle, etc., via verbal language rather than actually seeing it, as opposed to a production in which digital and/or filmic effects can depict a storm or pursuit by a bear. The argument that language might not be needed is a diversionary one: the language is needed, but there is also a need to 'read' the language of the play as both depicting character and action within the fictional world and framework of the play itself, to read it as referring to a construct outside the frame that is taking place in space and time and in which other connections are encouraged (our own previous experience of plays, contemporary events, our emotional states, etc.). But the main argument of Widdowson's essay is that elements of the context are 'unrecoverable': the linguistically pure experience of the Elizabethan or Jacobean staging cannot be reproduced if contemporary theatrical machinery overrides the words of the play (as, for example, if the storms in *The Tempest* and *King Lear* are so thunderous as to drown out the words). Such a position, however, seems irrelevant to the experience of a Shakespeare play if the director, designer and actors create a world in which the various elements of the play are integrated and which speaks to a contemporary audience.

These two essays from *Contextualized Stylistics* (Bex et al. 2000) reinforce the fact that stylistics, whether contextualized and/or formal, cannot get away from language as the central mode of communication and interest. They do not see language as one mode among several, but as the main mode of communication that suggests or evokes the other modes.

Rhetorical Stylistics

The next logical step in the design of a working theory of how poetry and poetics might be understood from a multimodal perspective is to see rhetoric as coming back into play, or more specifically, rhetorical stylistics.

A New Approach to Literary Study? 137

Thesleff (1975), in 'Notes on the Rise of Rhetoric as a Stylistic Genre' indicates the interest, but narrowly confines the discussion to how classical literary rhetoric, with its taxonomy of divisions and classifications, might be seen as a way forward for literary stylistics. In Thesleff's conception, for stylistics read 'early rhetoric style markers' applied to poetry (epic, tragic) and oratory. The positive contribution here is the emphasis on disposition (arrangement) as opposed to style in early rhetoric and the suggestion that study of different genres in classical literature might shed light on a new contemporary poetics. Disposition is about the larger structures at play in poetry as opposed to the surface features that often form the main focus of stylistic scholarship. Comparison with other genres is instructive as the effort is made to winnow the poetic expression and forms from poetics more generally. The important move is to see poetics as a sub-discipline of rhetoric and thus informed by social and political discourses in private and public life as well as by its own internal features. Such a move suggests that poems are arguments: they enter discourse as responses to existing bodies of poems and other literature, as well as ritual 'gifts' of new discourse in social exchange. Thesleff echoes the need for a move to rhetorical informing of poetics when he suggests,

> from a stylolinguistic point of view it is interesting to note that most of the generic markers considered here [derived from classical rhetorical oratory] are not empty clichés or mere 'embellishment'. Some reflect a tendency to systematization of thought [. . .] some a tendency to emphasis. Lucidity and dignity of expression is aimed at [. . .] not shock or surprise.
>
> (1975: 287)

Thus public speech can inform poetic expression. At this juncture, in the development of a contemporary multimodal poetics, surface features take on a diminished and limited role in literary study, to be replaced by a focus on the larger structures at play in the creation and reception of artworks, which in themselves are shaped by socio-political forces. This move does not mean to say that poetry or other art forms need to be any less personal but simply that the personal is informed by the economic, social and political contexts and communities in which individuals operate.

Towards Multimodal Poetics

The opening chapter of this book attempted to set multimodality and social semiotics within a wider and longer tradition of rhetoric. In the present chapter, the logical move has been from formal stylistics through contextualized stylistics to rhetorical stylistics. Thus, via different routes, the aim has been to arrive at the same theoretical place: multimodal poetics. Some of the initial arguments have been rehearsed in Chapters 7, 8 and 9; here,

138   *A New Approach to Literary Study?*

the argument is taken further. In order to focus the argument, the ground on which this theory is based is poetry, in all its forms.

First, it is important to identify the elements within multimodal discourse that might inform poetry and poetics. Taking the lead from Kress (2010), these include framing, modal resources, construction of meaning, design, naming and orchestration/collage.

Framing

Framing has been discussed elsewhere (e.g. Andrews 2011) so the exposition here will be brief and condensed. The act of framing—not reified 'frames'—is a key creative/critical act in the making of an artwork. It defines the parameters of the created work; it defines what is 'inside' the frame and what is 'outside' it. What is within the frame is the artwork itself, composed of one or more modes. What is outside the frame are the contextual worlds that affect and inform what is within the frame. The frame itself is permeable but well defined. It allows reference out from within the frame as well as reference in from without. The dividing line is there to denote the need to attend both to what is inside and outside. Each cannot live or have meaning without the other. The very act of framing creates meaning: it suggests denotation and definition. What is inside the frame is a selection, representation and distillation of what is outside. The elements that are placed within the frame have a unity of their own which 'speaks' to the phenomena, communities and audiences outside the frame.

Framing is everywhere evident in the arts. The original metaphor derives from the framing of paintings. All the graphic and visual arts depend on framing, not only (as was the original purpose) to protect and make portable the work itself but also to reflect it and separate it from surrounding walls to encourage a closer look at what is within the frame. The principle of framing can be applied to three-dimensional arts such as sculpture, or, to take a more extensive example, garden design.

But framing also applies to the performing arts: the edge of the stage, the dance floor, the circus ring. It applies to literary works, such as novels, short stories, plays and poems. Framing theory has also been applied via sociology and sociolinguistics to schemata that occur and re-occur in social exchanges.

The multimodal works that are created and received are themselves housed or conveyed by framed media: the television, the cinema screen, the computer screen and the mobile/cell phone. It should also be noted that framed works often occur in highly framed spaces, such as museums, art galleries, theatres and cinemas.

In other words, framing is an integral part of communication and especially so of communication which is intended to be intensely experienced, such as artworks. Every time the threshold of a museum is crossed, for example, and a person enters an exhibition and then looks at particular

A New Approach to Literary Study? 139

framed works within that exhibition, a number of lines are crossed, each of which asks the viewer to attend differently to what is experienced within the frames. The same is true of a poem, which might be accessed via a bookshop, library, online resource or some other method. Each time there is a move towards a particular poem in a particular collection, the reader is framed by those moves and is willingly transported to a mode of attention that is different—more intense, more focused—than is the case in everyday life and discourse.

Framing "provides *unity, relation* and *coherence* to what is *framed*, for all elements within the *frame*" (Kress 2010: 149). Although these affordances have been attributed to, and even erected as, principles of 'art', they are in fact brought about by framing. The implication is not that everything outside the frame is chaos; rather, that certain patterns have been identified in everyday life and discourse that are captured and highlighted within the frame, in space and/or time.

Two more points about framing and its centrality to multimodal poetics. The first is that the frame itself is often invisible, like the edge of a poem. There is no marked black line around a poem to say 'this is the edge of the poem'. Instead, the (printed) poem is set on the page with white space around it; the words 'do not go up to the right-hand edge of the page', and there are various forms of closure at the end of poems to suggest that the poem itself is a highly framed entity. In oral deliveries of poems, the framing is often a short period of silence before and after the poem itself, which is sometimes spoken in a tone different from that of everyday speech in order to distinguish itself from that mode.

The second is that within the poetic frame, it is no longer the case that words are the only allowed mode. Images, moving images, sounds, gestures and other modal resources can be included alongside words. The same principles of unity, relation and coherence apply.

Finally, it is important to note that framing exists beyond the world of artworks. Framing takes place in society to differentiate one kind of social encounter from another. Kress notes,

> *Frame, text* and *communication* are inextricably interwoven. Without *frame*, no *text*; without *framed entities*, no *communication*. Without *syntagms* no order; without *syntagms-as-arrangements* not sufficient stability for *communication*. Without *communication*, no renewal of *text* or *frames* or *meanings*.
>
> (2010: 154)

If framing exists in everyday life and discourse, as well as in the creation and reception of artworks, what is the difference? It is that framings in everyday life and discourse are so wired into our induction into social experience that they are almost invisible, even though they are observed carefully (as in, for example, attendance at a church service or at a dinner party). When they are

140 *A New Approach to Literary Study?*

used to delimit artworks, they are consciously deployed, even where there is no ostensible or visible frame.

Framing might, then, be seen as a better and more precise way of characterizing the boundaries of contexts. As such, the act of framing plays a key part in multimodal poetics.

Modal Resources

Examples of modes of communication include the following: speech, writing, music, gesture, movement, still image, moving image and material objects where they are used for representation and communication. They are socially and politically informed means by which communication is made—not the material ways in which they are delivered, which include mobile/cell phones, televisions, computer screens, books, galleries and museums in actuality, in print or in digital format. Multimodality is particularly concerned with the modes of communication and their affordances.

In a framed composition which includes more than one mode, it is usually the case that one mode is foregrounded. For example, a poem with illustration (see Blake's 'London' in Chapter 1) has the printed word as foreground and the image as 'illustration'—in effect shedding light on the verbal text ('verbal' here is used to mean 'of the word', not just of the spoken word). But there are occasions where two or more modes are of equal status and sit alongside each other in a complementary relationship and/or in tension.

One of the advances of research in multimodality is that it has brought into question the dominance of the word, of 'language' (more specifically it should be said of 'verbal language' in speech and writing). Whereas literary study, and especially stylistics, has concentrated on the affordances of the (largely) written word, it has devoted less critical space to spoken language and to the other modes that are either implicit or explicit within the poetic frame. If a range of different types of poems is looked at, it will be seen that the written word is still the dominant mode. On the other hand, if there is consideration of the white space that surrounds the poem, and the affordances of the written word in the broad genre of poetry, there will be recognition that more modes are crowding in than had been assumed.

Consider the difference between the poem in Chapter 5, 'This Is the Age of the Typewriter' as a printed and performed poem.

The poem is formulaic, starting most of the lines with 'it' in a list-like fashion and with each of the lines of the poem also being formed as a short sentence. In terms of the written/printed mode, its visual uniformity and the gap between the penultimate and last lines, suggest a) that it might have been composed on a typewriter and b) that there is a repetitious uniformity to its work and its outputs. If the poem were performed, it would be readily accessible as the repeated formulaic lines provide a handle for the audience: they know roughly what's coming next and can array one line after another. However, the gradual shift to garbled typographic language towards the end of the poem, made possible through the affordances of written language/print, are not easily accessible to the spoken voice. By the last line of the first sequence of lines, the language is unpronounceable. In spoken performance, on the other hand, more modes can be brought to bear in the communication of the poem: gesture, movement, facial expression and physical verve.

So even in the distinctions between oral and written verbal language—despite much common ground—there are affordances that are distinctive to each mode. An audience that only heard the oral performance would be hard pressed to write down the whole poem. Similarly, spoken performances of the same written script would be different from each other, just as performances from the same musical score can be radically different in rhythm, tempo and touch, as well as the overall balance of orchestration. The interesting common aspect of the written musical score and poem is that they both try to pin down the meaning they wish to convey. In doing so, they can only pin down the written template for the creation of meaning. It takes more than words on a page or marks on a score to create the experience of the poem or piece of music.

The Construction of Meaning

Let us consider what modal resources are available to the poet as he/she composes. The germ of the poem comes from a number of sources, sometimes combined: a rhythmic phrase (non-verbal); a sense of a pattern that emerges or suddenly presents itself; a verbal phrase; the desire to tell a story; a lyric impulse, born of memory and/or an immediate experience/thought/feeling, and taking the form of a rhythmic and/or verbal phrase or a sketch, a small note; in response to some existing artwork; and/or a songlike response to a political imperative.

As soon as the initial impulse is captured in some way, other modal resources come into play. Because the poem is primarily verbal, there is already the interplay between speech/song on the one hand and the written text on the other. These two modes of the verbal continually work alongside each other from near the start of the conception through the process of composition to the performance of the poem. As a working assumption in the development of the argument about the construction of meaning in a multimodal poetic, let us follow the path of the composition of a written poem.

Writing, in whatever medium (pencil or pen on paper, directly on-screen, a stick on a beach, a penknife into bark or a spray can on a wall) uses the ground on which it operates (paper, screen, sand, etc.) and makes marks upon that ground. Firstly, the ground defines the available space for composition. In conventional terms, the ground is the piece of blank paper. That piece of paper is a white space within which the marks (letters, words, lines, stanzas, strophes, paragraphs and other constituent linguistic elements) are made. Surrounding the words is white space. So, secondly, the poem is an imprint on the white space: it consciously creates a shape which 'does not

142   A New Approach to Literary Study?

go up to the right-hand edge of the page', as prose would, because it is surrounding itself with silence. The white space surrounding the poem is an additional frame that defines the text as 'poem'. The poem, therefore, has a visual quality that is not so evident or significant in prose. It stands out. It requires extra attention. It is saying, "If you enter the zone in which I operate, you need to read/respond in a different way than you would if you were using everyday discourse or reading prose".

The defining extra dimension of poetry is not only its visual shape but also the fact that the visual shape is derived from musical form and or choreographic principles. The words move in space, in relation to each other. If the rhythm is metrical, or a variation on metricality, it will share some of the time signatures and rhythmic relations of conventional music. If it is in freer form, it may follow the additive rhythms of jazz or contemporary dance.

Thus although it would be possible to see the constructed poem as simply a composition in words, there are more varied modal considerations at play in its composition.

Let us look also at the path of composition that is oral, rather than written. A poem is made from 'a mouthful of air' (Yeats), is as insubstantial as wind and has no life outside that of performance. But part of that compositional energy is physical. It can also draw on the forms that inhabit the oral world, such as song, and the sub-forms or features of such forms such as repetition, rhyme and metricality. Composition may be accompanied by walking up and down the room or the beach. The physicality or oral poetic composition refers to more than the voice(s) that are at play. Its rhythms may be defined by movement.

Both approaches have implications for their reception, by readers or listeners. Both approaches can mesh at times with the other, exploiting and drawing on the affordances of the verbal mode in speech and in writing. This dual nature of verbal language is a rich multimodal resource in itself, closely allied with other modes such as gesture, movement, physicality, still and moving images and sound/music.

Design

"*Design*," suggests Kress (2010: 132) "is the process of translating the rhetor's politically oriented assessment of the environment of communication into semiotically shaped material". Design in poetry is about making social semiotic and rhetorical choices: whether to work in conventional poetic genres and forms, whether to compose freely, which language(s) to use and whether to combine other modes explicitly within the composition or to use them implicitly. Because others have previously travelled the roads to composition, such design is both new and not new. Its newness and originally derive from the nature of the composition: what is put together with what? Its conventionality and tradition derive from the forms which it uses, whether it uses them in the time-honoured ways, or reacts against

A *New Approach to Literary Study?* 143

them. Design of poetry, therefore, works within a set of expectations which can be met or challenged.

In poetry, design is highly attuned. The design of words on the page or in the air is deliberate, carefully worked and meant to convey meaning in itself (musical, spatial meaning) in addition to the content of the words. These attendant forms of meaning interplay with the substantial meaning conveyed by the 'content' of the words. I question the notion of 'content' because words are inexact and have multiple associations, not all convergent. They are also phonemic fragments of sense that react with each other and with other modes to provide a rich tapestry of potential meanings. Poetry is particularly good at heightening the possible range of meanings because it exploits the ambiguity of words rather than trying to strip down meaning to definable certainties.

An understated dimension of poetry that is better understood from a multimodal perspective is typography. Particularly in free verse, the development of which could be said to be partly inspired by the typewriter's ability to space words and letters on the equivalent of a grid, the calibration of space between letters, words and lines is critical to the meanings conveyed. Such spacing could almost be called the geometry or choreography of free verse: spaces mean something. They are crucial in articulating the rhythm of the poem: the very quality that distinguishes all poetry from (most) prose. It is not so much a matter of the particular typefaces chosen, whether in print or on a screen. It is more a matter of the relative spaces between the verbal elements.

One last point about design. In their own ways, poems as texts signify 'completeness', as recognized socially by the makers and receivers of the poetic text. That completeness—known also as unity, cohesion and coherence, each with their different nuances—is specifically signified in the poem by at least three design features. One of these is the verbal 'sense of an ending' and 'closure' that the poem exhibits, for example, in a rhyming couplet at the end of a Shakespearean sonnet. Another is the visual framing of the poem on the page. It does not need to be reinforced by the (now largely archaic) note, 'The End', as sometimes appears in larger works. The end of a poem is always easily identifiable through its visual completeness. A third feature is the extent of white space that follows the ending of the poem, as well as surrounding the whole work.

Naming

Titles of poems are, in most cases, simpler than the poem which follows. They are indicative rather than descriptive or symbolic (not always the case with titles of novels or reports). Sometimes they are elliptical, and occasionally poems, like compositions in music, have numbered titles (e.g. in a sonnet sequence).

It is the poem itself which names and defines an experience or observation. This process is almost like labelling. But to name is to newly define.

144   *A New Approach to Literary Study?*

Many poems operate in the present tense, as if the act of composition was one of capturing a moment, as in a photograph.

Orchestration

If composition is the overarching term for making in a theory of multimodal poetics, it makes writing, creative writing, authoring and other more partial approaches seem inadequate to the task of describing the creative process. These more limited terms are all sub-categories of composition. There is always more than one mode at play in any composition. As well as the modes being contiguous and having a relationship of complementarity and/or tension, there is a further act in the process that requires defining: that of the orchestration of modes.

Even in a single mode, orchestration is important in that it selects and emphasizes certain aspects of the words that have been brought together. In the creation of a poem, it is particularly important because, as a consequence of the completeness that is required, each word must relate to all the other words in the composition. There is a balance to be sought so that the construct of the poem generates maximum resonance and multiple meanings, so that ambiguity is made possible and exploited and so that the musical qualities of the language are evident.

When more than one mode is implied or explicitly presented as part of a composition, their orchestration is even more pronounced. At some points in the contiguous relationship, some modes will need to be foregrounded and others backgrounded. If there is to be creative tension between them, that tension has to be managed so that, for example, word and image are equally weighted.

To develop the metaphor of orchestration yet further, in the composer's gift are a range of modes of expression and communication. He or she will choose which are to be present in a contiguous relationship in any one work. In Walcott's *Tiepolo's Hound* (Walcott 2000), for example, the edition in question brings together a numbered sequence of poems (I–XXVI) with 26 colour reproductions of Walcott's own paintings. The paintings seem subsidiary and illustrative. They are related thematically to the poems, but it is as if the poems come first. There is still considerable association between word and image: the words are characteristically visual:

> its cabin lights budded high over the lateen sails
> of tree canoes, it blocked the sun's orange disc,

and the paintings descriptive. But in Walcott and Doig's *Morning, Paramin* (2016) there is more equal status between poem and painting, each inspired by the other, each making it more evident that the composition of the book is not only multimodal but also any reading of the book of new poems is itself multimodal.

A New Approach to Literary Study?   145

This chapter has been about the fact that it is no longer sufficient to compose or read/listen to poems with singular modal attention. Even in the most apparently non-modal form of a poem printed on a blank page, there is a visual dimension to be reckoned with. That visual dimension—the surrounding of a poem with white space/silence—is significantly present, always, but perhaps taken for granted framings are adjusted in the reading or hearing of a poem. The composer is not always conscious of the white space around a poem, but uses it to focus more intensely on the words at the core of the poem. When he or she adds other modes, explicitly, the affordances of each mode are shown in high relief: what words can do, images can only partially do, and vice versa.

Thus multimodal poetics aims to enrich the context in which the composer works as well as to explore the implicit and explicit relations between modes. It is an extension of literary theory that affords as much attention to the composer as the reader/listener. In its own very different ways, it restores the balance between making and receiving, between writing and reading, between speaking and listening.

11 Poetry, Writing Process and the New Poetics

Introduction

This chapter broadens the aperture of the argument of the book yet further to look at the implications of a multimodal approach to poetics and rhetoric for art forms and aesthetics in general. It takes examples from different arts—painting, sculpture, installation art, video and dance—to look at how framing in the arts allows a range of modes to operate in relation to each other. It also looks at recent aesthetic theories to gauge to what extent they have taken on board advances in the understanding of communication and multimodality theory. O'Toole's *The Language of Displayed Art* (2010) will be referenced and discussed.[1] First, however, it looks at the creation of a poem in triptych form and relates it to other arts, developing the argument as to how the new poetics affects poetry and the writing process.

'Sudden Storm'

The following three-part poem was written in the Adirondack Mountains in July 2017:

I

Late July, 7pm.
Shucking corn on the back step.
A wind came out of nowhere
blowing the trees horizontal.

First, drops of rain, outriders of
an army of clouds from the north-west,
from Canada, across Rocky Ridge; and then
a downpour for twenty minutes.

During supper
we watched the rain ease up,

Poetry, Writing Process and the New Poetics 147

the lake returns to its flat, reflective blue,
skies open and a few late stragglers of cloud.

Now mist rises from the trees across the lake
drifting in different directions:
a Japanese print with loose orchestration of
the songs of the chickadee and whippoorwill.

Ghosts arise from the battlefield:
spirits heading off in different directions:
lost, looking for new air, for
redemption before dark, for any kind of direction.

II

And now light fades from the earth.
The clouds carry it away.
The surface of the lake mirrors them:
underwater carp in a Zen temple pool.

The last remaining ghosts hover
without motion.
All's growing dark: Rocky Ridge is edged in black,
the silhouette of a giant.

Sounds return:
the lake runs off its excess water to the stream
and the Northway rumbles to the east of here,
taking its evening traffic,

its own lost souls,
in carloads and truckloads
from New York to Montreal,
Montreal to New York.

III

Laughter in the trees
further along the shore.
Some children staying up late
at a board game, or adolescent jape.

Grey/pink clouds departing the scene.
The lake returning to its dark mirror.
The last wisps of ghost depart.
Darkness falls.

148 *Poetry, Writing Process and the New Poetics*

> Everything on the earth's mirrored in the sky.
> All above ground's replicated below it.
> As if we could ever have thought
> to live merely on the surface.

Weather tends to come in from the north-west, from Canada. The poem fell into triptych form from the start. It also marks a development in time from the first part to the third. It could have taken the form of a series of photographs, a film, a series of paintings, sketches and/or a sound recording. Instead, it takes written form.

There are allusions and references to the visual: Japanese prints of landscape and weather, Zen temple pools and the silhouette of Rocky Ridge (one of the high peaks to the north-west of the camp). There is a degree of 'painting with words' (*ut pictura poesis*) in the colouring, the chiaroscuro depiction of dark and light and the orientation on two planes ("blowing the trees horizontal"). It's a moving picture ("mist . . . drifting in different directions", "clouds departing the scene", "the last wisps of ghost depart") and suggests a theatrical staging. There are also sounds that are evoked ("the Northway rumbles to the east", "laughter in the trees").

One could argue that all these modes (still image, moving image, sound) and the dimension of staging are part of what language can do. It is referential. There is also literary cross-referencing: "laughter in the trees" echoes Eliot's "the leaves were full of children,/Hidden excitedly, containing laughter" from 'Burnt Norton' in *Four Quartets* (1963) and "as if we could ever" echoes Lowell's "as if in the end,/in the marriage with nothingness,/we could ever escape/being absolutely safe" from 'The Day' in *Day by Day* (1977).

One of the intriguing aspects of poetry is the use of metaphor, explored in Chapter 4. The heavily saturated/figurative nature of the English language makes it hard to distinguish description from metaphor. In one sense, the whole poem about a sudden storm is a metaphor (without labouring the point, a blowing away of preconceptions, a waking up to the multilevelled nature of consciousness). Within the poem, the first section is largely descriptive, but within the tradition of Gary Snyder and Buddhist poets where description itself is resonant of states of being (as if, to use a metaphor, the nature of the scene described *shimmers* with meaning). The metaphor that runs through the first section is that of an army on the move, a battlefield, stragglers and ghosts.

The first stanza of the second section is more metaphorically multi-levelled:

> And now light fades from the earth.
> The clouds carry it away.
> The surface of the lake mirrors them:
> underwater carp in a Zen temple pool.

The first line is seemingly descriptive, except that "the earth" can refer to both the ground and the planet. The second line contains a clear metaphor,

Poetry, Writing Process and the New Poetics 149

although it's close to the natural language in using the verb 'carry' to convey the agentive movement of the clouds; they carry the light with them. The third line presents a clearer metaphor from the material, civilized world: a mirror. The stanza then moves in its last line to build on this metaphorical momentum by providing an image couched in an analogy: "Underwater carp in a Zen temple pool". The earlier reference to Japanese culture (specifically the stillness of a Japanese print, of a Zen pool) is picked up and developed, providing a counterpoint to the violence and movement of the storm. As well as being located in the middle of the poem, this line also provides a pivotal point relating the experience of weather and landscape to a sense of the multi-levelled nature of existence. In terms of distance from the landscape of the poem, the line is the furthest away: the most extreme metaphor.

Triptychs and Polyptiques

The three-section form of the poem is akin to the triptychs of medieval iconography as well as the work of some contemporary artists in poetry (Heaney) and painting (Bacon). This particular poem consists of a five-, four- and three-stanza format, different from the typical pattern of a visual triptych where the panels may be of the same size, or the two outside smaller panels flank the central one. Visual triptychs do not have to be 'read' sequentially, although the classic medieval triptych draws the eye to the central (larger) panel first before it takes in the accompanying panels. There is, however, sequence in the aforementioned poem, as there would be in music or film or a play. As well as sequence, there is multi-panelled juxtaposition of sections. Each panel represents a different 'take' on the subject of the poem. The 'take' can be time-based and/or it can perspectival.

Finally, why does the poem take the form of unrhymed quatrains? The question can be answered from two standpoints. From a process point of view, the first (pencilled) notes for the first section of the poem fell into this four-line shape for its first two stanzas and then drifted into a section of five lines, then eight, then two. In the draft of the second section, the emergent stanzas took the form of nine lines each. In the third, there was reversion to four-line stanza form, with a final couplet. In the earlier version—a third draft—the four-line stanza form has established itself as the common standard across the poem as a whole, with some variation.

What is the nature of the unrhymed quatrain? It is long enough to allow development within the stanza, as evidenced by the first stanza of the second section discussed earlier. At the same time, it provides vignettes: twelve in all, all end-stopped, with only one instance of run over from one stanza to the next. The unrhymed nature allows for a rough-edged, unpackaged, 'prosaic', dynamic feel to each stanza.

What is demonstrated in the earlier example of a triptych-like poem can be scaled to other forms of multi-panelled works, from diptychs to many-panelled forms. Novels take chapter form; sonatas and symphonies can take

150 *Poetry, Writing Process and the New Poetics*

any number of movements; photomontages can piece together any number of individual photographs; plays can take a one act/scene, or they can take several. This polyptical structuring of a composition in any art form (or, say, in furniture, garden or architectural design) always brings together different elements into a unified composition; there is always complementarity and tension between the constituent parts; there is the possibility of not only multi-panelled works in the same mode but also of multimodal and multi-media composition. Such polyptical, multimodal design is now the norm. Even when the composition is in one or two modes, the referentiality of the work is more diverse. In composing and in receiving such works, our sensibility is now attuned to these possibilities and makes the act of communication both more 'real' (closer to everyday lived experience) and more highly constructed.

A Trope

A different perspective on the multimodal nature of literary composition is explored by Barrell (2017) in his essay 'The Meeting of the Waters', in which he traces the multiple references to the poetic notion of the meeting of streams and rivers or rivers and oceans, particularly (but not exclusively) in the Irish, English and American sensibilities. Essentially, his narrative traces the many variations on Moore's 1808 song, 'The Meeting of the Waters':

> The song proposed that the pleasures of landscape were best experienced in company, and that this preference for sociability over solitude was also a preference for the beautiful over the sublime [. . .] This turning away from the sublime was reinforced by the supposedly peaceful character of the confluence. [. . .] A literary tourist described the river below the confluence as "rapid and tempestuous in progress". But in Moore's account, there is nothing torrential about these rivers, which behave as quietly as all rivers will one day behave, when, as the song puts it, "the storms that we feel in this cold world should cease".
>
> (2017: 23)

As a song, it quickly gained popularity. Barrell records advertisements, sheet music, reviews of concerts, postcards and "540 performances of 'The Meeting of the Waters' between 1838 and 1900" (2017: 24). Barrell's argument is that the song permeated English, Irish and American consciousness as "a metaphor for comings together of almost every imaginable kind" (2017: 25). The essay is illustrated by four images, all entitled 'The Meeting of the Waters': an engraving, a print, an illustration and a painting by Turner, 'Junction of Greta and Tees at Rokeby'.

This trope of the meeting of the waters, with its associations of harmonic confluence, is further interpreted in the following poem, with due tribute to Barrell's essay:

Poetry, Writing Process and the New Poetics 151

'The Meeting of the Waters'

John Barrell's essay in *London Review*
(27 July, 2017, p. 23) is remarkable
not least for its narrative of the Irish origin
of the song, the deep exploration of the concept
'the meeting of the waters'.

Not far from Johns Brook Lodge
on 27 July 2017, 9am
I came across my own meeting of the waters:
an unnamed brook off Big Slide
meeting Johns Brook.

If the meeting of the waters
signifies a fluidity of souls
an invisible emergence of purity with itself
disembodied, pre-Eden like,
then this was of a different kind:

wild harmony, a turbulent marriage
dancing over and around rocks
deadwood cargo trapped in the confluence
sheer exuberance in morning sunlight
coming off the impregnable mountains.

This poem was inspired partly by a reading of the Barrell essay, partly by a moment during a walk in the mountains. When its composition is broken down and analyzed further, the multimodal nature of the poetic process and of the captured moment become evident.

I had walked for an hour or so from the garden car park near Keene Valley towards Johns Brook Lodge. The first mode to record is that of physical movement through forest: a combination of balance and forward momentum, driven by early morning energy in morning sunlight through the trees. The second mode is gradual awareness of the sound of streams, and in crossing several small streams coming down from the mountains to my right, an assumption that these met the larger brook (Johns Brook) to my left. I was thus drawing on knowledge of the map of the area, plus directional sense (walking gradually uphill as I walked alongside, but out of the sight of the brook). As that sounds of streams intensified, I drew on the third mode—sight, vision—to identify the meeting of one of the larger streams and Johns Brook. Whereas these modes of perception and communication are close to the senses, they are not synonymous with them. To suggest that the senses engaged in these three modes were touch, hearing and sight would be to over-simplify the nature of modes: the senses tend to

152 *Poetry, Writing Process and the New Poetics*

be perceived as receptive, whereas modes depend on a conception of communication that is two-way.

In this particular case of two-way communication, the vehicle or embodiment of the feeling/thought nexus was words, initially in the mode/medium of pencilled notes. Again, there needs to be a distinction between the mode and medium of communication. The mode is verbal, and the first question is whether speech (the oral version of the mode) and writing (the written version of the mode) are modes in themselves, or two different media manifestations of a single verbal mode. Usually in the multimodal literature, they are characterized as separate modes because of a) their scale and ubiquity and b) their different systems, despite their common vehicle in words. Given that the media in which the mode is expressed in the development of the poem, it is worth seeing them as separate modes which take pencilled-in-a-notebook and then typed-on-a-laptop-screen form. From such a position, the media provide the hardware and the modes provide the less tangible means of communication.

Concerned about the timing of the day (the goal of which was to climb Basin Mountain), I made no notes on the way into the mountains and, unusually, no directly perceived notes on the scene on the way down. Instead, later that day or the next morning, I quickly scribbled the pencilled notes. These initial notes fell broadly into three or four passages or sections. Later, in typing up the next draft of the poem, the five-line, four-stanza form established itself. The poem did not attain printed form until the publication of the present book.

The description of the composition of this poem and its partial inspiration by Barrell's essay is intended to show the multiple tributaries that make up composition: in this case, literary history encountered through an essay in the *London Review of Books*, the addition of another voice using the trope of the 'meeting of the waters', an actual encounter with a confluence of waters in the mountains and the modal complexity of the encounter and of the compositional process.

A New Look at the Writing Process

In the old poetics, writing poems was seen as part of a hallowed tradition of 'creative writing' that also included the writing of fiction and plays. The tradition is deep set in universities and schools so that 'creative writing' is set aside from other kinds of writing (functional, non-creative, documentary, etc.). There are hundreds of creative writing courses at universities from undergraduate to graduate and research degree levels, and it is enshrined in syllabi for examination boards at school level. Such writing is deemed 'creative' because it employs the imagination, is largely fictional and expresses feelings as well as thoughts.

Creativity is often associated (especially in poets and Romantic composers) with mood swings and specifically with bipolar disorders. Chiasson's

Poetry, Writing Process and the New Poetics 153

review (2017) of Jamison's *Robert Lowell, Setting the River on Fire: A Study of Genius, Mania and Character* [2017] explores the line between "elevated spirits and mania" (2017: 94), and although Chiasson holds back from too close an association between bipolar disorder and Lowell's poetry, he makes the general point:

> Mood disorders occur with staggering frequency in creative people, and writers seem to suffer the most. A 1987 study at the University of Iowa found that eighty per cent of the writers studied exhibited the diagnostic signs of mood disorders, with fifty per cent fitting the criteria for bipolar disorder [. . .] Poets might be the most susceptible of all. They count on a basic disorientation to do their work, which many report involves the temporary unshackling of the mind from ordinary semantic logic. There are various names for this willed receptivity to associations: flow, inspiration, the muse. These are not the names we assign to symptoms of mental illness.
>
> (2017: 96)

Such a connection between extreme mental states and poetry is particularly associated with the Romantic tradition in which society loosens its tempering effects and the individual soul/consciousness/being is exposed to a wider range of emotional states. Chatterton was an early example; Lowell, Plath, Crane and other mid-twentieth-century American poets were more recent examples, specialists in disconnection and thus making connections via a different 'semantic logic'. Late Romanticism seems particularly prone to the connection between poetry and states of mental disorientation, and it is not so much a *semantic* logic as a grammatical, rhythmic logic that differentiates poetry from other written genres and makes it susceptible to, and perhaps conducive to, the expression of altered states. To associate creativity with mood disorder, however, is to sideline a whole tradition of creative composition in balanced states of mind as well as unbalanced ones.

In a new poetic, creativity is a general characteristic of all writing and all composition rather than one confined to the genres (poetry, fiction, plays) or the states of disorientation mentioned above. It may exhibit the following qualities: arresting and new patterning, the bringing together of elements that are not associated in conventional semantic logic, exploration of new ground, a different look back over old ground, the development of a new voice or voices and the combination of different modes. All of the aforementioned include two main principles: framing and re-framing on the one hand and re-arrangement on the other, combining to create a transformation of perception (not always via metaphorical exploitation of levels of meaning).

If creativity is accepted as applicable to a wider range of genres that the fictional, dramatic and poetic, it can be seen that the following genres are themselves creative: travel writing, real world film documentaries, cookery (itself) and cookery publications (some), particularly inventive manuals,

154 *Poetry, Writing Process and the New Poetics*

essays and reviews. The list is deliberately eclectic. It includes what is oddly referred to as 'non-fiction' (a negative category to cover a wide range of genres) in writing and also in film, cooking and other modes, media and activities. To give just one example, I have on my desk *The Adirondack Atlas: A Geographic Portrait of the Adirondack Park* (Jenkins and Keal 2004). It contains sections on environments; animals and plants; war, settlement and industry; forest change; employers, jobs and income; town budgets and local taxes; etc. Each section is illustrated with copious maps, diagrams and tables, all in a range of coded colours. There is a plethora of mathematical and statistical data, often presented in graphic form. Jenkins "was trained in philosophy and mathematics and works as a botanist and geographer", and Keal "is a specialist in geographical information systems" (2004: inside back cover). This high-end book production (275 quarto-landscape pages, with probably 500 maps and diagrams) is a work of art. It is scientifically based and the result of a high degree of creativity, both in the original research and in the presentation of that work.

What are the implications for a new poetics and specifically for poetry? First, it must be accepted that poems are not merely the expression of feeling. They provide a vehicle for a range of states of being, including thoughts, feelings and expressions of states of being. Second, poems do not have a proprietary hold on the imagination: the imaginative faculty is shared with the sciences, the social sciences, the humanities in universities and research institutes and the operation of everyday social and political life. Third, poetry does not have a 'special relationship' with creativity, nor does poetic creativity with disoriented states of mind. Fourth, they are specific genres and text-types that foreground rhythm, framing and intensity. Fourth, as the present book as a whole demonstrates, they are permeable and open to other modes, both implicitly and explicitly.

Poetry, Music and Performance

Much of the present book has been concerned with poems on a page or screen: static and in need of interpretation via a 'lifting off the page' or in the act of composition. Reference was made in an earlier chapter to spoken word poetry or poetry in performance. In the following section, a comparison is made between the performance of poetry and the performance of music, both from a multimodal perspective.

The performance of poetry can range from improvised (or rehearsed improvised) creation of new work, as in rap or free form poetry (sometimes programmed with, and even performed with, music and thus bordering on song) at one end of a spectrum, to a simple reading of poems from a printed manuscript/typescript or published book at the other. At any point on the spectrum, the physical presence of the poet brings voice, timbre and resonance to the performance, as well as the (optional) contextual introductions. Before and after the reading, there is often the opportunity

Poetry, Writing Process and the New Poetics   155

to chat informally with the poet. The reading/performance itself is usually enshrined in a silence that frames the poem, marking the fact that it operates in a different space: sometimes in a late-Romantic precious cocoon, sometimes in the distant voice of the sage/oracle and sometimes (rarely) in the same voice or voices as those of everyday discourse.

Performance in music has similarities and differences. What is similar is the framing of the event and of the moments of delivery of the artwork itself. I attended a concert in August 2017 in the Adirondacks in Keene Valley.[2] It was typical of many such chamber concerts. First, there was a talk about the pieces to be played in an adjacent library: three of the five musicians talked about each of the works to be played and answered questions from the audience about the lives of contemporary musicians and the structuring of the evening's programming. The librarian who introduced the musicians framed the talk, the talk took place, questions and answers took place and there was applause and appreciation. Then the audience moved to the concert space in a church: milling around, the audience chatting. Silence fell. The musicians walked in to moderate applause. Tuning. A further moment of silence. The first piece was played by a cellist and pianist followed by rapturous applause. They walked off and back on while the applause continued. Then off again as the applause died down.

What are the differences? The musicians work from a score, or more rarely from memory. It is not their own compositions they play, but that of established composers or (in this case) a piece by a new composer, a friend. They are performers. Modally, the score is a transcription into notation of the original composition. It may have been composed directly into a notational program on computer, or more conventionally handwritten in the act of composition and then composed on-screen and printed. The score is re-translated (back) into sound via the instruments and playing of the musicians in the moments of performance, possibly to be filmed and recorded for a variety of media formats. There may be introduction of the pieces by the musicians, or explanation of variations. Such a performance is invariably multimodal and time limited.

In this particular concert, the music director talked about the programming of such events in her pre-performance talk. She compared it to cooking and presenting a dinner party. The choice of pieces to be played was partly dependent on the preferences of the director and the musicians (and instruments) she had available to her. The choice of pieces could be thematic or could be based on an anniversary or occasion, for example, but more often than not, they were based on pieces she thought would balance, complement and contrast each other. The sequencing would follow principles of dinner party design: starting with something to arrest the audience, then providing something more substantial in the middle of the programme and finishing with something lighter and delightful: a dessert. She also mentioned the practicalities that bear upon such decisions: the time available, the space for the performance, the personnel available and the nature of the audience.

156 *Poetry, Writing Process and the New Poetics*

Exhibitions

Exhibitions of static visual art do not qualify as 'performance', but they do involve time-limited, spatial presentation that is accompanied by catalogues, brochures, publicity, talks, private views and other interpretive genres and modes. The whole genre of exhibition also involves curation—a compositional process. I will cite two examples: an exhibition at the Hepworth Wakefield (1 July to 8 October 2017), *Howard Hodgkin: Painting India* and an informal exhibition in the School of Education and Lifelong learning at the UEA of the work of Mary Webb (April to August 2017).

At the core of the Hodgkin exhibition were over 35 works painted "since his first trip to the country in 1964. They—to quote the brochure—"characterize the warmth of India and capture the artist's sensory impressions of the country—including fierce blazing sunsets, heavy oppressive rain, landscapes, cities he visited, and portraits of people he befriended". They reflect, in line with Hodgkin's *oeuvre* as a whole, a movement ever further towards abstraction over a 50-year period. Characteristic of Hodgkin is the representation on canvas and wooden frames of emotion and memory in paint. Such compositions can take several years, both in the conception and execution. The static final product is often given a title that conveys the specific context, and the composition is time based. The 'work of art' is therefore the product of evolution over time. The particular exhibition is also time limited.

Experience of this exhibition involves more than looking at the paintings: it involves concentration of attention (cf. the 'economics of attention') for a limited period during a visit to the gallery and appreciation of both the works themselves and of their curation and display.

At the margins of the exhibition is an array of other texts, genres and modes that frame the experience. From the brochure alone, the following are advertised: a catalogue/book, edited by the curator, Eleanor Clayton (Clayton 2017); a rug designed by Hodgkin and produced in "hand-knotted Persian yarn in India"; various other books and postcards of Hodgkin's work; the card advertising the exhibition itself, showing Hodgkin's painting 'Mrs Acton in Delhi, 1967–71' on one side and contained in formation about the exhibition, its sponsor, a web link and other information on the other. There is also notice of a pop-up restaurant and Howard's Folly wine tasting:

> Join us for a three-course, India-inspired dinner in our pop-up restaurant [. . .] Each course will be paired with wines from Howard's Folly, an award-winning wine producer from Alentejo, Portugal [. . .] the limited edition wines feature labels by Howard Hodgkin and are available to buy in our shop.

Poetry, Writing Process and the New Poetics 157

Furthermore, in order to celebrate the exhibition, the gallery hosted a series of events under the title 'Indian summer', including a yoga and Indian music day; "a tranquil and immersive music experience for all ages, combining traditional Indian lullabies, Japanese instruments and 'lumisonic' visuals, which allow hearing-impaired individuals to interact with graphic representations of sound"; a music and dance performance; a summer bazaar; a yoga and climbing retreat; and an illustrated talk and film screening on textiles.

At one level, such a proliferation of possible purchases and events around an exhibition is a commercial venture. In terms of multimodal poetics, the range of modes and genres is indicative of the fact that not only is the core artwork creation itself a result of a range of modes (and memories, places, experiences, emotions) transformed and concentrated into expression into one or two modes (paint on wood) but also the experience of the exhibition is framed by a wider number of modes, genres and media, as well as by the time and place of the setting (summer, Wakefield, the Hepworth Gallery, the diverse Asian-British culture of West Yorkshire).

In another very different context, the School of Education and Lifelong Learning at the University of East Anglia worked with Calvin Winner, curator of the Sainsbury Centre for Visual Arts at UEA, to create a small exhibition of the work of Mary Webb in a grey breeze-block atrium that needed brightening up. Whereas the Hodgkin exhibition was mounted on large white walls, the Webb exhibition had to operate in a working building with extraneous objects and signs (a piano, tables and chairs, directional signs, etc.). Webb's use of colourful geometric, abstract forms in paintings and prints is in a modernist tradition: more angular than Hodgkin's, but equally redolent of experience, landscape and place. For example, in an interview with Sarah Bartholomew, Webb suggests the relationship between landscape, place and recollected feeling:

> This landscape that I see out of the window and walk in every day is so much in my bloodstream; it's so familiar that when I go somewhere different it's a terrible shock. Frequently I am trying to make sense of that difference, what I've seen and felt about a place over a period of time. It isn't what just what one felt at one moment, but the layers of feeling that accumulate over a period of reflection. One struggles to find the language, the vocabulary appropriate to that accumulation of thought and feeling.
>
> (Webb 2011: 58)

A good example of the translation of experience of a landscape is the following, 'Dunwich Study 2' (Dunwich is a 'sunken village on the coast of East Anglia'; Figure 11.1):

158 *Poetry, Writing Process and the New Poetics*

Figure 11.1 Mary Webb, 'Dunwich Study 2, 1977, Charcoal on Paper'

On occasion, the compositional process has been helped by photographs, for example, of Manhattan, that are used to jog the memory of the experience of colour, form and shape (Figures 11.2 and 11.3).

The geometric nature of the compositions asks the viewer's attention to be spread across the whole square canvas or print, thus not focusing on any one part or on the centre of the work: such geometric composition requires concentrated attention to the combination of colour, both in the composition of the work and in its reception. As Alastair Grieve notes in the introduction to the catalogue of a 2011 exhibition at the Sainsbury Centre for Visual Arts, *Mary Webb: Journeys in Colour*,

> in Mary Webb we have a rarity: a painter anchored in the life of East Anglia, with Constable country just down the road, who gives us an art

Figure 11.2 Mary Webb, 'New York 1980, Photograph'

160 *Poetry, Writing Process and the New Poetics*

Figure 11.3 Mary Webb, 'Circle Line Series: The Isle of Manhattan 18, 1984, Collage'

developed from the discoveries of the Continental pioneers of abstract art. With her art she evokes memories of places far removed from here.

What is also notable about Mary Webb's work is her embracing of two media: painting and printmaking. The latter was mostly undertaken in collaboration with Mel Clark of the Norwich School of Art and involved creative collaboration rather than the artist being seen as the composer and the printer as performer.

In terms of poetics, such collaboration suggests that a mode (painting) can become a medium and vice versa, and that such distinctions are partly maintained by the field in order to privilege some modes over others. In the second half of the twentieth century, the screen-print (seemingly a medium) became accepted as having equal status to the hand-created painting (a mode of expression), despite its more mechanistic processes. Such raising of the status of a medium to a mode of expression and communication indicates that the relationship between mode and medium is a fluid one, dependent on taste/aesthetics as well as the market, politics and socio-economic perception.

A further point about poetics is that as a visual artist, Webb (Figure 11.4) is inspired by musicians (series, pauses, intervals) and uses the language of words (not only in the interviews but also as a metaphor for the compositional process):

> I've got a wide-ranging *language* which I've accumulated over the years, and I like the idea of mixing the *vocabulary* up and bringing things that are opposite together in one context. Pushing the *vocabulary* around, raiding different contexts to see what will happen. But not based on a place necessarily, but just working with colour and taking from the *library* of colours that I've built up from different places.
>
> (Ibid., my italics)

Finally, it is notable that the small Webb exhibition in 2017 (and a follow-up in 2018) in the breeze-block atrium transformed the way that may of the users of that building saw it. What had been a bleak, grey, awkward space became integrated with the colourful abstract prints and painting, and thus appeared differently. Through a frame of a time-limited exhibition, the architectural qualities of the building itself were transformed.

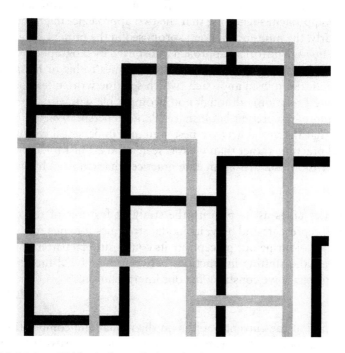

Figure 11.4 Mary Webb, 'Yellow, Black and White 1976, Oil on Canvas'

162　*Poetry, Writing Process and the New Poetics*

The Grammar of the Visual Arts

The use of 'language' and its sub-categories—grammar, vocabulary—as metaphors for discussing the visual arts is two edged. On the one hand, there is the promise of an interdisciplinary and multimodal connection between the various arts. On the other, there is the risk of the metaphorical transference of one set of precise meanings, in language study and linguistics, to a more ethereal set of meanings in the visual arts, dance or other modes.

O'Toole's *The Language of Displayed Art* (2010) investigates the 'grammar' of the visual arts, using three approaches: what is represented, how it engages us (modal) and how it is composed (compositional), deriving these categories form the work of Halliday and others in systemic functional linguistics. Of these three categories, the modal and compositional are of most interest to the argument of the present chapter and book, not least because 'representation' has been approached via the notion of possible worlds, thus re-defining the relationship between what is represented and what is created in the new artwork. As such, the present book does not go back to Hallidayan linguistics to set its foundation for new theoretical work (see Keefer 1996), but instead draws on Berger, Bakhtin and Pavel: a tradition more concerned with literary production within a social, rhetorical framework.

However, like O'Toole, the basis for the analysis of poetry and its implications for poetics in the present work is not historical. O'Toole makes it clear (e.g. p. 120) that his social semiotic approach is different from a traditional art history approach, suggesting that the two approaches might be compatible. Similarly, the multimodal poetic proposed in the present book is different from a literary-historical approach (most used by biographers or literary critics who wish to link the writer's life and times to his or her work), or from a practical criticism approach (which sees the written text *only* as the basis for interpretation), although not incompatible with either.

Furthermore, the present book shares Berger's perspective, and O'Toole's assertion, that the visual arts are best seen and understood within a frame of cultural practices rather than what is seen as an art history approach that tends to see the visual arts as an elite practice, characterized by the concept of 'fine art':

> Semiotics takes as its priority the study of features of the text itself: what it represents and how; its modal strategies for engaging our attention and colouring our perception; its compositional patterning; and the complex and shifting interactions between these [. . .] functions in the semiotic space we construct for our interpretation.
>
> (2010: 129)

The emphasis of the current book is on the modal and compositional, but with a focus, too, on the creation and production of artworks as well as their reception and interpretation. As such, it tends to align more with Kress

Poetry, *Writing Process and the New Poetics* 163

and van Leeuwen's notion of a grammar of visual design (and making) that is different from that of its original basis in linguistic categories.

Performance on Stage

The term 'language' is also used in theatre design and performance, not to the script of a play itself, but to the nexus of design in which the stage is used to put on a performance. Although performances can be recorded and/or broadcast live, the act of performance is one of the present, recreating (whether in music and/or theatrical performance) a score or script in multi-dimensional and multimodal ways.

The particular case to be discussed here is that of the Royal Shakespeare Company/Intel/Imaginarium Studios production of *The Tempest* in Stratford and London in 2017. This groundbreaking production used the notion of the elaborate masque from early seventeenth-century theatre, with its magical other-worldly associations, as a starting point. Then the character of Ariel was seen as central to the magical transformations in the play and as one in which the possibilities of digital projection and representation, live onstage, could be embodied. From this point, an avatar of the real-life Ariel was created to appear onstage, in various transmuted forms, alongside or instead of the real actor:

> The digital character you see on stage is not a recording but a live performance. Ariel is played by an actor, Mark Quartley. In his costume there are sensors picking up his movement, called "live performance capture". Data describing his movements is processed, rendered into the computer-generated character in real time by Intel processors, and fed through to video servers for projection, live on stage.
>
> (Programme notes, *The Tempest*)

What are the implications here for the poetics of literary text and for the wider applications of poetics to drama, theatre and performance?

The very act of lifting the text from the page in the rehearsal and performance of a play is a move from a two-dimensional text (in Shakespeare's case, itself the product of actors remembering their parts and compiling the first folio edition of the text) into a three-dimensional presentation involving speech, physical movement, exploration of space as well as time, visual representation in the form of costume and set design and an audience. With the addition of a digital dimension, the performed play adds a magical dimension in keeping with the spirit of the original text, in which both the real actor (Ariel) and his/her avatars appear onstage, concurrently and separately. Thus the constraints of physicality are transgressed. Combined with song, dance, the masque itself and the fourth dimension of representation afforded by the digital technology, the production is richly multimodal as well as using a range of media.

164 *Poetry, Writing Process and the New Poetics*

Sarah Ellis, head of digital development at the Royal Shakespeare Company and co-producer of *The Tempest*, concludes in the programme: "The show you'll see is made with the technology and tools of today in the hope of inspiring future generations. I hope you'll agree that, as Antonio in *The Tempest* says, 'What's past is prologue' ". In contemporary poetics, it is no longer possible to see even the most seemingly monomodal of artistic forms as limited to one mode. The written text has visual space around it; the spoken text is embodied. These are the multimodal principles and simple basics of a new poetic that take into account the multimodal nature of communication in framed aesthetic spaces, whether the works are in theatres, art galleries, concert halls, online and/or in print. The palette for the composer is multimodal; the economics of attention demand that the audience is receptive to a range of modes in combination. At the core of this new conception is the term from which 'poetics' derives: *poietikos*, meaning capable of making. It is fitting that poetry, with its multiple vertical layers of reference and its compressed compositional energy, is a literary genre via which exploration of the new poetic can take place.

Notes

1 O'Toole, M. (2010) *The Language of Displayed Art*. Abingdon: Routledge.
2 Lake Placid Sinfonietta's Pro-Musica chamber music series, directed by Navah Perlman from the piano, with Christine Lamprea. Luosha Fang, Amitai Vardi and Daniel Szasz, 7 August 2017.

12 Implications for Multimodality and Learning Theory

Introduction

What effect could a consideration of poetry, poetics and the arts in general in the present book have on studies in multimodality? To date, multimodality studies have founded themselves on a theory of social semiotics. This final chapter sums up the argument of the book as a whole, points forward to new practices in literary study and strengthens the case for a multimodal approach to poetics, aesthetics and rhetoric. Reference is made to dialogism, to design and aesthetics and to sociological and artistic framing. Examples of multimodal approaches to a performance of *The Waste Land* and to the reading of a Shakespeare sonnet are included. This chapter also provides guidance on the teaching of poetry within a multimodal framework, examines implications for situated learning theory and education policy and suggests further areas for research. It ends with a question about how a re-thinking of the relationship between multimodality, poetry and poetics might inspire new forms of creativity.

The Argument So Far

The present book is based on the premise that multimodality presents new challenges and new opportunities for poetics. Whereas poetics has a long history as a theoretical toolkit for the analysis of literary works, literary stylistics in the twentieth century has narrowed the field by concentrating on the language and forms of literary analysis. Its taxonomic drive has led it into encyclopaedic or manual-like categorization, like the cul-de-sacs of a narrow conception of rhetoric, divorced from actual practice. The argument put forward for a new approach to poetics is based on a number of principles or ground-shifting trends: a) that poetics needs to address creativity and production as well as analysis, b) that dialogism needs to be taken into account and c) that 'texts' are no longer to be full appreciated if seen as produced and received in a single mode.

166 *Implications for Multimodality*

Dialogism, Multimodality and Poetry

As discussed more briefly in Chapter 8, one of the most influential approaches to literary study over the last century has been that of dialogism, deriving from the work of Bakhtin (1981). Essentially, dialogism suggests that no literary work exists as the product of a single authorial voice in a void. Rather, each written or spoken work responds to an existing work or works through a process of heteroglossia. It is as if a novel, for instance, constituted the bringing together of different forms of speech: for example, that of the author(s), the narrator(s), the characters. In such an act of transduction from imagined speech to the written novel, not only does heteroglossia operate in the creation/orchestration of the novel but also in relation to existing works of art in a literary tradition or traditions, as well as to— theoretically—all previous utterances. In terms of the composer's and reader's (readers') positioning in relation to the produced 'work', the process is one of refraction of different voices through the mode of writing in order to contribute a new work to the kaleidoscope of existing works.

Although Bakhtin's thinking applies largely to the novel as an expansive, inclusive literary genre, the same principles apply to poetry. Let us address the two concepts—heteroglossia and dialogism—separately and then bring them together. Perhaps the best and most well-known example of a heteroglossic poem is *The Waste Land* (Eliot 1922), originally titled in its first full draft 'He Do the Police in Different Voices' (see Eliot 1971: 5). The final poem includes the voices of a shifting narrator (for example, Marie in the first section), quotations from unattributed voices, literary quotations, dramatic dialogue (in the second section), italicized snatches of song, dialogic question-and-answer, questions without answers and other forms of embedded citation and quotation. Gordon (2017a, 2017b) has shown how allusion, citation and quotation are woven into literary works, and into the discourse of teachers of literature in the classroom, and the implications of such heteroglossic discourse will be explored further later in the present chapter. The heteroglossic nature of *The Waste Land* suggests that writing is closely allied to reading, however implicit or explicit that connection is in the finished work of an author. It also reinforces the notion that literary works are not the product of a single expressive Romantic 'voice', but the orchestration, composition and distillation of a number of 'voices' into a seemingly single utterance. The simplicity of that utterance is likely to be more evident in relatively short lyric poetry and perhaps in narrative poetry than in epic, cinematographic, modernist poetry (like Pound's *The Cantos*). But on a spectrum of heteroglossic voices, the presence of other voices in any poetic work will be relatively implicit or explicit.

The Waste Land is also dialogic: a product of the 'dialogic imagination'. As well as being a distillation of a number of voices, it is Eliot's own response, long gestated in his own psychological, circumstantial, Geiger-counter-like reading of contemporary culture. The personal is meshed with

Implications for Multimodality   167

the literary, political, social nexus which his sensibility registers and reflects/ refracts. Even in the most seemingly monologic work, such as Beckett's *Not I* (for example, in Lisa Dwan's performance, excerpted at www.theguard ian.com/stage/video/2014/feb/03/samuel-beckett-not-i-lisa-dwan), with the existential, disembodied mouth uttering words from a script that is precise in its scoring and in which the particular performance adheres to closely; the single voice reflects at high speed on other voices, other experiences, other moments in time. *Not I* is Beckett's response to the personal socio-political and literary nexus which his sensibility inhabits.

When the heteroglossic (with Greek etymological origins in 'different' and 'languages', or translated in Russian as 'different speech-ness') and the dialogic (etymologically in Greek, 'through speech') combine, always with multimodal context and reference, the seemingly intact and mono-modal nature of the printed script, poem or novel is revealed as multi-dimensional, multi-temporal, multi-spatial, multimodal. When a play script such as *Not I* is performed by an actor like Dwan, the multimodal nature is obvious (heteroglossia becomes script, script becomes speech, speech becomes embodied/disembodied performance, performance is recorded in film and/or video media, the media are transported further via the Internet and onto a number of outlet devices, such as the laptop in which I am writing this book, books becomes print/e-book, etc.). Such is the case, too, when Fiona Shaw performed *The Waste Land* (see www.youtube.com/ watch?v=lPB_17rbNXk), first at Wilton's Music Hall, London, in 1997, then in subsequent filmed versions. Lyn Gardner's (2010) reference to the 'original' 1997 performance is telling in its sense of the multi-dimensional nature of the performance and of the way that live performance inhabits specific place, space and time:

It is London, a broken place full of ghosts, bones and ashes, that haunts the poem, and no more so than in Deborah Warner's staging in Wilton's Music Hall, still one of the capital's hidden gems.

First seen here in 1997 on the stage where Champagne Charlie toasted the girls, Fiona Shaw's 37-minute recitation of the poem is a perfect meeting of performance and architecture. There are moments when Shaw's turn as the charlatan clairvoyant Madame Sosostris or the drinkers in an East End pub has a sly music hall jollity, but mostly this is a quiet cry of spiritual despair, an eternal search for meaning in a jumbled world without meaning. I was intensely reminded of some of Sarah Kane's work in the dramatic use of a single, multi-voiced consciousness.

Twelve years ago Shaw was the first person to give a live performance here since 1880, and the place smelled of damp and rot. It has since been tidied up a bit—the candy cane pillars no longer look as if they are about to crumble away. Fortunately, nobody has tidied away the ghosts, which still lurk in every corner and in the stark shadows raised by Jean Kalman's lighting. The 37 minutes are more like a sighting than

168   *Implications for Multimodality*

a performance, a collective hallucination in which past, present and future mingle and the living and dead walk hand in hand.

In other words, the very nature of multimodality suggests a dialogic exchange between modes. If any seemingly single mode of poetic expression manifests itself, it is always with other modes implied ('in the wings') or explicitly juxtaposed. The notion of a single voice, too, is exploded into a heteroglossic range, variety and distillation of voices. Put more starkly: there is no such thing as a single mode of literary/poetic expression, nor of a single voice uttering itself to the void.

Implications for Multimodality

As discussed in Chapter 1, most studies in the field of multimodality have concentrated on the limitations of spoken and written language in contemporary communication, positing a new approach in which the affordances of different modes are used in combination in the act of communication. Such an approach is based on a theory of social semiotics and, as such, sits within a broadly social science framework. There are several implications for multimodality when art forms in literature and the other arts are brought into play: these include whether multimodality has reached the status of a theory, what relation it has to poetics and rhetoric, whether the arts and humanities basis for literary production and reception can be accommodated and what the aesthetic dimension of design and multimodality looks like.

Social semiotic theory remains important in any exploration of multimodality and poetics as the cultural zeitgeist continues to move away from a Romantic or late-Romantic conception of poetic creation. Drawing on thinkers such as Bakhtin, Vygotsky, Habermas, Halliday and Kress, the social remains prior to consideration of contexts, situations and forms of production for meaning—in the arts as well as in everyday discourse. In such a conception, framing remains an active agent in contributing to the making of meaning. Sociologically, framing retains its function in the development and consolidation of schemata in everyday life; in the arts, framing takes on an even more formal function in selecting aspects of everyday discourse for transformation and consideration, for providing a membrane which can be broken or transgressed and for heightening attention.

If theory is taken to be a high-level coherent set of ideas that is able to explain patterns, commonalities and differences between phenomena, then multimodality, from at least 25 years of development, has perhaps reached that status itself. It is more than a set of resources that can be deployed in making meaning; rather, as the kaleidoscope is turned for each new social situation, the crystals in the kaleidoscope and the patterns they create become themselves the ground for a new theory. As the field of multimodality matures and is explored for its applicability to contemporary

Implications for Multimodality 169

communication, the aesthetic (and as I will argue, the political) dimensions are just two further territories that are embraced by the power of the multimodal project.

The social dimension of creation and reception in the arts is not merely social; it is also economic and political. Resources for the arts are distributed unevenly. There is therefore an economic and political dimension to the argument for the arts. Such choices manifest themselves in right-wing emphases on elitist forms of art and a too-clear distinction between popular art and high art. Furthermore, such attitudes inform school curricula. The marginalization of the arts in school curricula in the decade since the coalition and then Tory governments have been in power in the UK is symptomatic of such attitudes. Such politicization of the imagination and sensibility enables us to see that even the so-called individualistic lyrical voice of Romantic and late-Romantic poetry is informed by social and political considerations. Thus rhetoric becomes an overarching theory of communication, approaching communication from a slightly different perspective from social semiotics (from the political and social perspectives), embracing poetics as a sub-section of its interests and linking consideration of rhetoric and poetics to their long history.

At the interface of the arts and humanities on one side, and the social sciences on the other, is an in-between space which rhetoric can inhabit. The arts of discourse are applicable to social interaction, building on work in sociolinguistics, pragmatics, conversation analysis and discourse analysis. Similarly, but more obviously, communication in the humanities is informed by rhetorical repertoire and choice and artistic production is informed by rhetoric *and* poetics.

Design remains key. As Kress suggests (2010: 132) "*Design* is the process of translating the rhetor's politically orientated assessment of the environment of communication into semiotically shaped material. In realizing the interests of rhetor and interpreter, *design* has moved to centre stage". Closing linked to the *act of framing* (not ready-made frames), design—always a factor in the arts, especially in production, making and re-making—become both a productive and interpretive action that is not only applied to interior design, furniture design, architectural design and fashion design (i.e. the applied arts) but also to the act of making itself in a wider number of genres.

Within design, *composition* takes on a new meaning. Rather than referring to adherence to the conventions of fixed genres, it now suggests something more akin to its etymological roots: putting together elements to generate meaning. These elements might be from one mode or from several. *Composition* (to make the process clearer) involves a number of moves: selecting the appropriate modes from according to rhetorical need; considering the affordances of each of the modes and their applicability in the socio-political situation; combining them accordingly; considering the juxtaposition of these elements, both with regard to harmony and tension; thinking about the challenges and sparks created by the very juxtaposition of elements;

170 *Implications for Multimodality*

being aware of the framing processes that are taking place and what these imply about what is inside and outside the frame; considering the relative permeability of the frame and whether transgression of the frame is part of the intention; and (returning to the overall rhetorical context) considering the audience and its own positioning in relation to the frames that have been created, including the frames it brings to the engagement.

From the perspective of the arts and humanities, it does not seem to me that writing is giving way to image in an overall economy of communication. Rather, that writing and speech are finding a new, more modest position in relation to the other modes of communication. Chapter 8 discussed the economies of the imagination and of attention. From the receiver's point of view, the demands on attention have to be managed during any hour, day, week or year. From the rhetor's or producer's point of view, the arrangement of choices in communication have also to be managed within an economy of available resources. These resources continue to include verbal language(s) as well as image, moving image, sound, colour, gesture and movement. It could be said that the surge of interest in the 'turn to the visual' in the wake of the Internet and the availability of media such as computer screens and mobile phones has now reach an equilibrium, with spoken language finding its irreducible affordances recognized alongside those of the other modes. As attention is crucial to the act of making and understanding meaning, so too is the imagination central to the act of design:

> A *design* is the imagined projection of a complex, closely interrelated social array in which the designed entity, object, process is used, has social effects, meanings; and produces affect.
>
> (2010: 137)

Design and Aesthetics

In all forms of written, visual and aural production, design is not just the operation of composition; it has the added dimension of elegance. Designers know this and know that good design is economical as well as beautiful. It fulfils purpose; it is coherent; it resonates so that the user of a well-designed object feels in harmony with the actions he or she is performing. Those qualities constitute 'beauty', whether that elegance is functional and/or purely experiential.

In poetry, such design is paramount. The edges of a poem—its parameters—are usually visible and thus the internal relations of the words and sounds can be addressed. Within the frame of the poem, principles of elegance include proportion, balance, propriety (or managed impropriety), rhythmic relations, choice of vocabulary, the relation between speech and writing and the degree to which imagery plays a part in the whole. Even when the poem is on a larger scale, architectural structures (as in *Paradise Lost*) are evident.

Implications for Multimodality 171

The danger with such a conception of elegance is that poetry and poetics would take on what happened in the late seventeenth, eighteenth and nineteenth centuries in English verse: a refinement and purification of the language of poetry to a more limited diction, a set of 'rules' whereby poetry should operate and the ascendance of taste over passion or affect. In each of these cases, poetry became for some writers a process of modulation, or variations on a theme. Each time there was a deracination of the poetic sensibility from that of the everyday sensibility.

However, the greater risk is for multimodality to be seen as merely the combination of modal resources. What the multimodality project enables us to see is that the principles of composition in any one moment and in any kind of social situation include the dimension of elegance. Often the aesthetic dimension is not noticed because the design has been so successful that the social transaction is completed without reflection or comment; it seems 'natural'. So poems, by their very compressed nature as formal artworks, and poetics—as the aesthetically driven sub-section of rhetoric—embody this extra dimension. The act of communication, from a producer's print of view, becomes one of choosing from the wide repertoire of modes and combining them elegantly for a particular function and situation. From a receiver's point of view, the act of communication is a seemingly natural one, with maximum clarity and impact.

A Return to Framing

In social semiotic theory, frames play a central role. They are conceptual ways of fixing the flux of social action so that pattern in social relations can be seen and therefore analyzed and better understood. The accent in the present book, in considering not only frames as an analytical but also as a productive tool, is on the *act* of framing. Frames can soon fossilize into conventions. In a world of flux and uncertainty, framings and re-framings make and re-make the parameters within which meaning is generated and understood.

An artist may work within conventional frames. In poetry, a writer may, for example, decide to use well-tried forms such as the sonnet, or rhyming quatrains, to frame his or her composition. But even within the conventional forms, there is room for innovation and frame breaking. Robert Lowell's sonnets are unrhymed, eschewing the various rhyming combinations (Petrarchan, Shakespearian) that had become conventional. These poems by Lowell are still recognizably sonnets; indeed, the poet himself consciously worked with the form in mind. They break to convention to an extent, but not to the extent of transgressing the boundaries of the form. An ode has a more capacious form, allowing different line lengths, different sections, different perspectives and voices as part of the ensemble that is created. Free verse, although it has its own conventions, is an even more open form that is not pre- or pro-scribed.

172 *Implications for Multimodality*

Although part of the creation of an artwork is to frame and therefore freeze the ongoing flux of experience in order for it to be examined, the nature of the framing can determine the degree to which the experience is 'fixed'. Improvisation in music, theatre or performance of a poem can re-invent in the light of the particular moment of communication the seemingly fixed score/script. There is, despite even heavy and fixed framing, space for interpretation from both the performers and the audience in the light of the rhetorical demands for clear, powerful and appropriate communication. Propriety—so much a consideration in the use of imagery in the Elizabe-than and late eighteenth-century poetics—is not so much an issue, however, when the force of the imaginative imperative breaks the conventional frame. Such was the case with metaphysical poetry in the early seventeenth century, Romantic poetry in the late eighteenth and early nineteenth centuries, and the free verse movement and Imagism in the late nineteenth and early twen-tieth centuries. Despite Yeats's dictum that 'ancient salt makes best packing', the formal inventions in the use of metaphor, in the individual voice and in the breaking of the pentameter revolutionized poetry and poetics.

In short, the act of framing within a new poetic is a central device for making meaning; for connecting between those outside the frame and the expression, juxtaposition of elements and their relations within the frame; for transgression across frames; for the concentration of attention; and for heightened profiling of image and rhythm within the frame. To return to the discussion of the image and the imagination and their function within poetry and poetics, discussed in Chapters 4 and 8, image operates in the vertical dimension that links the literal with simile, metonymy, metaphor and symbol through analogy; rhythm operates in the temporal and (largely, in Western conceptions of time) thus the horizontal dimension. Both key elements in the creation of poetry work within framing as a highly con-scious device in the making of meaning. The framing, therefore, is of a different order to imagery or rhythm: it enables their operation, asking us to consider their relations in an ensemble of words and other modes, whether implicit or explicit. Although a conscious part of the artwork, framing is largely unseen or invisible as concentration on the work itself in larger sociological and political acts of looking, listening and reflecting are considered. What is experienced in the making or reception of a poem can be writ larger in poetics as a whole. At this level, "aesthetics is the category which seems essential to make analytic inroads [. . .] about characteristics of the imagined readership, of the relation of [. . .] design and viewer/reader" (Kress 2010: 172). Thus aesthetics is "the politics of *style*" (ibid.) and, in my own conception, takes in place within an overarching theory of rhetoric as the domain of poetics. All the possibilities of modal choice and combination within this landscape of communication are available to the rhetor/maker as s/he creates an object of consideration and as the receiver/audience interprets it.

The Social Nature of Design and Framing

The ideas developed in this book—essentially that poetics needs to be informed by rhetoric, multimodality and social semiotic theory—does not derive from a Saussurian model of synchronic linguistic systems. Rather, it is informed, first, from a socio-political ground which sees cultural production as a read-off from social dynamics—and social dynamics as shaped, themselves, by economic and political forces. In this nested sense, contemporary poetics would be more accurately described as socio-economic and political poetics with an eye on both production and reception. Poetry is merely the particular object of focus in order to demonstrate and suggest some of the principles outlined in the book. Therefore, contemporary poetics (to use a shorthand) is more than 'political literary criticism' because it involves production (specifically composition) as well as reception (reading, criticism). If there is an overarching theory that embraces all these principles and perspectives, it is contemporary rhetoric: the arts of discourse.

I have argued elsewhere that contemporary rhetoric does not proliferate endless categories: devices, tropes and other machinery. It is does not lend itself to manuals. In these senses, it is not a science with multiple categories and sub-categories. Its interest is more in the vectors and frames that shape contemporary discourse. As Pavel (1986: 116) suggests,

> Seen as governed by semiotic conventions, literary texts do not describe real or fictional worlds, but merely manipulate an amorphous purport on which they impose their arbitrary rule. Mythic and realist discourse are equally conventional and unmotivated; Balzac's novels do not resemble reality any more than do chivalry novels; they just make use of a different semiotics, as conventional and artificial as any.

The "amorphous purport" might be translated as the motivational impulse that arises from the socio-political flux: the need to 'say something', usually in response to or in dialogue with existing utterances. The tenor of the passage is key to Pavel's thesis: that realist and highly fantastic worlds exist on the same spectrum of 'otherness', and that seeming 'non-fictional' genres, too, have a distance from the actual real world that places them on the fictional spectrum. Because this spectrum of possibility is also a material part of the real world, "no empirical evaluation of the argument would ever be possible" (ibid.). Hence such a world could be envisaged in which 'criticism' might wither on the vine, to be replaced by a more powerful response to a work of art—viz., another work of art.

Rhetoric assumes that the impulse to communicate (i.e. to produce and receive), grounded in socio-political experience, is more powerful than the systems it generates or could generate. Ironically, such a position brings us closer to the dynamics of everyday life and art than abstract monomodal

174   Implications for Multimodality

systems like literary stylistics. Pavel discusses Riffaterre's "intertextual theory of poetry" (1978) as an example of a sophisticated position: one that moves poetry further away from the real world because of its self-referential internal music, but which also fuses Aristotelian poetics with Saussurian semiotics. To an extent, Riffaterre's fusion is helpful: it explains why the internal dynamics of a poem are part of its meaning and why such internal synergies generate 'significance' (largely because the words resonate with meaning which rises like steam from a swamp, but which also have a tight horizontal, structural, web-like interdependence). Classicist 'imitation' is a long-forgotten principle in such a conception of literary and artistic significance, but the danger from Riffaterre's perspective is that poetry and the other arts might speak only to themselves in a surfeit of self-referentiality.

With regard to frames: these are akin to agreed social-artistic conventions for the transference of meaning. If you are unable to read the frame in which communication is trying to take place, you are likely to misunderstand the tenor of the intended communication. This is where criticism can be helpful: it is a corrective to mis-reading the frames in which the communication is taking place. However, as soon as the frames fossilize into rigid conventions, they can be transgressed and broken, and new frames of reference can be created. At the early stages of the creation of such new frames, communication can be tentative and exploratory. As frames establish themselves, the mutual understanding is easier, although the danger again ensues of conventionality exceeding and overpowering new meaning. Such potential fossilization is why the emphasis in the present book is on framing rather than frames.

Shakespeare's sonnet 129 demonstrates that a conventionally accepted form—the sonnet—carries the personal and romantic associations of that form, but can also carry the burden of a powerful and abstract argument:

> Th'expence of Spirit in a waste of shame
> Is lust in action, and till action, lust
> Is perjud, murderous, blouddy full of blame,
> Savage, extreame, rude, cruell, not to trust
> Injoyd no sooner but dispised straight,
> Past reason hunted, and no sooner had
> Past reason hated as a swallowed bayt,
> On purpose layd to make the taker mad.
> Mad in pursuit and in possession so,
> Had, having, and in quest to have extreame,
> A blisse in proofe and prov'd a very wo,
> Before a joy proposed, behind a dreame,
> All this the world well knows yet none knowes well,
> To shun the heaven that leads men to this hell.

There are a number of elements of context that affect the reading of the poem: its position in a series or array of sonnets that deal with love, death, the fleeting nature of time and existence, absence and beauty; the sonnet form itself, derived from Renaissance romance and from song; and the 'personal' or intimate dimension, in contrast to the plays. Yet this, and the other sonnets by Shakespeare, break the frame of the form by engaging in a moral excursion—a compact argument. In this particular case, the excesses of lust are captured in past, present and future in two sentences. The poem deals in abstract concepts that are themselves highly physical: it is threaded through with antinomies. The point of its inclusion and brief discussion here is to suggest that the balance between the conventional frame and the breaking of the frame is itself an act of delicate framing and that the intimate and general can be balanced in the composition and reception. Multimodally, the poem is resonant with sound, physicality, song and dance movement.

The fallacy that art imitates nature is often more evident in the reading fiction than in that of poetry—*viz* that fictional works are to be tested in the degree to which they reflect 'reality'. As Pavel suggests, the relationship is rather the other way round: real experiences are tested against the hypotheses of fiction. The relationship is slightly different in poetry. Because poems are more obviously formally constructed than novels or short stories, there is never any sense that they are direct imitations of the real world, or conversely that they are hypotheses against which the real world can test itself. Rather, their form or genre or text-type (ode, sonnet, free verse, etc.) suggests a different kind of fallacy: that they 'express' an inner voice, an inner autobiographical motive and that the 'I' of the poem is that of the poet. The conventions of poetry would suggest the opposite: that these musical or quasi-musical forms are constructs for the generalized representation (through imagery, rhythm and internal verbal harmonies and discordances) of patterned meaning which is 'suggestive'.

The social nature of design and framing itself suggests that learning to navigate and understand these new conventions is central to leaning to create, to read and thus to find one's way through the semiotics of everyday life and its relation to the possibilities afforded by fiction, poetry and the other arts. It could be said that exposure to such art forms helps to orient audiences, viewers and readers to the choices that are made every day: moral choices in a post-religious world, practical choices and personal and affective choices. The situatedness of such learning is the topic to which this chapter now turns.

Situated Learning and its Relation to Multimodality, Poetry and Poetics

Lave and Wenger's notion of 'situated learning' sits closely with theories of contemporary rhetoric. Both have in common an assumption that the social is prior (albeit informed by the economic and political in a more Marxist, Russian-European tradition). Both assume that a cognitivist or 'brain science' model is inadequate to account for thought and action in

176   *Implications for Multimodality*

everyday life and learning. Both move beyond the structuralist assumption that systems explain how communication works, irrespective of the contexts in which communication takes place. Both emphasize the social over the individual experience, resulting in a more process-oriented view of human development; both subscribe to a more Vygotskian direction of travel (from the social to the cognitive) rather than, to put it over-simply, a Piagetian/Romantic journey from the embryonic self to the social). Thus, to quote Rogoff (1992), learning is an effect of community rather than of individual growth.

The title of Rogoff's 1992 work is *Apprenticeship in Thinking*. In the UK in the 2010s, one of the most sustainable ideas in higher education has been that of degree apprenticeships. In other words, these degrees are born from social and economic need, and operate via an apprenticeship model in which 'legitimate peripheral participation' is valued as part of a learning trajectory. What implications might legitimate peripheral participation have for the learning and teaching of poetry and poetics?

First, it could be said that apprenticeship in poetry and poetics (to condense the nature of the challenge) is not just an apprenticeship in shaping verbal language. In the light of the perspective that the present book takes, it is more a matter of understanding and practising in the contexts in which poetry and poetics manifest themselves. For example, a poetry reading, with all its physical properties (presence, audience, volume, voice(s), interaction with other modes and arts forms) is a characteristic setting for the *performance* of poetry, just as the solitary composition of poetry means, at the very least, a pen and paper or laptop, even in the most remote of locations (or, at least, in moments of reflection and the capturing of a half-formed thought that comes like a rhythmic phrase into the mind).

Second, it is seeing the act of reception as closely allied to the act of production. Apprentice writers gain much from trying out a form before they encounter a fully achieved work in that form. To work on the constituent elements of a sonnet, whether rhymed or unrhymed, gives the feel of working to a 14-line form before encountering a polished final version from an established writer. This is the reverse of the classic imitatory pedagogy of 'copying' the form of established work. The advantage of trying the form first is that there is an emotional and compositional *investment* in learning and, ideally, a realization that the achieved works in the form have gone through the same processes of composition that the novice writer goes through.

Third, working with established writers gives an insight into the process of writing poetry and the more general practices of poetics. Teachers can demonstrate the process of writing by trying out what they are asking the class to do, and they can share their difficulties with starting writing, writing blocks, technical issues and multiple drafts.

Fourth, in the digital age, 'publication' is a more open and accessible dimension of poetry and poetics. Publication means a degree of 'setting' and

Implications for Multimodality 177

finishing of the work as well as making it available to a wider audience. It 'freezes' the work in time.

Further Areas for Research

The exploration of multimodality, poetry and poetics in the present volume is not complete.

Further areas of research include the possibility of a general classification of rhetorical and poetic 'moves' for the twenty-first century. Although I have argued that such a project leads in the direction of fossilization and over-categorization, the activity would be useful in mapping the range of multimodal relations that is possible.

Another area for research would be to measure the degree to which theoretical deliberation is useful in providing an overarching explanation of the poetic compositional process. New or resurrected terms have emerged in the writing of this book: *composition* as a central creative act, *framing* rather than frames and design and the *elegance* of design. These form the pillars of a new edifice of theory that emerges from the application of multimodality to poetry and poetics.

The present book has focused on poetry to explore the relationship between multimodality and poetics. It could equally have focused on film, documentary, the novel or short story, plays and other fictional and 'non-fictional' genres. Many of the same principles would apply, but there would also be significant differences because of the particular multimodal make-up of each of the genres, as well as the principal media in which they are conveyed. Multiple media platforms have become the norm for the dissemination of poems as well as of other art forms and news/features. To what degree does the choice of medium of communication backwash on the multimodal forms that can be used to convey meaning?

Finally, but not with any sense of an ending, what new creative possibilities are offered by a multimodal approach to poetry and poetics?

References and Bibliography

Alghadeer, H.A. (2014) 'Digital landscapes: rethinking poetry interpretation in multimodal texts', *Journal of Arts and Humanities (JAH)*, 3, 2: 87–96

Andrews, R. (1995) *Teaching and Learning Argument*, London: Cassell

Andrews, R. (2009) *Argumentation in Higher Education: Improving Practice Through Theory and Research*, New York: Routledge

Andrews, R. (2011) *Re-Framing Literacy*, New York: Routledge

Andrews, R. (2014) *A Theory of Contemporary Rhetoric*, New York: Routledge

Andrews, R. (2016) *A Prosody of Free Verse: Explorations in Rhythm*, New York: Routledge

Apel, W. (1970) *Harvard Dictionary of Music*, London: Heinemann Educational

Aristotle (1965) 'On the art of poetry' in *Classical Literary Criticism*, translated and edited by T.S. Dorsch, Harmondsworth: Penguin

Aristotle (1982) *The 'Art' of Rhetoric*, translated John Henry Freese, Loeb Classical Library, London: William Heinemann Ltd

Bakhtin, M.M. (1981) *The Dialogic Imagination: Four Essays*, edited by M. Holquist and translated by C. Emerson and M. Holquist, Austin, TX: University of Texas Press

Barnes, D. and Barnes, D. (1983) 'Cherishing private souls' in Arnold, R. (ed.) *Timely Voices: English Teaching in the 1980s*, Melbourne: Oxford University Press

Barrell, J. (2017) 'The meeting of the waters', *London Review of Books*, 39, 15: 23–8 (27 July 2017)

Bateman, J. and Schmidt, K-H. (2011) *Multimodal Film Analysis: How Films Mean*, New York: Routledge

Bateman, J. and Wildfeuer, J. (2014) 'A multimodal discourse theory of visual narrative', *Journal of Pragmatics*, 74: 180–208

Bateson, G. (1972) 'A theory of play and fantasy' in *Steps to an Ecology of Mind*, Northvale, NJ: Jason Aronson

Benjamin, W. (1970) *The Work of Art in the Age of Mechanical Reproduction*, London: Cape

Berger, J. (1972) *Ways of Seeing*, London: Penguin

Berger, J. (1996) *Pages of the Wound: Poems, Drawings, Photographs 1956–94*, London: Bloomsbury

Berger, J. and Christie, J. (1999) *I Send You This Cadmium Red: A Correspondence Between John Berger and John Christie*, Barcelona: Actar

Berger, J. and Christie, J. (2016a) *Lapwing and Fox: Conversations Between John Berger and John Christie*, Framlingham, Suffolk: Objectif Press

References and Bibliography   179

Berger, J. and Christie, J. (2016b) 'Looking beyond: conversations between John Berger and John Christie', exhibition at the Sainsbury Centre for Visual Arts, University of East Anglia, Norwich, 7 May to 27 November 2016

Berger, J. and Mohr, J. (1995) *Another Way of Telling*, New York: Vintage

Bex, T., Burke, M. and Stockwell, P. (eds) (2000) *Contextualized Stylistics: In Honour of Peter Verdonk*, Amsterdam/Atlanta, GA: Rodopi

Bicecci, V.G. (2017) catalogue write-up in *Transartation!* See also www.vernicagerberbicecci.net

Blake, W. (1970) *Songs of Innocence and Experience*, London: Oxford University Press, with an introduction and commentary by Geoffrey Keynes

Brône, G. and Vandaele, J. (2009) *Cognitive Poetics. Goals, Gains and Gaps*, Berlin: Mouton de Gruyter

Bruns, G. (1974) *Modern Poetry and the Idea of Language: A Critical and Historical Study*, London: Dalkey Archive Press

Burke, M. (ed) (2014) *The Routledge Handbook of Literary Stylistics*, Abingdon: Routledge

Burn, A. (2013a) 'The kineikonic mode: Towards a multimodal approach to moving image media' in Jewitt, C. (ed.) *The Routledge Handbook of Multimodal Analysis*, London: Routledge

Burn, A. (2013b) 'The kineikonic mode: towards a multimodal approach to moving image media', National Centre for Research Methods Working Paper, 03/13, Southampton: NCRM.

Burn, A. (2013c) https://mode.ioe.ac.uk/2014/06/11/multimodality-and-the-moving-image accessed 19 June 2017

Burrow, C. (2016) ' "You've listened long enough": a review of *Aenied: Book VI*, translated by Seamus Heaney (London: Faber)', *London Review of Books*, 38, 8: 13–14 (21 April 2016)

Buxton Forman, H. (ed) (1917) *The Poetical Works of John*, Keats, London: Oxford University Press

Carey, J. (1971) *Milton: Complete Shorter Poems*, London: Longman

Caridad Casas, M. (2009) *Multimodality in Canadian Black Feminist Writing: Orality and the Body in the Work of Harris, Philip, Allen, and Brand (Cross/Cultures)*, Amsterdam: Rodopi

Chiasson, D. (2017) 'The illness and insight of Robert Lowell' *The New Yorker*, issue 20 March 2017, accessed online August 2017

Cicero (1989) *Rhetorica ad Herennium*, translated Harry Caplan, Loeb Classical Library, London: William Heinemann Ltd

Clayton, E. (ed) (2017) *Howard Hodgkin: Painting India*, London: Lund Humphries

Coleridge, S.T. (1971) *The Collected Letters of Samuel Taylor Coleridge*, edited by Alethea Hayter, Harmondsworth: Penguin

Davie, D. (1952) *The Purity of Diction in English Verse*, London: Chatto and Windus

Derek Jarman Lab (2016) *The Seasons in Quincy: Four Portraits of John Berger*, London: Birkbeck, University of London and Pittsburgh PA: University of Pittsburgh

Doležel, L. (1998) *Heterocosmica: Fiction and Possible Worlds*, Baltimore, MD: Johns Hopkins University Press

Domingo, M. (2011) 'Analyzing layering in textual design: a multimodal approach for examining cultural, linguistic, and social migrations in digital video', *International Journal of Social Research Methodology*, 14, 3: 219–30

180   *References and Bibliography*

Dvorák, C. (2016) *John Berger: The Art of Looking*, film, London: BBC accessed January 2017 at www.bbc.co.uk/iplayer/episode/b082qynq/john-berger-the-art-of-looking?suggid=b082qynq

Eco, U. (1984) *The Role of the Reader: Explorations in the Semiotics of Texts*, Bloomington, IN: Indiana University Press

Eliot, T.S. (1922) *The Waste Land*, New York: Horace Liveright

Eliot, T.S. (1963) *Collected Poems 1909–1962*, London: Faber and Faber

Eliot, T.S. (1971) *The Waste Land: A Facsimile and Transcript of the Original Drafts Including the Annotations of Ezra Pound*, edited by Valerie Eliot, London: Faber and Faber

Ellestrom, L. (2010) *Media Borders, Multimodality and Intermediality*, Basingstoke: Palgrave Macmillan

Feng, G.F. and English, J. (1973) *Tao Te Ching*, London: Wildwood House

Friedlander, B. and Cato, B. (1972) *Cookbook for the New Age: Earth Water Fire Air*, New York: Palgrave Macmillan (Collier Books)

Gardner, L. (2010) Review, 'The Waste Land', posted on 6 January 2010 and accessed 3 March 2017 at www.theguardian.com/stage/2010/jan/06/the-waste-land-fiona-shaw

Gardner, S. (1968) *Blake* (Literature in Perspective series), London: Evans Brothers Limited

Gavins, J. and Steen, G. (2003) *Cognitive Poetics in Practice*, London: Routledge & Brighton and Portland: Sussex Academic Press

Gibbons, A. (2008) 'Multimodal literature "moves" us: dynamic movement and embodiment in *VAS: an opera in Flatland*', *hermes—Journal of Language and Communication Studies*, 41: 107–24

Gibbons, A. (2013) 'Multimodal metaphors in contemporary experimental literature' in Hidalgo-Downing, L. and Angeles Martinez, M. (eds.) *Metaphor and Creativity Across Modes and Across Cultures*, Amsterdam: John Benjamins

Gibbons, A. (2014) *Multimodality, Cognition and Experimental Literature*, New York: Routledge

Gordon, J. (2017a) 'The turn of the page: how teachers guide literary reading using spoken quotation of study texts', unpublished ms, submitted to *Linguistics and Education*

Gordon, J. (2017b) 'Reading from nowhere: assessed literary response, practical criticism and situated cultural literacy', unpublished ms, submitted to *English in Education*

Grierson, H.J.C. (1949) *Criticism and Creation, with Some Other Essays*, London: Longman

Grierson, H.J.C. and Bullough, G. (1934) *The Oxford Book of Seventeenth Century Verse*, Oxford: The Clarendon Press

Grishakova, M. and Ryan, M-L. (eds) (2010) *Intermediality and Storytelling*, Berlin: De Gruyter

Halliday, M.A.K. (1994) *Introduction to Functional Grammar*, 2nd ed., London: Edward Arnold

Händel, G.F. (1859) *Georg Friedrich Händel's Werke*, Bd: 6, 'L'Allegro, Il Pensieroso [sic] ed Il Moderato', Leipzig, 1859, accessed 9 January 2017 at http://daten.dig itale-sammlungen.de

Harrison, T. (1985) *V*, Newcastle-upon-Tyne: Bloodaxe Books

Heaney, S. (1979) *Field Work*, London: Faber and Faber

References and Bibliography 181

Hiraga, M. (2004) *Metaphor and Iconicity*, Basingstoke: Palgrave Macmillan

Hodgkin, H. (2017) *Howard Hodgkin: Painting India*, exhibition at The Hepworth, Wakefield, 1 July to 8 October 2017

Horace (1965) 'On the art of poetry' in *Classical Literary Criticism*, translated and edited by T.S. Dorsch, Harmondsworth: Penguin

Hughes, T. and Baskin, L. (1975) *Season Songs*, New York: The Viking Press

Hughes, T. and Baskin, L. (1978) *Cave Birds*, London: Faber and Faber

Hughes, T. and Godwin, F. (1979) *Remains of Elmet*, London: Faber and Faber

Hughes, T. and Keen, P. (1983) *River*, London: Faber and Faber

Illeris, K. (2007) *How We Learn: Learning and Non-Learning in School and Beyond*, Abingdon: Routledge

Illeris, K. (ed) (2009) *Contemporary Theories of Learning: Learning Theorists . . . in Their Own Words*, Abingdon: Routledge

Ishiguro, K. (1982) *A Pale View of the Hills*, London: Faber

Jakobsen, R. (1960) 'Linguistics and poetics' in Sebeok, T. (ed.) *Style in Language*, New York: Wiley, 350–77

Jamison, K.R. (2017) *Robert Lowell, Setting the River on Fire: A Study of Genius, Mania and Character*, New York: Penguin Random House

Jenkins, J. and Keal, A. (2004) *The Adirondack Atlas: A Geographic Portrait of the Adirondack Park*, Syracuse, NY: Syracuse University Press & the Adirondack Museum

Jennens, C. (1740) Georg Friedrich Händel, *L'Allegro, Il Penseroso ed Il Moderato: An Ode* sourced at opera.stanford.edu/iu/libretti/allegro.htm, 8 January 2017

Jewitt, C. (ed) (2009) *Handbook of Multimodal Analysis*, London: RoutledgeFalmer

Jones, P. (ed) (1972) *Imagist Poetry*, Harmondsworth: Penguin

Keefer, D. (1996) 'Review of *The Language of Displayed Art* (O'Toole)', *The Journal of Aesthetics and Art Criticism*, 54, 3: 304–6

Kisselgoff, A. (1990) 'Review/dance: Mark Morris interprets Handel', *The New York Times*, October 8th, 1990, accessed 9 January 2017 at www.nytimes.com

Knottenbelt, E.M. (2000) 'What was John Donne hearing? A study in sound sense' in Bex, T. et al. (2000), 113–29

Koskimaa, R. (2007) 'The challenge of cybertext: teaching literature in a digital world', uocpapers, issue 4 (available at www.uoc.edu), March 2007

Koskimaa, R (2014) *Digital Literature: From Text to Hypertext and Beyond*, thesis accessed at users.jyu.fi/koiskimaa/thesis/htm

Kress, G. (2003) *Literacy in the New Media Age*, London: London: Routledge

Kress, G. (2010) *Multimodality: A Social Semiotic Approach to Contemporary Communication*, Abingdon: Routledge

Kress, G. and van Leeuwen, T. (2001) *Multimodal Discourse: The Modes and Media of Contemporary Communication*, London: Edward Arnold

Kress, G. and van Leeuwen, T. (2006) *Reading Images: The Grammar of Visual Design*, 2nd ed., London: RoutledgeFalmer

Lanham, R. (2006) *The Economics of Attention: Style and Substance in the Age of Information*, Chicago: The University of Chicago Press

Latham, A. (2003) 'L'Allegro, il Penseroso ed il Moderato', in *The Oxford Dictionary of Musical Works*, Oxford: Oxford University Press, 5

Lauveng, A. (2013) *The Road Back from Schizophrenia: A Memoir*, New York: Skyhorse Publishing

Lave, J. and Wenger, E. (1991) *Situated Learning: Legitimate Peripheral Participation*, Cambridge: Cambridge University Press

182 References and Bibliography

Lowell, R. (1970) *Notebook*, London: Faber and Faber

Lowell, R. (1973) *History*, London: Faber and Faber

Lowell, R. (1977) *Day by Day*, New York: Farrar, Straus and Giroux

Mark Morris Dance Group (2014) *L'Allegro, il Penseroso ed il Moderato*, DVD of performance at Teatro Real, Madrid, Bel Air Classiques and Thirteen Productions (Bel Air Media)

Milton, J. (1911) *The Poetical Works of John Milton*, London: Macmillan and Co.

Morgan, E. (1972) *Instamatic Poems*, London: Ian McKelvie

Morgan, E. (1982) *Poems of Thirty Years*, Manchester: Carcanet New Press Limited

Morgan, E. (1988) *Themes on a Variation*, Manchester: Carcanet Press

Nørgaard, N. (n.d.) *Multimodal Stylistics: The Happy Marriage of Stylistics and Semiotics*, Hauppauge NY: Nova

Norris, S. and Maier, C.D. (eds) (2014) *Interactions, Images and Texts: A Reader in Multimodality*, Berlin: Mouton de Gruyter

Nwulu, S. (2016) 'A strange kind of beauty', *RSA Journal*, Issue 1: 50 and accessed in an animated version at www.a newdirection.org.uk/a-strange-kind-of-beauty

O'Connell, M. and Powell, J. (1978) 'Music and sense in Handel's setting of Milton's *L'Allegro* and *Il Penseroso*' (Autumn 1978)', *Eighteenth-Century Studies*, 12, 1: 16–46

O'Halloran, K. and Smith, B. (eds) (2012) *Multimodal Studies: Exploring Issues and Domains*, New York: Routledge

O'Toole, M. (2010) *The Language of Displayed Art*, 2nd ed., Abingdon: Routledge

Page, R. (ed) (2009) *New Perspectives on Narrative and Multimodality*, New York: Routledge

Pavel, T. (1986) *Fictional Worlds*, Cambridge MA: Harvard University Press

Paz, O. (1974) *Alternating Current*, London: Wildwood House Ltd.

Peacham, H. (1577/1977) *The Garden of Eloquence*, New York: Scholars Facsimiles and Reprint

Pirsig, R. (1974) *Zen and the Art of Motorcycle Maintenance: An Inquiry into Values*, New York: William Morrow and Company

Pound, E. (1964) *The Cantos of Ezra Pound*, London: Faber and Faber

Powers, A. (2013) *Eric Ravilious: Artist and Designer*, Farnham: Lund Humphries, p. 39

Ray, J. (n.d.) 'Build: aspects of construction' in *Catalogue 13*, York: Janette Ray Rare and Out of Print Books

Rensselaer, W. L. (1967) *Ut Pictura Poesis: The Humanistic Theory of Painting*, New York: Norton

Riffaterre, M. (1978) *Semiotics of Poetry*, Bloomington, IN: Indiana University Press

Ringbom, H., Inberg, A., Norrman, R., Nyholm, K., Westman, R. and Wikberg, K. (1975) *Style and text: studies presented to Nils Erik Enkvist*, Stockholm: Språkförlaget Skriptor

Rogoff, B. (1992) *Apprenticeship in Thinking*, New York: Oxford University Press

Royal Shakespeare Company (2017) *The Tempest*, production and programme notes, in collaboration with Intel and Imaginarium Studios

Ryan, M-L. (2013) 'Possible worlds', accessed at www.lhn.uni-hamburg.de/article/possible-worlds on 9 February 2016

Scott, J. (2014) 'Creative writing and stylistics' in Burke, M. (ed.) *The Routledge Handbook of Literary Stylistics*, Abingdon: Routledge, ch26.

Segal, E. (2011) 'Cognitive poetics: goals, gains and gaps', *Poetics Today*, 32, 3: 607

References and Bibliography   183

Semino, E. (1997) *Language and World Creation in Poems and Other Texts*, Longman—reissued by New York: Routledge in 2014

Semino, E. and Culpepper, J. (2002) *Cognitive Stylistics: Language and Cognition in Text Analysis*, Amsterdam: John Benjamins

Shackelford, L. (2014) 'Migrating modes: multimodality in e-poetics as another kind of language', *Mosaic: A Journal for the Interdisciplinary Study of Literature*, 47, 4: 99–118

Shelley, P.B. (1840) 'A defence of poetry' in *Essays, Letters from Abroad, Translations and Fragments*, London: Edward Moxon

Stockwell, P. (2002) *Cognitive Poetics: An Introduction*, London: Routledge

Stockwell, P. (2007) 'Cognitive poetics and literary theory', *Journal of Literary Theory* 1, 1: 135–52

Thesleff, H. (1975) 'Notes on the rise of rhetoric as a stylistic genre' in Ringbom et al. (1975), 278–88.

Transartation! (2017), 'Transartation!: wandering texts, travelling objects', exhibition at The Byre Theatre, University of St Andrews, Abbey Street, St Andrews (31 March–8 April 2017) and The Shoe Factory Social Club, St Mary's Works, St Mary's Plain, Norwich (12 April–6 May 2017)

Tsur, R. (1992) *What Makes Sound Patterns Expressive: The Poetic Mode of Speech-Perception*, Durham, NC: Duke University Press

Tsur, R. (1998) *Poetic Rhythm: Structure and Performance*, New York: Peter Lang

Tsur, R. (2003) *On the Shore of Nothingness: Space, Rhythm, and Semantic Structure in Religious Poetry and Its Mystic-Secular Counterpart*, Upton Pyne: Imprint Academic

Tsur, R. (2008) *Toward a Theory of Cognitive Poetics*, Second, expanded and updated ed., Brighton: Sussex Academic Press

Ventola, E., Charles, C. and Kaltenbacher, M. (2004) *Perspectives on Multimodality*, Amsterdam: John Benjamins

Verdonk, P. (2002) *Stylistics*, Oxford: Oxford University Press

Walcott, D. (2000) *Tiepolo's Hound*, New York: Farrar, Straus and Giroux

Walcott, D. and Doig, P. (2016) *Morning, Paramin*, London: Faber and Faber

Walsh, R. (2007) *The Rhetoric of Fictionality: Narrative Theory and the Idea of Fiction* (Theory and Interpretation of Narrative Series), Columbus: Ohio State University Press

Walsh, R. and Stepney, S. (eds) (2016) *Narrating Complexity*, Dordrecht: Springer

Webb, M. (2011) *Journeys in Colour*, Norwich: Sainsbury Centre for Visual Arts, University of East Anglia

Widdowson, H.G. (1975) *Stylistics and the Teaching of Literature*, London: Longman

Widdowson, H.G. (2000) 'The unrecoverable context' in Bex, T. et al. (2000), 229–41

Index

Adirondack Mountains 110, 146
Aeneid: Book VI (translated by
    Heaney) 47–8
aesthetics 107, 109, 146, 161, 165,
    170–2; and design 170–1; and
    framing 172
Allen, Woody 75
Alternating Current (Paz) 45
Anderson, Kirsteen 32
Another Way of Telling (Berger) 121
Apollinaire, 'Les Fenêtres' 32–3
applied linguistics 133
Apprenticeship in Thinking (Rogoff) 176
Aristotle 1–2, 6–8, 60, 76–7, 93;
    Poetics 1–3, 76; on rhetoric 14;
    Rhetoric 1, 6–7
arrangement, multimodal 8–9
art, political/rhetorical context of
    119–20; see also visual art
'Art in York' map 78–80, 80
attention, economics of 114–16
'Au Cabaret-Vert' (Rimbaud) 36
'Au Cabaret-Vert' (Scott) 36–7
audience 1, 5, 7–9, 14, 18, 22, 30, 33,
    51, 56, 60, 73, 75, 96–101, 103,
    109, 112, 117, 128, 130–1, 133,
    135–6, 138, 140–1, 155, 163–4,
    170, 172, 175–7; experience of
    18, 103, 112, 130, 136, 141, 172;
    imagination of 109; implied 101;
    reaction of 5, 30; relationship with
    actors/readers 5, 60, 73, 75, 109,
    112, 117, 128, 130, 155, 170; role of
    9, 14, 56, 97, 163
Austen, Jane, *Pride and Prejudice* 106

'Bach in California' 54–5, 73–4
Bakhtin, Mikhail 33, 62, 77, 162, 166,
    168; *The Dialogic Imagination* 116;
    theory of poetics 116–18

ballads 90, 107–8
'Bangaon India July 1971' (Morgan)
    93–4
BBC 88–9, 121
beauty 1, 19, 47, 53, 89, 170, 175
Beckett, Samuel, *Not I* 167
Behn, Aprha, 'Love Arm'd' 68–9
Belarus Free Theatre (BFT) 128–31
Berger, John 14, 119–22, 125, 127,
    162; *Another Way of Telling* 121;
    contribution of 126–7; letters to
    Christie 122–5; multimodality
    in works of 127; *Ways of Seeing*
    119–21
Bicecci, Verónica Gerber 33, 34;
    'Exhumation' 44
Biographia Literaria (Coleridge) 57
bipolar disorder 153
Blake, William 1, 10–11, 13, 18–19,
    90; 'London' from *Songs of
    Experience* 9–13; as poet and artist
    11; 'The Poison Tree' 68; 'The Sick
    Rose' 12, 18–19, 53, 68; *Songs of
    Innocence and Experience* 9–13, 19;
    'The Tyger' 19
blank verse 5, 41
blogs 15, 126
Blomberg, Sven 119
border crossing 112–13
Bronte, Charlotte 75
Brooklyn Academy of Music 30
'Build: Aspects of Construction' 77–8
Burns, Robert, 'My love is like a red,
    red rose' 53
Burrow, Colin 47–8

'Canto XLIX' (Pound) 134
'Catédrale de Quimper' 58, 59
Centre of Ceramic Art 78, 79, 189
Charlie, Champagne 167

Index 185

chorus 101, 103, 112
Christie, John 122; Berger's letters to 122–5; 'Poem, Print, Note' 123
Clark, Mel 160
Clayton, Eleanor 156
'Closing' 110–11
cognition 16n3; embodied 15, 45
Coleridge, Samuel Taylor 52, 57; *Lyrical Ballads* 90
collaboration 97, 119, 121–2, 128, 129, 160
Combi, Linda 84–8, 191–5; 'Flexible Language' 87–8; 'Herb Garden Melody' 84–5; 'Mosque' 85–6; 'Politics and Rhetoric' 86–7; 'Shipping Forecast' 88–9
communication 1–2, 5–6, 14, 31, 34, 51, 60–2, 76–7, 89–92, 95–7, 100–1, 106, 108, 112, 115, 119, 121–2, 124–5, 131, 133, 135–6, 138–42, 144, 146, 150–2, 160, 164, 168–72, 174, 176–7; economy of 170; framing in 138; and language 117–18; mode and medium of 139, 152; multimodality in 76, 89–90, 95–7; new theory of 115; personal and private 119; public 119; theory of 169
composition 2, 6–9, 15, 17, 23, 25, 30, 33, 41, 44–5, 50, 56, 59–60, 62, 73, 75–8, 81, 86–7, 89, 95, 98, 100–3, 111, 114, 121, 125–6, 128, 131–3, 140–4, 150–6, 158, 161–2, 164, 166, 169–71, 173, 175–7; compact 59; creative 153; and design 169–70; filmic 128; framed 2, 140, 171; inside/outside 111; internal 121; literary 150; multimedia 150; multimodal 9, 15, 28, 60, 62, 78, 150; musical 17, 23, 25, 33, 45, 62, 143, 155; oral 142; pattern in 7; poetic 8, 41, 56, 95, 101, 141, 142, 144, 150–2, 164, 166, 173, 175–6, 177; polyptical structuring of 150; principles of 171; process of 6, 152, 154, 156, 161, 162, 177; rhythmic 44, 50, 125; silence in 45; sub-categories of 144; of texts 133; in visual art 81, 86, 87, 156, 158
compression 4, 19, 42, 47, 53, 61, 75, 77, 86, 95, 109, 111, 113–14, 117, 131; of language 19, 53, 86, 111; in poetry 4, 42, 47, 61, 75, 77, 95, 109, 113, 117, 171; of time 131–2

contextualized stylistics 135–6
cookbooks, multimodality in 81, 82
creation, social dimensions of 169
creativity 31, 34, 96, 152–4, 165, 177
cross-referencing 148
cultural mystification 120
curation 156

dance 17, 21, 30–1, 39–43, 47, 50, 61–2, 76, 86, 88, 95, 138, 142, 146, 157, 162–3, 175; music and 41–2; music for 39–40
Delaunay, Robert 33
De Poetica (Aristotle) see *Poetics* (Aristotle)
design 142–3, 169; and aesthetics 170–1; elegance of 170–1, 177; social nature of 173–5; see also composition
Dialogic Imagination, The (Bakhtin) 116
dialogism 116–18, 165; and multimodality 166–8
dialogue 2, 8, 62, 102, 103, 117, 119, 120, 124, 166, 173
Dibb, Michael 119
diegesis 91
digital technology 163–4
digitization 15, 89
'Dimanches' (Laforgue) 36
'Dimanches' (Scott) 35, 36–7
discourse 173
distance 3, 47, 52, 55, 56, 66, 91, 109, 110, 111, 112, 116, 149, 173
Doležel, L. 4
Donne, John 42, 44, 47–8, 66–8, 135–6; 'Good Friday, Riding Westward' 47; 'The Good-Morrow' 42–3; *Songs and Sonnets* 42; 'A Valediction: Forbidding Mourning' 66–8
Dwan, Lisa 167

'Easter Wings' (Herbert) 65–6
East London National Health Service Trust 131
Eco, Umberto 3
editing 62
ekphrasis 32
Eliot, T. S. 33, 44–5, 59, 63, 148, 166; *Four Quartets* 44–5; 'The Waste Land' 61, 166–7
Ellis, S. 164
embodied cognition 15, 45
enjambement 49

186 Index

'Eve of St. Agnes, The' (Keats) 90–1
exhibitions 156–61
'Exhumation' (Bicecci) 44
explicity 3, 12–13, 15, 17–19, 41, 51–64, 65, 67, 76, 91–2, 101, 109, 112, 117, 133, 140, 142, 144–5, 154, 166, 168, 172

fantasy, framing of 109
Ferrante, Elena 113
fiction 15, 75, 102, 105–13, 115–16, 118, 126, 152–4, 175; vs. non-fiction 105–6; rhetorical take on 105–6
film 14, 21, 30, 45, 59–60, 62, 75, 92, 100, 102, 125, 127–32, 148–9, 153–4, 157, 167, 177; as medium 128; multimodality in 60–2, 153–4
'Flexible Language' (Combi) 87–8
formalism, Russian 76–7, 133
Four Quartets (Eliot) 33, 44–5, 148
Fox, Chris 119
frame breaking 75
framing 11–12, 19, 22, 42, 56, 60, 92, 95, 138–40, 168, 169–70, 177; and aesthetics 172; of fantasy 109; in free verse 73–5; in performing arts 138; of a poem 68–75; and re-framing 153; rhetorical take on 108–9; social nature of 173–5; in social semiotic theory 171–2
framing theory 65
free verse 39, 41, 46–7, 49–50, 57–8, 70, 94; framing in 73–5
French Revolution 11
fugue, imagery in 62–4

Garden of Eloquence, The 52
Gardner, Lyn 167–8
genres 1–5, 8, 47, 62, 75–6, 96, 99, 101–3, 105–6, 110, 113, 117, 127, 134, 137, 142, 153–4, 156–7, 169, 173, 177; poetic 1, 15, 117, 142
genre theory 4–5
'Good Friday, Driving Southwards' 48–9
'Good Friday, Riding Westward' (Donne) 47
'Good-Morrow, The' (Donne) 42–3
Gorgias 5
graphic design, multimodality in 77–80
Grieve, Alastair 158

Halliday, M.A.K. 135, 162
Handel, George Frederic 22, 24, 25

'Heavenly Rain, The' (Lowell): in *History* 71–3; in *Notebook* 69–70
Herbert, George, 'Easter Wings' 65–6
'Herb Garden Melody' (Combi) 84–5
heteroglossia 64, 77, 117, 118, 166–8
History (Lowell) 69, 71
Hollis, Richard 119
Horace 3, 55–6, 60
Howard Hodgkin 75, 94, 156; *Painting India* (exhibition) 156–7
hybridity 22, 102

'Il Penseroso' (Milton) 21–3, 30–1; choreography by Morris 22; setting to music by Handel 22, 24–5
image and imagery 18–19, 67–8; in fugue 62–4; function of 54–5; implicit and explicit 59–60; moving 60–2; in poetry 51; and word 77–80
imaginary, economics of 114–16
imagination 57, 96, 100, 105, 109, 154, 172; multimodal 69
Imagist movement 57–9, 61, 64
implicitly 19, 59–60, 62–3, 76, 109, 142, 154
improvisation 172
incompleteness 113–14
Industrial Revolution 12
Instamatic Poems (Morgan) 93–5
International New York Times (8 May 2016) 81
Internet access 14–15, 89, 127, 167, 170
'I Send You This Cadmium Red: A Correspondence Between John Berger and John Christie' (Berger and Christie) 121–3, 126

Jennens, Charles 23–5, 31
journalism, multimodality in 81, 83–4, 83

kaleidoscope 21, 166, 168
Kalman, Jean 167
Keats, John 52; "The Eve of St. Agnes' 90–1; 'On First Looking into Chapman's Homer' 56–7
Knottenbelt, E.M. 135–6
Kress, Gunther 13–14, 95–6, 138–9, 142, 162, 168–9, 172

Laforgue, Jules 57; 'Dimanches' 36
'L'Allegro' (Milton) 21–3; choreography by Morris 22, 30–1; setting to music by Handel 22, 24–5

Index 187

'L'Allegro, Il Penseroso ed Il Moderato'
22–31; choreography by Morris 22,
30–1; Handel's composition process
25; libretto by Jennens 23–5, 31; live
performances 25, 30; opening bars
(score) 26–9
language 1–2, 4, 8–9, 12, 16n3, 17–21,
23, 25, 30–1, 34, 36–7, 41, 43, 47,
50–4, 56, 59–62, 69–70, 76–7,
85, 87–91, 96, 105, 109, 111, 113,
115–16, 118, 121, 124, 127–9, 131,
133–6, 140–2, 144, 146, 148–9,
157, 161–3, 164n1, 165, 167–8,
170–1, 176; compression of 19,
53, 86, 111, 114; definition 163;
figurative 53–5; and imagery 54–5;
literary 91; poetic 51–2, 76–7, 91;
written 52
language in education movement 77
Lanham, R. 114–15
*Lapwing and Fox: Conversations
between John Berger and John
Christie* 119, 121–2, 125
Lauveng, Arnhild 128–30
learning, situated 175–7
learning theory, and multimodality
165–77
Leonardo, 'The Virgin and Child with
St Anne and St John the Baptist' 120
'Les Fenêtres' (Apollinaire) 32–3
'Les Fenêtres Simultanées' (Delaunay) 33
Lightman, Ira, 'Vista' 32–3, 32
linguistics, applied 133
listener 5, 33, 46–7, 60, 114, 145;
attention of 46–7; demands on 114;
range of possibilities for 61
literary analysis 15
literary stylistics 76–7, 90, 105, 133–5,
165; history of 76–7
literary theory 127
loathed melancholy 23–4
'London' (Blake), in *Songs of
Experience* 9–13
'Looking Beyond: Conversations
between John Berger and John
Christie' (exhibition) 119, 125–6
'Love Arm'd' (Behn) 68–9
Lowell, Robert 171; 'The Heavenly
Rain' 69–73
Lyrical Ballads (Wordsworth and
Coleridge) 90

Mallarmé, Stéphane 52
Manhattan 158, 160, 198

Marriage hearse 10, 13
Marxism 131
Mary Webb: Journeys in Colour
(exhibition) 158, 160
meaning 2, 4–6, 9, 12–13, 15, 17–19,
25, 43, 46–7, 50–4, 56–7, 60–1,
63, 69, 72–3, 76, 92–3, 95–8,
100, 120–1, 125, 127, 134–5, 138,
141–3, 148, 153, 164, 167–9,
170–2, 174–5, 177; construction of
141–2, 172
media 1–2, 5, 11, 13–14, 17, 21, 30–1,
33, 46, 87, 90, 93, 102, 106, 119,
121–2, 126–9, 138, 152, 154–5,
157, 160, 163, 167, 170, 177; modes
and 13–14; multimodality and
127–8
'Meeting of the Waters, The' 150–1
metaphor 18–19, 52, 53–4, 115–16,
148–9, 161, 172
metonymy 51, 54, 115–16, 172
Milsom, Anna 33, 34, 186
Milton, John 17, 21–5, 30–1, 38,
63, 102–4; 'Il Penseroso' 21–3;
'L'Allegro' 21–3; *Samson Agonistes*
102–4; 'Of That Sort of Dramatic
Poem Called Tragedy' 103
mimesis 76, 91, 108
minimal departure 4, 113
modal logic 3–4, 15n1, 107–8
modal resources 140–1, 171
modes 3–4; and the arts 14; combining
62; and media 13–14; relationship
between 100, 122; as rhetorical
choices 109; as semiotic resources 13
Mohr, Jean 121
Monro, Harold 61
Morgan, Edwin 93–5; 'Bangaon India
July 1971' 93–4; *Instamatic Poems*
93–5
Morris, Mark 17, 22, 30–1
'Mosque' (Combi) 85–6
multimedia 13–14, 21, 31, 150
multimodal arrangement 8–9
multimodal construct 1
multimodality 1–16, 119–132,
165–177; in Berger's works
127; in Blake's poetry 12–13; in
communication 76, 89–90, 139;
and contemporary communication
95–7; in cookbooks 81, 82; and
dialogism 166–8; dynamic 100–1;
in film and video 60–2; in graphic
design 77–80; implications for

188 *Index*

168–70; in journalism 81, 83–4, 83; in 'L'Allegro, Il Penseroso ed Il Moderato' 22, 25–31; and learning theory 165–77; in Linda Combi's work 84–5; and media 127–8; vs. multimedia 13–14; and poetics 14–15, 92, 95–7, 138–9, 165; in poetry 60; and situated learning 175–7; and the spoken or performed poem 96, 100–1; in *Transartation!* exhibition 31–7
multimodality theory 15
multimodal presentations 17–37
music 2, 6, 21–2, 24–5, 30–1, 33, 39–42, 46–7, 50–1, 55, 61–2, 67, 70, 91, 100, 103, 122, 125, 128–9, 136, 140–3, 149–50, 154–5, 157, 163, 164n2, 167, 172, 174; composition of 17, 23, 25, 33, 45, 62, 143, 155; for dance 39–40; and dance 41–2; performance of 154–5; and poetry 154–5; rhythm in 39–41
'My love is like a red, red rose' (Burns) 53

naming 143–4
narrative 6–7, 91, 108, 127–8; limits of 107–8
narrative theory 108
narratology 2, 7
Neo-Classicism 30, 107
neo-Marxism 131
New York Daily Graphic 81
New York Times (8 October 1990) 30
non-fiction 154; vs. fiction 105–6; rhetorical take on 105–6
Notebook (Lowell) 69–70
Not I (Beckett) 167
novels 33, 38, 42, 45, 91, 106–7, 112, 114, 126–7, 138, 143, 149, 173, 175; Bakhtin's treatises on 116–17; of Balzac 173; Berger's observations on 127; chapter form of 149; differences from poetry 113–14, 117, 175; each reading as renewal 126–7; fiction in 106, 107, 109; frame breaking in 75; framing in 138; heteroglossia and dialogism in 166–7; historical 102; imagetext 15; by Ishiguro 111; manipulation of time in 45, 47, 131; multimodality in 8, 105, 177; narrative in 107, 108, 117; poetics in 105; possible worlds in 111, 112; reading of

111–12, 113, 114, 126–7; real-world 4; rhythmic shape of 38; rhythm in 42, 45; silence in 33; titles of 143; use of language in 118; use of past tense in 126; of Virginia Woolf 91
Nwulu, Selina 19, 21, 89; 'A Strange Kind of Beauty' 19–22

Official Preppy Handbook, The (Ms Birnbach) 83
'On First Looking into Chapman's Homer' (Keats) 56–7
On the Art of Poetry (Aristotle) see *Poetics* (Aristotle)
On the Art of Poetry (Horace) 55–6
opacity 91
orchestration 144–5
O'Toole, M. 146, 162; *Language of Displayed Art, The* (O'Toole) 162

paean 6
Pages of the Wound: Poems, Drawings, Photographs 1956–94 (Berger) 121
Pale View of the Hills, A 110–11
Pavel, T. 3–4, 107–8, 109, 112, 113, 114, 115, 173–4, 175
Paz, Octavio, 'Recapitulations' 45
performance, on stage 163–4
personification 69
photography 2, 21, 34, 81, 93–5, 127, 131
Pirsig, Robert, *Zen and the Art of Motorcycle Maintenance* 106
plays 163–4; by Berger 127; compared to poetry 19; as 'creative writing' 152; framing in 138, 140; herbs in 84; interface with the audience 112, 130; manipulation of time in 45, 47; multimodality in 4; *Not I* 167; rhythmic shape in 38, 40; scenes in 150; sequence in 149; by Shakespeare 2, 63, 136, 163; silence in 33; *Tomorrow I Was Always a Lion* 128–31; turning points in 114
'Poem, Print, Note' (Christie and Turnbull) 123
'Poem for Emily' 98–100
poems 5, 7, 9, 11–13, 15, 17, 19, 21–2, 24–5, 33, 40, 42, 47, 56, 59, 61–3, 65, 68–70, 74, 76, 84, 89–90, 93–6, 103, 107–14, 116, 121, 134–5, 137–40, 143–5, 152, 154, 171, 175, 177; borders of 112; and the

construction of meaning 141–2; design of 142–3; framing 138–40; modal resources for 140–1; naming 143–4; orchestration of 144–5; titles of 143–4; see also poetry
poetic genres 1, 15
poetic prosodies 133–4
poetics 2, 76–92, 93–104, 119–132, 134, 146–64; cognitive 14; and collaboration 160–1; dynamic multimodal 100–1; elements of a new poetics 101–4; and the everyday 89–92; multimodal 61–2, 61, 92, 97, 136, 137–8; multimodality and 14–15, 95–7, 165; and poetry 127; relation of rhetoric to 131–2; and rhythm 45; and situated learning 176–7; social dimension of 97; social semiotic approach 162; and theatre 163–4; theory of 117; widening the range of 90
Poetics (Aristotle) 1–3, 76
poetry 17–37, 38–50, 51–64, 146–64; as argument 137; border crossing in 112–13; in the canon 47; compared to prose fiction 109–12; compression in 4, 42, 47, 61, 75, 77, 95, 109, 113, 117; dramatic 2; epic 2; and the everyday 89–92; experimental 93; as fiction or non-fiction? 107; found 122; framing of 68–75, 95, 140–1; imagery in 51, 67–8; as imitation 1–2; incompleteness in 114; intertextual theory of 174; lyric 126; metaphor and imagery in 18–19, 52–5; metrical feet 40; modal resources for 171; movement in 15, 66; multimodality in 60; multimodal potential of 17–19; multimodal taxonomy for 61; and music 41–2, 154–5; narrative 107–8; performance of 17, 141, 154–5, 176; as poetics in action 2; popularization of 89; possible worlds of 109–12; post-Romantic 113; and the present tense 109–10, 126; as public voice 1; rhythm in 43–5, 118; selectivity in 19, 22; shift to free verse 46–7; and situated learning 176–7; social dimension of 97; spoken or performed 96, 100–1; as text-type 4–5; translations of 33–7, 34–6; use of figurative language in 115–16; use

of metaphor in 115–16; verticality of 115–16; visual dimensions of 12, 17, 32–3, 37, 40–1, 44, 54, 65–7, 77–8, 84–6, 88, 89, 94, 96, 97, 100, 133, 140, 142, 143, 145, 149, 164; see also poems
'Poison Tree, The' (Blake) 68
'Politics and Rhetoric' (Combi) 86–7
polyptiques 149–50
possible worlds 108–9; in poems 110–11; size of 113–14
possible world semantics 3–4
Pound, Ezra 61, 63; 'Canto XLIX' 134
Prague School 133
Pride and Prejudice (Austen) 106
Prufrock, Alfred, J. 59
publication 176–7
Purity of Diction in English Verse, The (Davie) 90
Purple Rose of Cairo, The (film) 75

quatrains, unrhymed 149

reader 1, 5–6, 8, 12, 14–15, 18–19, 33, 46–7, 51, 58, 60, 67–9, 72–3, 75, 79, 81, 96–7, 100, 109, 111–14, 117, 120, 126, 134, 136, 139, 145, 172; attention of 46–7; demands on 114; range of possibilities for 61
re-arrangement 153
'Recapitulations' (Paz) 45
Renaissance 79, 106, 175
repetition 40, 45, 46, 63, 74
research, further areas for 177
rhetoric 2, 5–8, 14, 169; contemporary 131, 173–4; and delivery 7; and poetics 131–2; three kinds of 5
Rhetoric (Aristotle) 1, 6–7
rhetorical stylistics 136–7
rhetorical theory 5–6
rhythm 2, 19, 22, 33, 62; in Donne's poetry 135; isometric 39–40, 41; modal 40–1; multimetric 40, 41; in music 39–41; in oratory 5; and poetics 45; in poetry 43–5, 118; in translation 38–9
Riffaterre, M. 174
Riley, Denise 37
Rimbaud, Arthur, 'Au Cabaret-Vert' 36
Road Back from Schizophrenia, The: A Memoir (Lauveng) 128
Romanticism 153

190 *Index*

Romantic movement 57, 62, 90–1, 97, 101, 107, 152, 153, 155, 166, 168, 169, 172, 176
Romantic tradition 107, 153
Royal Shakespeare Company 163–4
Russian formalism 76–7, 133

Sainsbury Centre for Visual Arts (UEA) 119, 121, 126, 132n1, 157–8
Samson Agonistes (Milton) 102–4
schizophrenia 128–9, 131
Scott, Clive 34–5; 'Au Cabaret-Vert' 36–7; 'Dimanches' 35, 36–7
Seasons in Quincy, The: Four Portraits of John Berger (film) 127–8
selectivity 18, 19, 22
semiotics 13, 17, 19, 31, 33, 74, 88, 125, 162, 173, 175; Saussurian 174; see also social semiotics
Shakespeare, William 2, 53, 136, 165, 175; Sonnet 18 53; Sonnet 129 174; sonnets by 174–5
Shaw, Fiona 167
Shcherdan, Vladimir 131
Shelley, Percy Bysshe 52
'Shipping Forecast' (Combi) 88–9
short stories 33, 42, 46–7, 102, 105, 107–8, 112–13, 126–7, 138, 175, 177; Berger's observations on 127; compared to other forms 46; construction of 175; each reading as renewal 126–7; multimodality in 177; narrative in 33, 42, 47, 107–8; poetics in 105; reference worlds of 112; single theme in 113; as sub-genre 102, 107
'Sick Rose, The' (Blake) 12, 18–19, 53, 68
sign language 123–5
silence 33, 69; see also white space
similes 51, 53, 55, 115, 172
situated learning 175–7
Skyros 63–4
Snyder, Gary 54, 148
social media 90, 126
social networks 97
social semiotics 17, 73, 81, 95, 97, 135, 137, 162, 165, 168, 169, 171–2, 173; see also semiotics
software interfaces, multimodal 15
Songs and Sonnets (Donne) 42
Songs of Innocence and Experience (Blake) 9–13, 19

'Sonnet 18' (Shakespeare) 53
'Sonnet 129' (Shakespeare) 174
sonnets 41–2, 53, 69–73; by Shakespeare 53, 174–5
spatial arrangement 6
speech-act theory 108
'Strange Kind of Beauty, A' (Nwulu) 19–22
stylistics 2, 4, 8, 14, 45, 52, 76–7, 90, 105, 107, 109, 134, 136–7, 144, 116–17, 133–7, 140, 165, 174; contextualized 135–6; literary 76–7, 90, 105, 133–5, 165; rhetorical 136–7
Stylistics (Verdonk) 134
'Sudden Storm' 146–8
suspension of disbelief 111, 113
Swinton, Tilda 127
symbol 53–4
symbolism 59, 89, 115, 127
Symbolistes 57–8

theatre, radical 128–31
theory of literary composition 132
theory of poetics 117
theory of possible worlds 91
Thesleff, H. 137
'This is the Age of the Typewriter' 73–4, 140–1
time 2–4, 6–7, 11–13, 15, 18–19, 22, 25, 31, 33, 38–9, 50, 52, 56, 60–3, 70, 72, 81, 85, 90, 93–5, 100, 103–4, 125–7, 155–7, 161, 163, 167, 171–2, 175, 177; articulation of 45; compression of 131–2; manipulation of 45, 47, 110, 131
Tomorrow I Was Always a Lion (play) 128–31
tragedy 103–4; six elements of 2
Transartation! exhibition 31–7
transduction 21, 25, 38, 94–5, 129, 166
translation(s) 129; of *Aeneid* 47–8; of poetry 33–7, 34–6; rhythm in 38–9
Translation Games: Still in Translation (Vidal) 37
transparency 91
Treadaway, Sam 37
tropes 150–2
tryptychs 149–50
Turnbull, Gael 122–5; 'Poem, Print, Note' 123
'The Tyger' (Blake) 19
typography 15, 87, 143

Index 191

University of East Anglia 119, 125, 132n1, 157
unrhymed quatrains 149
ut pictura poesis 55–7

'A Valediction: Forbidding Mourning' (Donne) 66–8
Verdonk, P., *Stylistics* 134, 135
vers libéré 134
vers libre 39, 134
Vidal, Ricarda 37
video 60, 126, 129–30, 146, 163, 167; multimodality in 60–1; in stage plays 130
'Vista' (Lightman) 32–3, 32
visual arts 75, 127, 138, 156, 162–3; exhibitions of 156–61; grammar of 162–3
visual imagery 6, 11, 12, 13, 51–2, 59, 62, 64, 67, 71, 73, 148; visual dimensions of 69

Warner, Deborah 167
'Waste Land, The' (Eliot) 61, 166–7
Ways of Seeing (BBC production) 119
Ways of Seeing (book by Berger et al.) 119–20
Webb, Mary 156–61; 'Circle Line Series: The Isle of Manhattan 18,

1984, Collage' 160; 'Dunwich Study 2' 157, 158; exhibition of works 156, 157–61; 'New York 1980, Photograph' 159; 'Yellow, Black and White 1976, Oil on Canvas' 161
white space 5, 12, 17, 33, 44–5, 59, 65, 68–70, 73, 74, 81, 96, 99, 100, 102, 112, 139, 140, 141–2, 143, 145; see also silence
Whitman, Walt 63
Widdowson, H.G. 133, 136
Williams, William Carlos 63
word, and image 77–80
Word and Image: A Journal of Verbal-Visual Enquiry 77
words 3–4, 6–7, 11–13, 25, 30, 50–2, 77–9, 84–9, 100–2, 108, 112, 114–15, 120–1, 152, 161, 167–8, 170, 172, 174, 176; juxtaposition of 41; in visual art 84–9, 84–8
Wordsworth, William 57; *Lyrical Ballads* 90
worldwide web 89
writing process 152–4, 176

Zen and the Art of Motorcycle Maintenance (Pirsig) 106

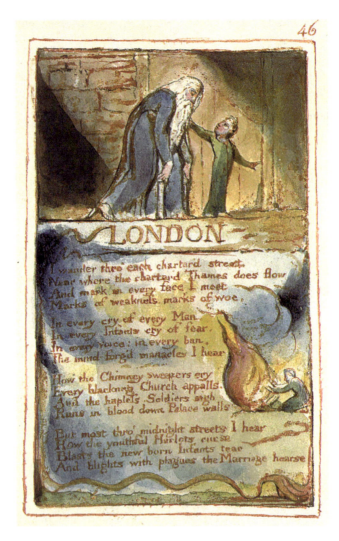

Plate 1 William Blake, 'London' From *Songs of Innocence and Experience* (1794)

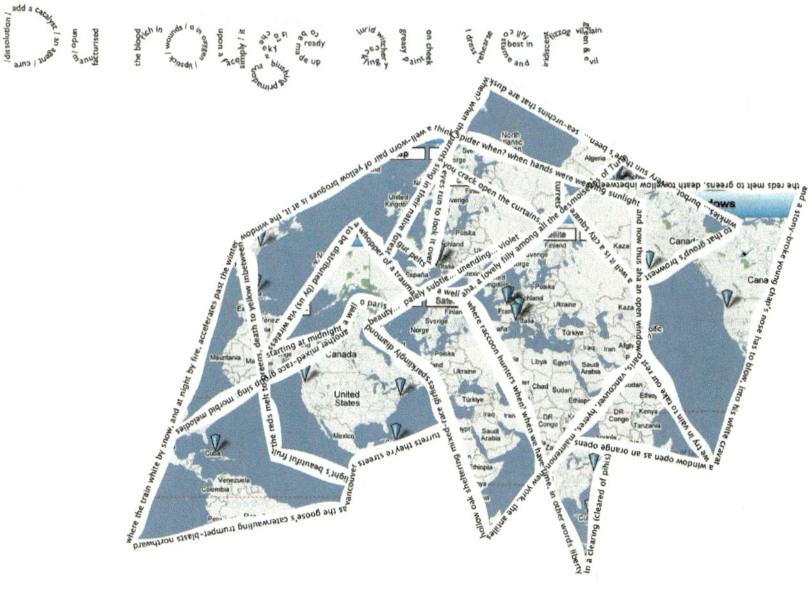

Plate 2 Ira Lightman, 'Vista'

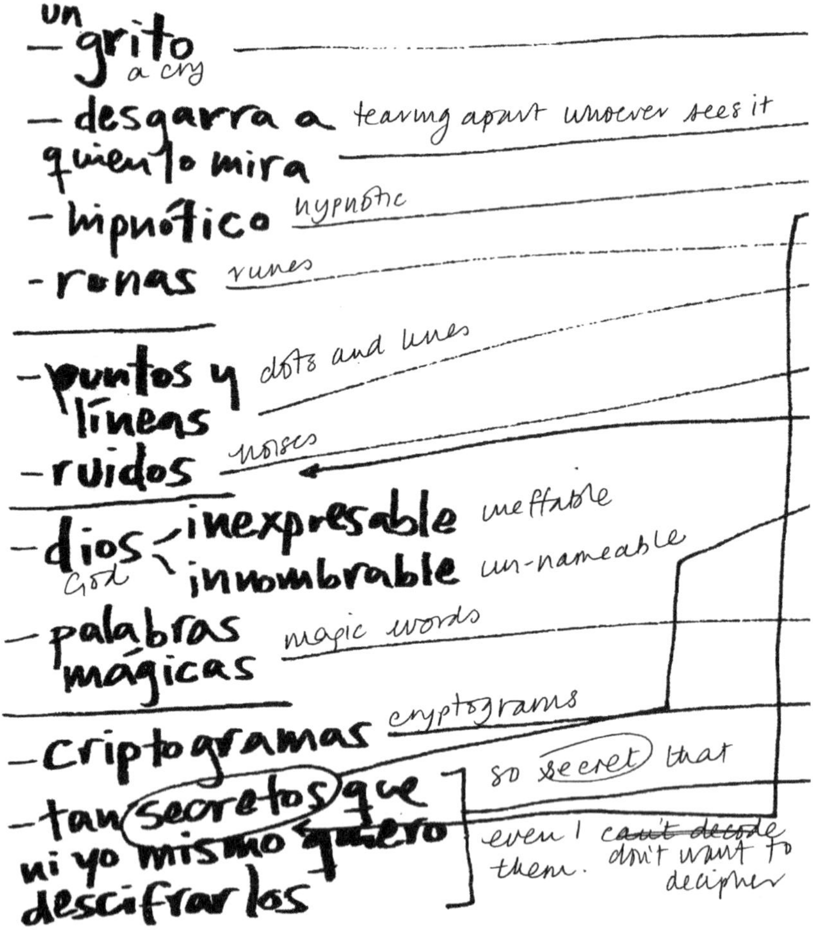

Plate 3 Verónica Gerber Bicecci and Anna Milsom, Inverted (and Translated) Poem (2017) Visual Essay

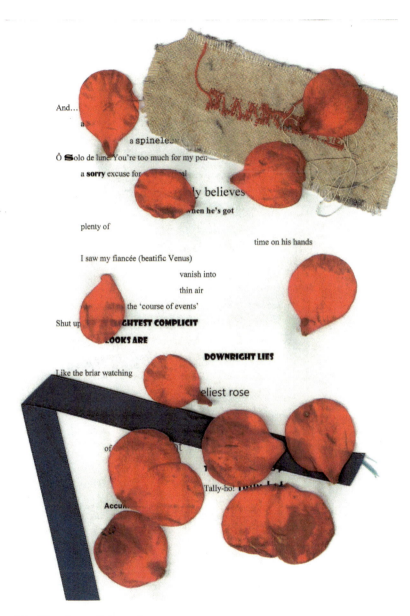

Plate 4(i) Clive Scott, 'Dimanches'

Au Cabaret-Vert, at five o'clock in the afternoon

FOR a week or more I'd walked

    my boots to bits

        on rough roads; I

Came into Charleroi: *Au Cabaret-*

Vert: I ordered

Buttered *tartines* and ham

    just halfway cold.

Cloud nine: legs stretched out under the green

Table, idly scanning the tapestry, its artless

Images – and it was gilt

    on my gingerbread

      when the barmaid

What a pair and eyes to curl your **toes**

- Not one, that girl, to miss out on a clinch –

Bubbling with merriment, brought me buttered *tartines*

    on a gaudy plate, and warmish

Ham, ham pink **and** white, perfumed

    with a garlic-clove – and filled my roomy

Beer-jar to the brim, its fluffy

head burnished

by the late

afternoon

sun.

RHYTHM OF LOVE

EXQUISITE PARURE

Plate 4(ii) Clive Scott, 'Au Cabaret-Vert'

Plate 5 Centre of Ceramic Art Brochure: Cover

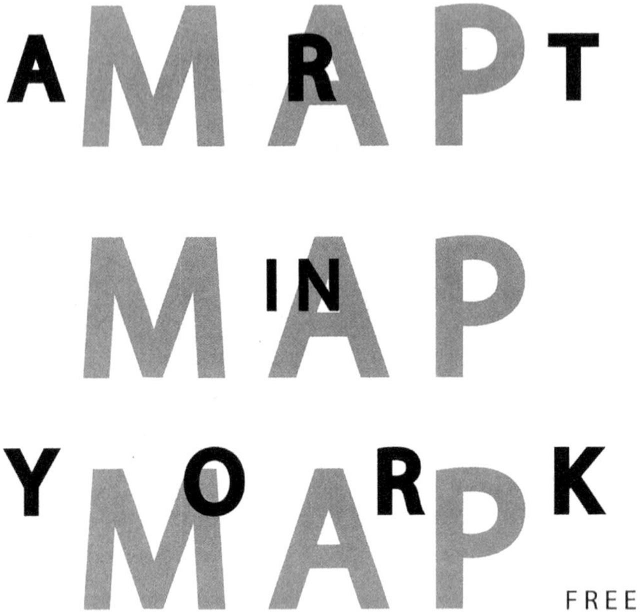

Plate 6 Art in York

Plate 7 Linda Combi, 'Herb Garden Melody'

Plate 8 Linda Combi, 'Mosque'

Plate 9 Linda Combi, 'Politics and Rhetoric'

Plate 10 Linda Combi, 'Flexible Language'

Plate 11 Linda Combi, 'Shipping Forecast'

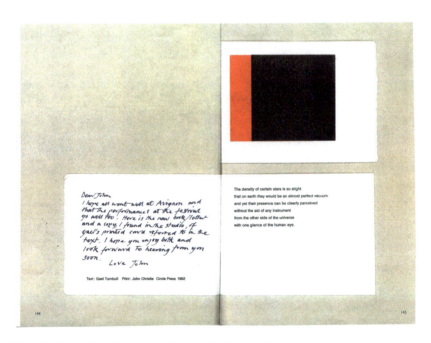

Plate 12 John Christie and Gael Turnbull, 'Poem, Print, Note'

Plate 13 Mary Webb, 'New York 1980, Photograph'

Plate 14 Mary Webb, 'Circle Line Series: The Isle of Manhattan 18, 1984, Collage'

Plate 15 Mary Webb, 'Yellow, Black and White 1976, Oil on Canvas'

PGMO 04/16/2018